Inclusion and Diversity

In their important book, Grace and Gravestock offer practical tips for those committed to enhancing student learning. The authors offer useful case scenarios for readers to ponder, thoughtful questions for teachers to reconsider their assumptions, and believable advice that acknowledges the diverse backgrounds of students. Readers will surely find this volume particularly helpful in their efforts to maximize learning outcomes.

Stephen John Quaye, Assistant Professor, College Student Personnel Program, University of Maryland

This thought-provoking and practical book is tailored for those involved in teaching and learning in higher education. It takes a holistic view of learning, as occurring both within and outside the classroom, and successfully brings together theoretical perspectives and practical suggestions, to the benefit of all students.

Dr. Helen May, Senior Adviser, Higher Education Academy, UK

In this one volume, both new and experienced university teachers will find an impressive range of rich and comprehensive suggestions about how to better meet our students' increasingly diverse needs. The authors do this in a sympathetic and practical way, recognizing the complexities and challenges now facing academics not only in the UK but in universities internationally. They clearly draw on a depth and breadth of experience about all aspects of student life and academics' work.

Dr. Janette Ryan, Senior Lecturer in Education, Monash University, Australia

How should you prepare for the first day of class? How can you encourage all students to participate in discussions? How do you ensure disabled students can take part in fieldwork? Increasingly, universities are drawing from a less traditional group of students – international students, disabled students, part-time students and mature students. This book offers specific, practical advice on the issues that teachers encounter when teaching in a diverse classroom.

Inclusion and Diversity highlights good practice for all students, and provides a helpful structure around the day-to-day experiences of staff and students as they make contact with each other. With reference to the international literature, and discussing some of the educational principles that underpin an inclusive curriculum, this book covers a wide range of useful topics so that teachers will have quick access to guidelines on different aspects of teaching and learning:

- small and large group teaching
- e-learning
- work placements
- students' lives out of the classroom

- personal tutoring
- skills agenda
- assessment
- employability and further study

Addressing a range of themes, including student age, ethnicity, disability, sexuality and gender, this book aids all practitioners in higher education today – particularly those new lecturers meeting their students for the first time – to develop a better understanding of the issues involved in teaching a diverse range of students.

emic Practice at the University of York, UK.

g Enhancement and Technology Support at the

Key Guides for Effective Teaching in Higher Education Series
Edited by Kate Exley

This indispensable series is aimed at new lecturers, postgraduate students who have teaching time, Graduate Teaching Assistants, part-time tutors and demonstrators, as well as experienced teaching staff who may feel it's time to review their skills in teaching and learning.

Titles in this series will provide the teacher in higher education with practical, realistic guidance on the various different aspects of their teaching role, which is underpinned not only by current research in the field, but also by the extensive experience of individual authors, and with a keen eye kept on the limitations and opportunities therein. By bridging a gap between academic theory and practice, all titles will provide generic guidance on teaching, learning and assessment issues, which is then brought to life through the use of short, illustrative examples drawn from a range of disciplines. All titles in the series will:

- represent up-to-date thinking and incorporate the use of computing and information technology (C&IT) where appropriate
- consider methods and approaches for teaching and learning when there is an increasing diversity in learning and a growth in student numbers
- encourage reflexive practice and self-evaluation, and a means of developing the skills of teaching, learning and assessment
- provide links and references to other work on the topic and research evidence where appropriate.

Titles in the series will prove invaluable whether they are used for self-study or as part of a formal induction programme on teaching in higher education (HE), and will also be of relevance to teaching staff working in further education (FE) settings.

Other titles in this series:

Assessing Skills and Practice
  – Sally Brown and Ruth Pickford
Assessing Students' Written Work:
  Marking Essays and Reports
  – Catherine Haines
Designing Learning: From Module
  Outline to Effective Teaching
  – Chris Butcher, Clara Davies and
  Melissa Highton
Developing your Teaching: Ideas,
  Insight and Action
  – Peter Kahn and Lorraine Walsh
Enhancing Learning Through Formative
  Assessment and Feedback
  – Alastair Irons

Giving a Lecture: From Presenting to
  Teaching
  – Kate Exley and Reg Dennick
Inclusion and Diversity: Meeting the
  Needs of all Students
  – Sue Grace and Phil Gravestock
Small Group Teaching
  – Kate Exley and Reg Dennick
Using C&IT to Support Teaching
  – Paul Chin
Working One-to-One With Students:
  Supervising, Coaching, Mentoring,
  and Personal Tutoring
  – Gina Wisker, Kate Exley, Maria
  Antoniou and Pauline Ridley

Inclusion and Diversity

Meeting the Needs
of All Students

Sue Grace
and
Phil Gravestock

Routledge
Taylor & Francis Group

NEW YORK AND LONDON

First published 2009
by Routledge
270 Madison Ave, New York, NY 10016

Simultaneously published in the UK
by Routledge
2 Park Square, Milton Park, Abingdon, Oxon OX14 4RN

Routledge is an imprint of the Taylor & Francis Group, an informa business

© 2009 Taylor and Francis

Typeset in Perpetua by
Florence Production Ltd, Stoodleigh, Devon
Printed and bound in the United States of America
on acid-free paper by
Edwards Brothers, Inc.

Library of Congress Cataloging in Publication Data
Grace, Sue.
Inclusion and diversity: meeting the needs of all students/
Sue Grace and Phil Gravestock.
p. cm. – (Key guides for effective teaching in higher education
series)
Includes bibliographical references and index.
1. College teaching. 2. Effective teaching. 3. Inclusive education.
4. Multiculturalism. I. Gravestock, Phil. II. Title.
LB2331.G665 2008
378.1'2—dc22   2008014930

ISBN10: 0–415–43044–5 (hbk)
ISBN10: 0–415–43045–3 (pbk)
ISBN10: 0–203–89038–8 (ebk)

ISBN13: 978–0–415–43044–9 (hbk)
ISBN13: 978–0–415–43045–6 (pbk)
ISBN13: 978–0–203–89038–7 (ebk)

Contents

Illustrations

FIGURES

TABLES

Series Preface

The *Key Guides for Effective Teaching in Higher Education* were originally discussed as an idea in 2002 and the first group of four titles were published in 2004. The series has grown in popularity and size, now boasting ten volumes and a topic spread that recognises both the variety and richness in the modern teacher's role in Higher and Further Education. This latest volume, focussing on issues of student diversity and inclusivity in teaching, is a timely and appreciated addition.

The series includes:

- *Giving a Lecture: From Presenting to Teaching*, Exley and Dennick (2004)
- *Small Group Teaching: Seminars, Tutorials and Beyond*, Exley and Dennick (2004)
- *Assessing Students' Written Work: Marking Essays and Reports*, Haines (2004)
- *Using C&IT to Support Teaching*, Chin (2004)
- *Designing Learning: From Module Outline to Effective Teaching*, Butcher, Davies and Highton (2006)
- *Assessing Skills and Practice*, Brown and Pickford (2006)
- *Developing your Teaching: Ideas, Insight and Action*, Kahn and Walsh (2006)
- *Enhancing Learning Through Formative Assessment and Feedback*, Irons (2007)
- *Working One-to-One with Students: Supervising, Coaching, Mentoring and Personal Tutoring* Wisker, Exley, Anoniou and Ridley (2008)
- and this volume, *Inclusion and Diversity*, Grace and Gravestock (2009).

It was intended that the books would be primarily of use to new teachers in universities and colleges. It has been exciting to see them being used to support Postgraduate Certificate programmes in teaching and learning for new academic staff and clinical teachers and also the skills training programmes for postgraduate students and Graduate Teaching Assistants (GTAs) who are beginning to teach. A less anticipated, but very valued, readership has been the experienced teachers who have dipped into the books when reviewing their teaching and have given the authors feedback and made further suggestions on teaching approaches and examples of practice.

KEY THEMES OF THE SERIES

The books are all attempting to combine two things – to be very practical and to provide lots of examples of methods and techniques and also to link to educational theory and underpinning research. Articles are referenced, further readings are suggested and researchers in the field are quoted.

There is also much enthusiasm here to link to the wide range of teaching development activities thriving in the disciplines, supported by the excellent work of the Higher Education Academy Subject Centres and the Centres for Excellence in Teaching and Learning (CETLs). Indeed both the Subject Centres and the CETLS are frequently recommended as further sources of information and suggested as useful points of contact, throughout the volumes. The need to tailor teaching approaches to meet the demands of different subject areas and to provide new teachers with examples of practice that are easily recognisable in their fields of study is seen as being very important by all the authors. To this end the books include many examples drawn from a wide range of academic subjects and different kinds of Higher Education Institution in the UK, USA and Australia in particular.

Although diversity is the particular focus for this volume, the theme of inclusive teaching is embraced in the other titles of the series too. Authors have considered the heterogeneous groups of students we now teach and have recognised their different expectations, approaches to study and learning needs. Student cohorts include people of different ages, experience, ability, culture, language, etc., and all the books include discussion of the issues and demands this places on teachers in today's universities. Where appropriate this may include guidance on current legislation and shared and developing views on the nature of good practice.

Series authors have also attempted to gaze into their crystal balls and look towards the future – what will our student groups look like in the future? What will lectures and seminars look like in ten or twenty years time? How will we assess and support our students? How will student expectations, government policy, funding streams, and new technological advances and legislation affect what happens in our learning spaces in the future? The books try to see beyond our current situation and think of the needs of tomorrow. One of the first books to be published in the series is currently being revised and we hope that the second edition of *Giving a Lecture*, with exciting new additions on podcasting and e-lectures, interactive handsets and the role of the lecture in a problem-based curriculum and the latest in audio visual aids, will be on the shelves very soon.

So these were the original ideas underpinning the series, and I and my co-authors have tried hard to keep them in mind as we researched our topics and typed away. We really hope that you find the books to be useful and interesting whether you are a new teacher, just starting out in your teaching career, or you are an experienced teacher reflecting on your practice and reviewing what you do.

Kate Exley
Series Editor

Acknowledgments

We would both like to thank the teachers and students who have genuinely informed our practice and our views on teaching and learning over the years.

We would like to thank Dr Jean McKendree, Hull York Medical School, for presentations to the University of York Postgraduate Certificate in Academic Practice (PGCAP) that helped structure and inform the content for Chapter 2; Professor Sue Mendus, Philosophy Department, University of York, for discussion on equity and fairness; colleagues in the northern network of PGcert leaders; and Wendelin Romer for looking at early drafts of the chapters.

For support in our 'day jobs' we are profoundly grateful to Lesley Catt, Dr Sylvia Hogarth and Professor Kristine Mason O'Connor.

Thanks too go to the team at Routledge–Taylor & Francis Group: Helen Pritt, Sarah Burrows, Meg Savin, Heather Jarrow and to other colleagues who have offered us timely and helpful advice on progressing this project. Particular thanks must go to Dr Kate Exley, the series editor. Without her wisdom, cheerfulness and sound advice this series would not have happened.

The data used in Chapter 1 are presented with permission from the Universities and Colleges Admissions Service (UCAS) and the Higher Education Statistics Agency (HESA). (HESA student records 1996–2006. Please note that HESA cannot accept responsibility for any inferences or conclusions derived from the data by third parties.) Microsoft product screen shots in Chapter 5 are reprinted with permission from Microsoft Corporation.

Last, but very definitely not least, to our children Justin and Theo (Grace) and Rebecca (Gravestock) and to our extremely supportive spouses Andrew and Penny. Without their patience and active support there would be no book.

Introduction

This volume of the *Key Guides for Effective Teaching in Higher Education* series is of critical importance to any discussion of learning and teaching in universities. Yet it is one of the most complex to address well. The main purpose of the volume is to encourage staff who are relatively new to higher education teaching (new lecturers, learning support staff or postgraduates who teach) to think through their teaching and carry it out in a manner that will minimise the risk of any student being disadvantaged for reasons beyond his or her control. The notion of fair treatment is explored throughout the text.

The terms *inclusion* and *diversity* have become suffused with specific and often politically loaded meaning. They have frequently become associated with particular aspects of higher education, such as widening participation initiatives, international or disabled students. However, we have used the terms in their broadest sense to mean issues relating to *all* students and to types of teaching and learning that fully and equitably include everyone in the classroom or in the programme cohort.

Clearly it is only practical for university support offices, such as a disability office or a widening participation office, to send out separate lists of requirements or guidelines; however, academics often struggle to deal with a plethora of separate instructions from different offices. From both the ideological and the practical points of view, we believe it is better for new academic staff to think holistically about inclusion and not just about dealing with one particular group of students or with any deficit model of student need. Having said this, we also recognise that there are times when particular features must be highlighted separately – such is the nature of identifying and embedding good practice.

1

We have used both terms (inclusion and diversity) because we believe that working inclusively is not quite the same as dealing with 'diverse' student groups. We cannot be 'difference blind' and we need to recognise the diverse needs of the different students in our programmes in order to help any student with a particular need. But we also need to celebrate and truly engage with these differences in a positive and constructive way. *Inclusivity* or *inclusion* implies this more positive dimension and a more all-embracing approach to our teaching.

It will be seen throughout the book that what is often extremely important is simply that there is a clear articulation of what is expected of, and what is offered to, students. Universities have long been shrouded in mystique; indeed the phrase 'ivory towers,' often used pejoratively about universities in the UK, US and elsewhere, implies isolation, perhaps even wilful isolation. Students who have little experience of the particular university culture they are in may struggle to understand and to find a way through unspoken, often long-established customs. Clearly some, such as international students or first generation students, are likely to find it still harder. An explanation of systems and processes is therefore essential if we are to reduce undue distress and uncertainty.

Having said this, universities around the world are working ever harder each day to attract, welcome and retain students. Academics often feel overwhelmed by the number of documents they are now expected to produce in order to clarify and articulate processes. We see the protection of space – both physical and intellectual – for academics as vital. The protection of research capacity for academics is an essential duty for universities if new academics are not to feel stretched beyond their limits. In our book we have tried to maintain an understanding that good teaching in universities cannot mean 24/7 availability to students of individual academics. Therefore, we have also tried to highlight the need for teachers to protect themselves if they are to work effectively.

We said in our first paragraph that this topic is immensely complex. In the UK there have recently been high-profile discussions about aspects of multiculturalism and teaching. Some of these – such as the wearing of the Muslim veil by female teachers in schools – have involved discussion at the very highest level and have led to court cases. These cases have demonstrated how utterly complex and contentious the interpretations and applications of 'inclusion' and 'diversity' can be. They relate to some of the most deeply rooted and emotive situations in society. Yet, at the other extreme, comments from individuals about how texts such as this are only 'common sense' or are aimed at 'spoonfeeding' students and reducing the intellectual rigour of university work are sometimes heard emanating from a small minority of cynical professionals. We therefore recognise the complexities and limitations of a text such as this. We also realise that readers are likely to range from those with world-leading knowledge in their academic field but little experience of teaching, to those with expert academic knowledge and experience of some aspects of this book. Thus the danger of seeming to oversimplify is large in a handbook of this size and range, but it is one that we are very much aware of. Our aim with what we have written is to stimulate enquiry and further study and critique.

Even those of us who, perhaps because of disciplinary expertise or personal politics and beliefs, are very aware of the philosophical issues relating to inclusion and diversity can still manage to forget to work inclusively while in the midst of hectic teaching, research and administration schedules. Throughout the process of writing this book the authors taught, and on more than one occasion realised they had omitted some appropriate action that might have helped them offer more inclusive teaching. As reflective professionals it is incumbent upon us to think through such omissions and rectify them for the next time. Sometimes even the dreaded 'tick boxes' help with this! This is one reason why we have offered a number of lists that can be used as aides-memoires should they be helpful – suspicious though we all tend to be of tick-box approaches.

There are often no correct answers for being inclusive in our teaching. Frequently, an action aimed at being more inclusive can inadvertently disadvantage another student. Our approach in this text is to offer information and guidelines on which to base best judgments. Our critical purpose is to ensure fairness and equity, but of course these very notions are often individually and culturally specific. Essentially this book is aimed at helping us all to think through specific situations and to make fair decisions.

We have said less about disciplinary differences in this book than we would have liked to, and we hope that staff will apply our ideas to their own disciplines as appropriate. Many of the Higher Education Academy Subject Centres (www.heacademy.ac.uk/ourwork/networks/subject centres) have published helpful guides with a specific disciplinary focus relating to issues of inclusion and diversity, and we hope that, in conjunction with this book, these additional resources will provide an appropriate disciplinary perspective to issues relating to inclusion.

Most of our material will need to be amended for your own situation – we are rarely prescriptive about the 'right way' to do something.

Perhaps the only situations where we are more prescriptive is where we speak of statutory obligation or institutional regulations. As academics we realise that even these should be open to debate – and in the long term may well be changed – but unless we wish to land ourselves and our institutions in deep trouble we will need to conform in those instances.

Throughout this book we have used the social model of disability as a way of underpinning our discussions in relation to all areas of inclusion and diversity. The social model proposes that the actions of society have imposed barriers that are responsible for disabling some people, and that changes in society's attitudes and actions may reduce, or remove, some of these disabling barriers. We discuss this issue in more detail in Chapter 1, and throughout the book we will describe practices that are easily implemented and do not require much cost – in terms of finances, time or effort – but that can have a potentially significant impact on students' ability to participate in higher education.

The book has been based upon the UK higher education system, since this is what has predominantly informed our backgrounds and experiences. However, we have tried to be aware that this does not mean they should be the dominant approaches. We have used research from worldwide sources to inform our thinking. It is clear that there are a number of nations whose thinking and experience on certain aspects of this book, such as multiculturalism, might be said to be more sophisticated since their experiences are wider and over a longer timescale. We feel there is much to learn from such places. We have been acutely aware of the realistic need to find the acceptable balance between pragmatism and principle – this is the very issue that faces teachers every day as they go about trying to work inclusively. Nonetheless, we hope that the broad principles in this book will be of relevance for staff in all global contexts.

STRUCTURE OF THE BOOK

In each chapter we offer an introduction to the general issues of teaching in an inclusive way for a diverse range of students. We offer some ideas to pursue in more depth and some guides to sources of additional and more specialised advice and more expert debate of issues. In order to follow the social model it was decided to approach this book by looking at the student life cycle, from the first days to the final days of the students. Our aim was to avoid tokenistic mentions of particular 'conditions' and to stress that most of what we advocate is good practice for all students. However, it was also clear that in a book of this nature readers may wish to use this resource as a reference text and use the index to check out particular features. For example, a reader may suddenly find they have a blind/vision-impaired student in their class, and the index will lead them to discussions on this in the chapters on small-group teaching, assessment and so on. What it cannot do is act as a comprehensive guide to all aspects of disability or other topics related to inclusion. Readers with such interests should think through our general principles and search the widely available specialist literature in these areas.

Chapters are interspersed with 'Pause for thought' sections, where it is hoped readers will stop and think through their own situation and apply some of the principles they have just read.

We hope that our introductory book on the topic of inclusion and diversity in higher education will help institutions and individuals to continue on the increasingly well-trodden path to a fair provision of university education for ALL students.

Chapter 1

Starting Off

Preparing to Meet Our Students

STUDENT DIVERSITY IN THE CLASSROOM

We would like to start this chapter by considering the range of students that we currently teach. In order to do this, let us picture one of our teaching sessions and consider the diversity within our student cohort. (If you have not had much experience of teaching to date then reflect on some of your own experiences as a student and remember one of your student classes.) Try to split the student group on the basis of identities – such as gender, age, ethnicity,[1] disability – and calculate the proportion of these identities. What is the range of diversity that you are aware of in the group?

Now consider what it is like when we walk into our first session with a new group of students. By scanning the room we may be able to determine some groupings based on visible individual identities such as gender and age. Some students' religious beliefs may be identifiable by the clothes or jewellery that they are wearing. Others may have a visible impairment, such as a wheelchair user or a student with a white stick and/or a guide dog. On the basis of these identities we might start to make a number of assumptions about our students' background, nature of prior learning and anticipated degree of participation; however, there are some potential problems with these assumptions.

What We Cannot See

Reflect upon what we cannot determine about our students, based on visual identities. For example, we may not be able easily to identify whether students are part-time or full-time, or whether they have a hidden impairment (e.g. dyslexia, dyscalculia). We might also find it hard to determine students' sexual orientation, religious beliefs or ethnicity.

Returning to your original estimation of diversity within your student group, you may know about some students with hidden impairments because you have been notified about this by your institution; however, what about students who have a hidden impairment but have not disclosed this to your institution? Some students may not wish to disclose an impairment, on the basis that they may feel – rightly or wrongly – that they will be discriminated against. Possible scenarios could include students with mental health difficulties, or perhaps epilepsy that is being controlled by medication.

Based on this possibility, do we need to reconsider the proportions of identities in our group? Are we still sure that we are aware of all the relevant identities?

Given the situation outlined above, it is sensible to assume that within our student cohort we will have students representing a number of identities and that we will not be able to identify them all visually. It is therefore important that the curriculum that we develop, the language and visual aids that we use, the materials that we distribute and the methods we use to engage students should be appropriate for a wide range of student identities.

Stereotyping

The *Oxford English Dictionary* describes stereotyping as 'something continued or constantly repeated without change'. It can be easy to make assumptions about groups of students, based on stereotypical characteristics that we may assign to particular identities, but we must not mindlessly assume that all our students conform to these images. These stereotypes might reflect our perception as to what the students will be able to do, or what their needs will be. These stereotypes could be based on our own previous experiences, impressions gained by characters in films or television programmes, or discussions with family, friends and colleagues. For example, we might assume that blind students will need handouts transposed into Braille, or that Chinese students are unlikely to challenge us because they respect the word of experts. Although there may be some students for whom these attributes apply, for example, we might have a blind student who does requires handouts to be transcribed into Braille, there will be many others for whom this is not applicable.

There may be, however, genuine differences in traditions that may mean our students are struggling to adapt, and these need to be addressed. Our students will need to understand, and have explained to them, the expectation that they will challenge the academic ideas of those seen to be prestigious scholars. We must check precisely where the individual students concerned are located intellectually on all this and not simply assume.

 PAUSE FOR THOUGHT

Consider your own ethnicity. Would you say that everyone who shares your ethnicity is the same? How do you react to stereotypes based on your ethnicity? Do you conform to the stereotypical view? If you don't – and we strongly suspect that this is the case – how do you think it feels to your students if you impose similar assumptions on them?

Hopefully it should be clear why it is important to consider all our students as individuals. In time we are likely to get to know their names and may get to know some of them well. The more we know about our students the more we will realise that they all bring their own individual attributes to the classroom and the more we will begin to appreciate how inappropriate it is to make assumptions based on broad categories and identities.

DIVERSITY STATISTICS

Hopefully, by reading through the previous sections you have started to consider the range of different identities in your own classroom, but how likely are we to have a diverse classroom and how are the proportions of identities that you identified at the start of this chapter reflected in the statistics?

Figures from the UK Higher Education Statistics Agency (HESA) show that the percentage of undergraduate disabled students and students from ethnic minorities in UK higher education institutions has generally been increasing for a number of years, probably as a result of national widening participation agendas. Figure 1.1 demonstrates some of these trends.

Similar trends can also be seen in the data for postgraduate students, although the percentage figures for disabled students and ethnic minority

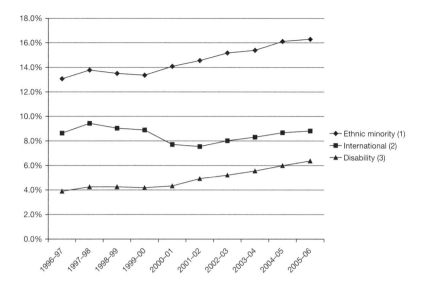

FIGURE 1.1 Percentage trends for UK undergraduate students in relation to ethnic minority, international students and disabled students. Data from HESA (www.hesa.ac.uk/)

Notes:
1   Data for ethnic minority students are based on first year UK domiciled undergraduates and are taken as a percentage of those students for whom ethnicity is known.
2   Data for international students are based on figures for all undergraduates in UK higher education institutions and include students from European and non-European countries.
3   Data for disabled students are based on first-year UK domiciled undergraduates and are taken as a percentage of those students known to have a disability. Note that these data will be an under-representation of first-year UK domiciled undergraduate students, as some students will not disclose that they are disabled.

students are slightly lower than those for undergraduates (2005–2006 data: disabled students – 5.1 per cent compared with 6.4 per cent; ethnic minority students – 15.1 per cent compared with 16.3 per cent).

The percentages for female/male undergraduate students and full-time/part-time undergraduate students are shown in Figure 1.2, and clearly show that there has been a general decrease in the number of full-time students and an increase in the proportion of female students entering higher education.

In terms of the age range of our students, Table 1.1 shows the percentages of different age groups for accepted applications to higher education institutions for a five year period.

9

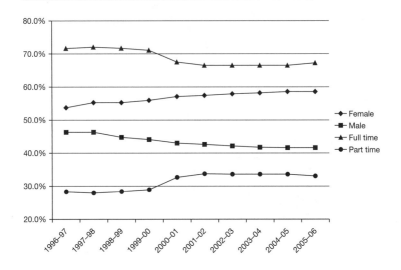

▓ **FIGURE 1.2** Percentage trends for UK undergraduate students in relation to gender and type of study. Data are all undergraduates in UK higher education institutions and include students from European and non-European countries. Data from HESA (www.hesa.ac.uk/)

Although it is clear from Table 1.1 that the greatest proportion of students entering higher education is in the 20 and under category, it is worth remembering that approximately 20 per cent of all applicants would be classed as 'mature' and are likely to bring with them a range of experiences that may not be directly related to academia.

▓ **TABLE 1.1** Age of accepted applicants, taken at the end of the September before entry to higher education (%)

	2002	2003	2004	2005	2006
20 and under	79.8	79.7	80.1	80.3	79.8
21–24	9.9	9.8	9.6	9.5	9.7
25–39	8.1	8.3	8.1	8.0	8.1
40 and over	2.1	2.2	2.2	2.2	2.3

Data from UCAS (www.ucas.ac.uk/he_staff/stat_services1/)

TABLE 1.2 Percentage of female/male and UK-domiciled/
international students studying different discipline areas in UK higher
education institutions for 2005–2006 (%)*

Subject	Female students	Male students	UK domiciled students	International students
Medicine & dentistry	57.8	42.2	86.1	13.9
Subjects allied to medicine	82.1	17.9	93.9	6.1
Biological sciences	64.1	35.9	90.7	9.3
Veterinary science	72.8	27.2	87.1	12.9
Agriculture & related subjects	58.0	42.0	87.7	12.3
Physical sciences	42.0	58.0	87.7	12.2
Mathematical sciences	37.7	62.3	82.5	17.5
Computer science	23.2	76.8	82.2	17.8
Engineering & technology	15.8	84.2	70.3	29.7
Architecture, building & planning	30.6	69.4	84.5	15.5
Social studies	62.0	38.0	85.2	14.8
Law	59.2	40.8	82.3	17.7
Business & administrative studies	49.2	50.8	72.5	27.5
Mass communications & documentation	58.9	41.1	85.6	14.4
Languages	67.5	32.5	85.4	14.6
Historical & philosophical studies	54.7	45.3	91.6	8.3
Creative arts & design	60.7	39.3	89.1	10.9
Education	74.1	25.9	93.8	6.2

*The percentages are based on data for postgraduate and undergraduate students.

Data from HESA (www.hesa.ac.uk/)

Figures 1.1 and 1.2 and Table 1.1 show overall trends for higher education students, but they do not demonstrate the differences that may be present between different disciplines. The nature of different discipline subjects will mean that they will appeal to particular groups of students, and may even put off others. As an example, Table 1.2 shows the breakdown of data for female/male and UK/international students in different discipline areas for the 2005–2006 academic year.

The data clearly show that if we are teaching in one of the subjects allied to medicine (Anatomy, Physiology, Pathology, Nursing, etc.) then we are likely to have a larger proportion of female students in our class, whereas if we teach engineering or technology subjects we are more likely to encounter a higher proportion of male students and a higher than average proportion of international students.

BARRIERS TO LEARNING

Having looked at the range of diversity that may be present in our student cohort, it would be sensible to consider what barriers exist in relation to students' learning and participation in higher education.

The activity below demonstrates that many students will encounter some form of barrier to learning during their time in higher education, and that some of the barriers that we may typically attribute as issues relating to particular groups of students, for example, disabled students or international students, may also be present for other groups of students. By recognising these barriers, we should be able to reduce, or remove, their impact on student learning through careful design and delivery of our courses.

In focusing on barriers, it is useful to consider the social model of disability (Oliver, 1996; UPIAS, 1976). The social model considers disability as an issue related to the attitudes and the actions of society as a whole. This differs from the medical model of disability that considers the issue of disability in terms of the individual, that is to say an individual has an illness or disability that is the subject of medical scrutiny in terms of looking for a 'cure'. The medical model does not consider other aspects of the individual, such as intelligence, potential for achievement or ability to communicate. Thus, in terms of the social model, society has imposed barriers upon some people that could be removed, or the impact of them could be reduced. Examples of barriers could include the impact of stairs or roadside kerbs on wheelchair users; by putting in place ramps and dropped kerbs society has removed these potential barriers. Something

ACTIVITY

The following are quotes from disabled and non-disabled students in response to the question 'Are there any barriers to learning that you have experienced?' Try to identify which quotes were made by disabled students and which were made by non-disabled students:

1   I have had difficulty with understanding what is expected of me for some assignments and even when I asked the lecturers it wasn't any clearer at all.

2   I have had one assignment back – the lecturer's comments were written in such appalling handwriting I was not able to read it. This is not useful . . . we have to word process our work so it's easy to read.

3   Lecturers tend to remove notes from the overhead before I get time to finish copying.

4   Sometimes lecturers don't explain fully some of the jargon that they use.

5   In some of the rooms it has been difficult to hear staff.

6   I can sometimes have too much information to take in.

7   Three hour lectures without a break.

8   I just find reading and writing assignments very hard, it seems to take me longer than everyone else. I have to try very hard!

9   Some lecturing staff put comments on work that I would find it hard to improve on. For example, 'grammar and comprehension need improving'.

10 It makes it quite difficult when notes for lectures are not on the server prior to a lecture. It is far easier to make notes on the handout.

11 Sometimes lecturers' accents can get in the way of understanding the subject.

12 Participation in a seminar when understanding of material is required within a time constraint, for example, research papers given during seminars with the expectation of discussing it in detail during the same seminar.

13 Ambiguous questions are asked, hindering the process of completing the tasks because it takes time understanding what is required.

14 I am slow at writing and written exams are not to my benefit.

Student quotes from research undertaken by Professor Mary Fuller, Dr Andrew Bradley and Professor Mick Healey, University of Gloucestershire, and funded by the Economic and Social Research Council and the Teaching Quality Enhancement Fund.

Answers: (D = disabled student, ND = non-disabled student) 1 – ND; 2 – ND; 3 – D; 4 – D; 5 – ND; 6 – ND; 7 – ND; 8 – ND; 9 – D; 10 – ND; 11 – ND; 12 – D; 13 – ND; 14 – ND.

From Gravestock (2006a: 15–16)

that should also become apparent throughout this book, in relation to barriers associated with teaching, learning and assessment, is that the removal of barriers for one group of people often benefits others. The removal of the barriers in the example given above would also be of benefit to parents with children in a pushchair. However, it is worth noting that while some adjustments will assist some users, they may cause new, or additional, problems for others. In terms of teaching, learning and assessment issues, it is therefore important that we evaluate all adjustments to ensure that they are having the desired impact on all students.

Our use of the social model of disability results in the terminology used throughout this book to describe disability. The term *disabled people* is used, as this describes the way that society has created the disabling barriers, that is to say that people are being disabled. Disabled people have *impairments* rather than *disabilities*, for example, a vision impairment. It should be noted, however, that some disabled people prefer the term *people with disabilities*, as this puts the person first. Our advice would be to use the social model terminology in your classroom literature and discussions, as there is a basis for this phraseology, but accept the fact that some of your disabled students may have a personal preference for alternative terminology.

The social model itself has become a contentious issue, with some writers (e.g. Shakespeare, 2006) suggesting that by focusing on the barriers created by society the model ignores the real lived experience of people with impairments. Some of these impairments may cause severe pain that cannot be easily reduced by the removal of barriers by society. While acknowledging that physical and mental impairments will have a very real impact on the everyday lives of students in higher education, we feel that consideration of teaching, learning and assessment issues in terms of the social model allows us to reflect on whether we are unintentionally creating a barrier that could be removed or have its impact reduced.

COMMUNICATING WITH YOUR STUDENTS

The nature of our communication has the potential to act as a barrier to enabling full participation from a diverse student group. The language that we use in class or in our course materials, either relating to academic processes of discipline-based issues, can have a large impact upon the level of engagement and participation of students in our curriculum. We need to be able to express our ideas and instructions in a language that all students are able to understand if we are to develop an inclusive curriculum. The issue of communication will also be discussed in subsequent chapters, but at this point it is important to consider more general issues relating to communication such as academic terminology.

Academic Terminology: What Do You Want Your Students To Do?

Prior to the introduction of widening participation agendas and the general expansion of the higher education system, it might have been reasonable to assume that the majority of students enrolling onto our courses would be straight out of school or college, perhaps having taken a year off. Given this background, it might also have been reasonable to assume that the students would be arriving into higher education with a certain level of skills and disciplinary knowledge, based on syllabuses set by the examination boards. Armed with this information, a lecturer could design their curriculum based on a reasonable assumption of the students' prior experiences, skills and disciplinary knowledge.

Depending upon the nature of the institution where you teach, this may no longer be the case. We have already started to consider the diverse range of students present in our classrooms, and this brings with it an equally diverse range of prior skills, disciplinary knowledge and experiences, either in general terms or in relation to teaching and learning strategies used prior to entry into higher education. We are therefore not able to assume that students, from any particular group, will be familiar with all our academic terminology, conventions and procedures. For example, our classes may contain a high proportion of students who have recently left school with good grades in their examinations, but they may also contain some mature students who may not have been academically successful when they were at school but who may have a wealth of relevant experience from the workplace (see Table 1.1). The former set of students may be familiar with some of the academic procedures used in higher education, as these may be similar to their experiences at school; the latter set of students may not. It is therefore important that we do not assume that all our students will understand what we mean when we introduce particular terminology.

Related to the above, consider the language that we use to describe what we want the students to do. Something that may seem fairly self-explanatory to us may not be as clear to all students. This is particularly important in relation to questions set for assessment (see Chapter 9).

15

PAUSE FOR THOUGHT

Take a moment to reflect on the curriculum that you intend the students to study. What existing level of skills is assumed? For example, is it assumed that students are aware of the following?:

- Effective methods of taking notes.
- The purpose of, and difference between, a tutorial and a seminar.
- How to structure an essay.
- The difference between collaboration and collusion.
- Referencing and citing sources.
- Obtaining relevant information from books, journal articles and online sources.
- Time management procedures in relation to the preparation and submission of course work.
- What is required from them during fieldwork.
- How to use a computer, for example, for word-processing.

These are just a few examples of some assumptions that might be made. Some students will be aware of these issues and distinctions, but certainly not all.

How can we help our students to deconstruct what we want them to do for an assignment? Do they really know what we mean by 'critically analyse' or 'reflect'? A clear explanation of process and a willingness to engage in discussion with students about these processes are essential to ensure that all our students are able to participate to the full extent of their ability. As noted by Haggis (2006) this is not 'spoon feeding', as 'only content information can be delivered by the spoonful' (Haggis, 2006: 532).

In addition to language associated with general academic procedures, there is the issue of disciplinary discourses. We may be familiar with this discourse, owing to our own immersion in the discipline over a period of years, but it may not have much meaning for all our students; for example, some of the discourses may be country-specific and may not mean much to international students. We all want our students to be fluent in the disciplinary discourse by the time that they leave higher education, but there are ways in which this can be introduced gradually so that all students are able to engage with, learn and use the language appropriately.

16

Preparation of Materials

Specific issues relating to the preparation and production of materials will be introduced in subsequent chapters. At this point we would like to introduce some general issues to consider when producing accessible materials. The main aim when creating and designing any materials for students is to be flexible. For example, how easy will it be for us to convert our materials to another format, change the point size or the font? The vast majority of materials presented to students nowadays are produced in electronic format, and this makes it easy to convert these resources into other formats, such as Braille or for scanning by a screen reader. It also means that, if the electronic document itself is available to students, then they will be able to make the required changes to the style of the document and can use online translation software to convert the text to other languages if necessary.

General points to consider when producing materials are as follows:

1 Restrict your use of different fonts within a single document.
2 The point size should not be too small (11 or 12 point is the standard minimum, depending upon the font).
3 Use left alignment of paragraphs, as this maintains a regular spacing between words. Do not use justified paragraphs (i.e. alignment of left and right sides), as this distorts the lengths of words and spaces.
4 Allow wide margins and spaces between paragraphs and do not be afraid of white space on a page.
5 Use lists to reduce the density of text on a page. If there are several items in the list consider using numbered lists, rather than bullet points, as this makes it easier to refer to specific items (e.g. the fifth point).
6 Avoid overuse of italics and underlining, as these can make words 'flow together'.
7 Use lower, or mixed, case text, as a block of words in upper case can be difficult to read.

(Adapted from Gravestock, 2006b)

Course Publicity and Marketing

The way in which we advertise our courses can have an impact on the nature of the students who subsequently enrol. The use of language, images and photographs may provide some subtle clues about the students to whom we hope the course will appeal. For example, in a study of exclusionary features relating to the participation of disabled students in fieldwork, Hall *et al.* (2002) noted the content of photographs used in publicity literature for geography field trips. Many of these photographs depicted young, active, non-disabled male students striding up steep hills and abseiling off bridges. Although such images may be appealing to a particular, although possibly small, group of students, it is likely that they would have been off-putting for disabled students, female students or mature students, who may have felt that such trips were not appropriate for them. It is therefore important that the images used in marketing courses show an appropriate range of students, without being tokenistic towards particular identities. Similar arguments can be made regarding the language used to accompany such images.

It is also worth noting that some aspects of legislation, for example, the UK Disability Discrimination Act, include a requirement for accessible and appropriate publicity in relation to attracting students onto courses:

> Education providers need to consider carefully what information should be included in advertisements and promotional materials and where they should be placed. This is necessary both to encourage disabled applicants and to avoid breaching the discriminatory advertisement provisions.
>
> (DRC, 2007a: 28, para. 2.27)

The Act says that, when advertising a course, it is unlawful for the education provider offering the course to publish an advertisement (or cause an advertisement to be published) which indicates, or might reasonably be understood to indicate:

- that the success of a person's application for the course may depend to any extent on his not having any disability, or any particular disability; or
- that the person determining the application is reluctant to make reasonable adjustments.

> (DRC, 2007a: 141, para. 8.15)

Other aspects of legislation may mean that marketing materials, for example, relating to admissions, do not make references to very specific criteria. An example of this may relate to age: the marketing materials for an institution or course would be safer to state 'the institution/course welcomes applications from people of all ages' rather than stating specific minimum and/or maximum age limits (ECU, 2006).

WHAT ABOUT YOU?

So far this chapter has concentrated on the range of identities in our student groups, but the other important factor to bear in mind is *you*. What are your identities?

We all come with 'baggage', for example, our own cultural beliefs and feelings, the way in which we have been taught at school, college and university and personal interactions with diverse groups of people. It is important to recognise these experiences and to reflect on how they interact with the way we design and develop our curriculum and the way in which we teach.

By thinking through some specific questions (see Pause for Thought, overleaf), we hope that you will be able to reflect on issues relating to inclusivity that have affected you in the past. We also hope that you will be able to reflect on your personal teaching and learning philosophy and to consider the aspects of your past experiences that have contributed towards this.

OTHER ISSUES

It is worth mentioning that, in addition to some of the diversity issues discussed above, something that will affect all students' behaviour, concentration, attitude and ability to learn are issues from outside the classroom. Higher education is not a closed system, and we may find that we have students who, for example:

1   are worried about financial issues, or who may have been the victim of identity fraud;
2   recently lost a close friend or relative;
3   act as a carer for a relative or partner;
4   have relationship problems;
5   have left home for the first time and are home-sick;
6   are considering whether to come out to their friends;
7   have a temporary illness or injury;
8   are considering disclosing an impairment;
9   are drinking excessively, or are taking drugs, possibly owing to peer pressure.

PAUSE FOR THOUGHT

Consider the following questions and prompts, and reflect on your own 'baggage':

General

- How would you describe your own identities, such as gender, ethnicity, religious beliefs and so on?
- Would you say that your identities changed over time? If so, how?
- How would you describe other aspects of your life (if not included above), such as family role, interests and abilities, occupation, voluntary roles?
- What experiences do you have of interacting with people from other ethnicities?
- Do you have any personal experiences of discrimination (either relating directly to you, or members of your family, friends, colleagues, etc.)? How did these experiences make you feel? Have they affected the way that you interact with other people?

Teaching and Learning

- How have your identities, interests and abilities influenced the way that you:
  - behaved as a student?
  - behave as a lecturer?
- How were you taught as a student? How is this reflected in your current, or intended, teaching methodologies?
- What assumptions have you made/do you make, regarding students and their abilities (either as individuals or groups)?
- What is your personal philosophy for teaching, learning and assessment? How has this been influenced by your life experiences?

Questions adapted from Apthorp *et al.* (2006) and OpenLearn (2006)

It is useful to reflect on the fact that we all encounter situations in our lives when we are not able to concentrate, work or study to our full ability. Thankfully such situations are often temporary and can be caused by a range of situations, including personal issues, illness – even a bad hangover – through to a broken limb or even issues associated with mental health difficulties (e.g. stress). It is therefore important to remember that sometimes a student's behaviour may be related to situations outside the classroom, and this topic will be addressed in more detail in Chapter 7.

A QUICK NOTE ABOUT LEGISLATION

To end this chapter, we thought it would be useful to outline some of the current legislation relating to inclusion and diversity issues in the United Kingdom. Much of this information comes from the Equality and Human Rights Commission (www.equalityhumanrights.com/) and the Equality Challenge Unit (www.ecu.ac.uk/), which provide information and guidance in relation to the legislation, along with links to resources and projects.

Age

The Employment Equality (Age) Regulations 2006
(www.opsi.gov.uk/si/si2006/20061031.htm)
The age equality legislation prohibits discrimination, harassment and victimisation on the grounds of age. Discrimination is classed as either: direct, where an individual or group is treated less favourably than others because of their age; or indirect, where institutional criteria, provision or practice disadvantages people of a particular age (ECU, 2006). In terms of student admissions, it is important to note that the legislation does not distinguish between admission to an institution and admission onto a course. This means that an institution could be liable to legal action if it allowed a student into the institution, but then did not allow them onto a particular course for a reason relating to age.

Some courses may require a certain level of physical fitness, for example, for fieldwork or sports-related activities. For such courses it is advised that the regulations state the fitness level necessary to participate in the course, rather than assuming that people over a certain age will not be at the required level.

It is possible that the institution where you teach may state a limit for the minimum age at entry, for example, 17 years. Such limits need to be justified, particularly as students from some countries may be younger than this minimum age limit because of the nature of the school/qualification structure in their country of study.

21

Disability

The Disability Discrimination Act (DDA) 2005
(www.opsi.gov.uk/acts/acts2005/20050013.htm)
Under the terms of the DDA, a person is disabled if they have:

> a physical or mental impairment which has an effect on his or her ability to carry out normal day-to-day activities. That effect must be:
> * substantial (that is, more than minor or trivial);
> * adverse;
> * long term (that is, it has lasted or is likely to last for at least a year or for the rest of the life of the person affected).
> (DRC, 2007a: 31–32)

People with conditions such as human immunodeficiency virus (HIV), cancer and multiple sclerosis are covered by the Act from the point of diagnosis, rather than the point at which the condition starts to impact on their day-to-day activities.

The aim of the DDA is to:

> * prohibit discrimination and harassment against disabled people;
> * ensure that 'reasonable adjustments' are put in place for disabled people;
> * ensure full and equal participation in learning and public life.
> (DRC, 2007b: 17)

Part 4 of the DDA applies to education and identifies four types of discrimination:

1   Direct discrimination, that is to say less favourable treatment of a disabled person on the grounds of their disability.
2   Failure to make a reasonable adjustment. Under the Act, 'the duty to make reasonable adjustments arises where:

> (a) a provision, criterion or practice, other than a competence standard, applied by or on behalf of the education provider; or
> (b) any physical feature of premises occupied by the education provider places disabled persons at a substantial disadvantage compared with people who are not disabled' (DRC, 2007a:

62). A 'competence standard' is 'an academic, medical, or other standard applied by or on behalf of an education provider for the purpose of determining whether or not a person has a particular level of competence or ability' (DRC, 2007a: 98).

3   Disability-related discrimination, that is to say less favourable treatment of a disabled person for a reason relating to their impairment.

4   Victimisation and harassment. The Act prohibits victimisation against anyone, regardless of whether or not they have a disability or impairment, and aims to protect all students who make, or support, a claim for discrimination from reprisal. Harassment may relate, for example, to the use of derogatory terms used to describe a disabled student that would humiliate them. It would still count as harassment even if the student was not present to hear the terms being used (DRC, 2007a,b).

The distinction between direct discrimination – on the grounds of a disability – and disability-related discrimination – for a reason relating to a disability/impairment – is important. An example of the former could relate to a stereotypical viewpoint about what a student will or will not be able to do; for example, an assumption that blind students cannot use computers. The latter is discrimination relating to a specific impairment; for example, not allowing a student with mental health difficulties to bring their medication onto university property because there is a policy that prohibits any drugs on the premises (DRC, 2007a).

It is possible that you may encounter references to the Special Educational Needs and Disability Act (SENDA) (2001). This Act has effectively become Part 4 of the DDA (2005), and it is therefore appropriate to refer to the DDA when discussing disability legislation, rather than SENDA.

Gender

The Sex Discrimination Act 1975

(www.opsi.gov.uk/acts/acts1975/PDF/ukpga_19750065_en.pdf)
The Act prohibits any discrimination on the grounds of sex, and relates to existing students within an institution and to offers made to prospective students.

23

Race

The Race Relations Act 1976 (Amendment) Regulations
2003 (www.opsi.gov.uk/si/si2003/20031626.htm)
The Act requires higher education institutions to:

- eliminate unlawful discrimination;
- promote equality of opportunity;
- promote good race relations between persons of different racial groups.

There are four types of discrimination under the Act:

1. *Direct*. Direct discrimination occurs when a person is treated less favourably on racial grounds compared with someone from a different racial group who has been, or would have been, treated more favourably in a similar situation. Racist abuse and harassment are forms of direct discrimination.
2. *Indirect*. Indirect discrimination can occur on the grounds of:

    (a) colour or nationality; for example, Sikh men who wear a turban could be exempt from regulations that prohibit the wearing of headgear in classes;
    (b) race, ethnic or national origin; for example, when provision, criteria or practice that appear to have nothing to do with race are applied equally to everyone and put people of the same race or ethnic or national origins at a particular disadvantage when compared with others.

3. *Victimisation*. In a similar manner to the DDA (see above), victimisation occurs if a person is treated less favourably than others because they have complained about racial discrimination, or supported someone who has.
4. *Harassment*. Under the Act, harassment is based on the grounds of race or ethnic or national origins, but not colour or nationality. Harassment occurs when someone violates a person's dignity or creates an intimidating or hostile, degrading, humiliating or offensive environment for them.

(Equality & Human Rights Commission,
www.equalityhumanrights.com/)

Religion and Belief

Religious freedom is covered by a number of Acts that include the:

- **Employment Equality (Religion or Belief) Regulations 2003** (www.opsi.gov.uk/si/si2003/20031660.htm)
- **Racial and Religious Hatred Act 2006** (www.opsi.gov. uk/acts/acts2006/pdf/ukpga_20060001_en.pdf)
- **Equality Act 2006** (www.opsi.gov.uk/acts/acts2006/pdf/ ukpga_20060003_en.pdf)

Under the Equality Act 2006, *religion or belief* applies to 'any religion, or religious or philosophical belief'. The Act also covers issues such as student accommodation and dietary requirements.

Sexual Orientation

The Equality Act (Sexual Orientation) Regulations 2007
(www.opsi.gov.uk/si/si2007/uksi_20071263_en_1)
The Act prohibits any discrimination on the grounds of sexual orientation and relates to existing students within an institution and to offers made to prospective students.

Transsexual

Gender Recognition Act 2004
(www.opsi.gov.uk/acts/acts2004/20040007.htm)
This Act provides legal protection for anyone over the age of 18 who makes an application for a gender recognition certificate. Certificates are granted if the applicant:

- has, or has had, gender dysphoria;
- has lived in the acquired gender for two years ending with the date on which the application is made;
- intends to continue to live in the acquired gender until death;
- complies with the requirements imposed by section 2 (which are formal evidence requirements) or with any requirements imposed by the Panel under section 2 (which is any further additional evidence required by the Panel).

(Equality Challenge Unit, www.ecu.ac.uk/guidance/trans/legislation.htm)

The Sex Discrimination (Gender Reassignment) Regulations 1999 (www.opsi.gov.uk/si/si1999/19991102.htm)
These regulations provide legal protection for those students who:

- intend to undergo gender reassignment;
- are undergoing gender reassignment;
- have at some time in the past undergone gender reassignment.

CONCLUSION

Hopefully this chapter has provided some prompts for us to consider the nature of our student cohort, and to reflect upon the range of diversity that may be present in our classes. Also, by considering our own background it is hoped that we will be able to reflect upon the way that we work with our students. Do we react in the same way to all our students? Are there situations where we think that we might react in a particular way because of a lack of knowledge about a subject, for example, a particular impairment, and a fear that we might do something, or say something, wrong? How does this relate to our own background and experience, or perhaps a lack of experience working with particular groups of students?

What we would suggest, on the basis of the information presented in this chapter, is not to make assumptions about students' needs and requirements. Although we need to be anticipatory in our duty to all students, there is no substitute for talking to students themselves and discussing their requirements. Providing students with opportunities to discuss and identify strategies that may assist them in participating and learning to their full potential could assist in establishing an atmosphere that encourages disclosure and discussion about issues relating to diversity and inclusion.

NOTE

1 Ethnicity can depend upon a number of factors that include:

1 country of birth;
2 nationality;
3 language spoken at home;
4 parents' country of birth in conjunction with country of birth;
5 skin colour;
6 national/geographical origin;
7 racial group;
8 religion.

(Office for National Statistics, 2003)

FURTHER READING

The following publications provide information about issues related to inclusion and diversity in higher education:

Adams, M. and Brown, S. (eds) (2006) *Towards Inclusive Learning in Higher Education: Developing curricula for disabled students*, Abingdon: Routledge.

Arshad, R. (2006) 'Race Equality Toolkit: Learning and teaching', Edinburgh: Universities Scotland. Available at www.universities-scotland.ac.uk/raceequalitytoolkit/.

Carroll, J. and Ryan, J. (eds) (2005) *Teaching International Students: Improving learning for all*, Abingdon: Routledge.

Cavanagh, S. and Dickinson, Y. (2006) 'Disability Legislation: Practical guidance for academics', London: Equality Challenge Unit and The Higher Education Academy. Available at www.ecu.ac.uk/publications/.

Duke, C. (ed.) (2005) *The Tertiary Moment: What road to inclusive higher education*, Leicester: NIACE.

Gallacher, J. and Osborne, M. (eds) (2005) *A Contested Landscape: International perspectives on diversity in mass higher education*, Leicester: NIACE.

Hale, F. (ed.) (2004) *What Makes Racial Diversity Work in Higher Education: Academic leaders present successful policies and strategies*, Sterling, VA: Stylus Publishing.

Landsman, J. and Lewis, C.W. (eds) (2006) *White Teachers/Diverse Classrooms*, Sterling, VA: Stylus Publishing.

Law, I., Phillips, D. and Turney, L. (eds) (2004) *Institutional Racism in Higher Education*, Stoke-on-Trent: Trentham Books.

Ouellett, M.L. (ed.) (2005) *Teaching Inclusively: Resources for course, department and institutional change in higher education*, Stillwater: New Forums Press.

Parry, E. and Tyson, S. (2007) 'The Impact of Age Discrimination Legislation on the Higher Education Sector: A literature review'. Available at www.ecu.ac.uk/publications/guidancepublications/200701-ImpactofAgeDiscrimination.pdf.

Pollak, D. (2005) *Dyslexia, The Self and Higher Education: Learning life histories of students identified as dyslexic*, London: Trentham Books.

Powell, S. (ed.) (2003) *Special Teaching in Higher Education: Successful strategies for access and inclusion*, London: Kogan Page.

Riddell, S., Tinklin, T. and Wilson, A. (2005) *Disabled Students in Higher Education: Perspectives on widening access and changing policy*, Abingdon: Routledge.

Talbert, C. (2004) *Equality, Diversity and Inclusivity: Curriculum matters*, SEDA special 16, Birmingham: Staff and Educational Development Association.

Turney, L., Law, I. and Phillips, D. (2002) 'Institutional Racism in Higher Education Toolkit Project: Building the anti-racist HEI', Leeds: Centre for Ethnicity and Racism Studies. Available at www.leeds.ac.uk/CERS/toolkit/toolkit.htm.

 ## USEFUL WEB RESOURCES

Inclusive Curriculum Project (Geography Discipline Network)

A series of ten guides (nine for staff, one for students) designed to support disabled students. The guides are aimed at staff in the Geography, Earth and Environmental Sciences disciplines, but the information contained within them will be useful to a broader audience. Also, although primarily aimed at supporting disabled students, many of the practical suggestions will be of benefit to other student groups: www2.glos.ac.uk/gdn/icp/gdlist.htm.

Strategies for Creating Inclusive Programmes of Study (SCIPS)

A resource primarily aimed at teachers and trainers in higher education that offers strategies for promoting inclusive teaching, learning and assessment. Although aimed at disabled students, the advice presented is relevant to a broader group of students: www.scips.worc.ac.uk/.

 ## Statistics

Australia

- Australian Government Department for Education, Employment and Workplace Relations: www.dest.gov.au/sectors/higher_education/default2.htm.

USA

- National Centre for Education Statistics, located within the US Department of Education and the Institute of Education Sciences: http://nces.ed.gov/index.asp.

UK

- Higher Education Statistics Agency (HESA): www.hesa.ac.uk/
- Universities and Colleges Admissions Service (UCAS): www.ucas.ac.uk/.

Chapter 2

Some Educational Principles Underpinning Inclusive Learning and Teaching

By way of a contrast to our preceding chapter, in this section we will consider a number of general educational principles and theories. These will serve as our rationale for suggesting an inclusive approach to teaching. While many academics do not have time or inclination to study educational theory to a high level, neither do they generally want prescriptive or ill-conceived educational models imposed upon them. Clearly most academics wish to know how a certain approach can be justified. We cannot, in this text, focus on educational research in depth, but in our summary we will flag up themes and further reading that you can pursue and critique if you are interested.

The educational principles identified in this section underpin much of the practice suggested elsewhere in the book. We have often connected them to small-group teaching in preparation for the subsequent chapter, but they also support our approaches to academic and personal supervision and to teaching large or online groups.

HOW DO SOME WELL-KNOWN THEORIES AND PRACTICES OF LEARNING SUPPORT THE NOTION OF INCLUSIVE LEARNING?

It has been clear from what we have said so far that the learning of the individual – staff and students – is at the heart of the approach to this book. Our approach is underpinned by a number of theories about learning. For example, small-group teaching 'can clearly support a "constructive" approach to learning'. Constructivism has at its heart the view that individual students construct or build their own knowledge and understanding rather than simply acquiring it 'pre-packaged and ready made' (Phillips, 2000, cited in Exley and Dennick, 2004b: 5).

This book is also particularly concerned with learning that is transformational – that is to say, learning that goes beyond gaining factual knowledge to creating real change in the learner. It is learning that involves questioning assumptions, values, beliefs and so on.

A survey of the UK Quality Assurance Agency subject benchmarks suggests that most higher education learning in the UK actually aspires to be transformative. Freire (1972), Habermas (1984) and Mezirow (1991) and have all produced theories that relate to this notion, and although there are debates over precise meanings and differences that need not be explored here it is sufficient to say that, even at its simplest, it is a useful notion for higher education. The notion of critical reflection as part of the learning process is also key to the work of Mezirow and others (Mezirow, 1991). Reflective learning, at its most basic, means asking oneself questions about the process that one has undertaken in order to learn something. One must then determine and act upon these learning points for the future in order to continue to develop and learn more effectively. Such a process is more than mere introspection because, in order to learn most effectively, we need to link our critical self-evaluations of how we are learning to 'evidence' of what we are achieving. In relation to learning that might be that we are remembering key points or we understand a concept that we did not understand previously. This process is a form of self-assessment. We link this to effective use of feedback with students in Chapter 9, and such self-evaluation is critical in learning. We can help our students enhance this process.

Action learning is as above, where the student interrogates his or her own learning processes and builds on that experience to learn more. The learner is not simply a passive recipient in the process. Thus action learning is another term that is often associated with transformational learning and in turn with small-group work. Small-group teaching is, these days, generally taken to be synonymous with an interactive experience of learning. We will also see that, in these respects, the small group/large group distinction can be a false one. Based on the educational philosophies outlined above, large groups can and should also be interactive; it is probably just that the balance of transmission of knowledge and interaction is significantly different. However, in a small group the expectation that all learners in the group will be fully engaged is normally far higher.

Linked to the above learning concepts has often been the notion of andragogy. Do we consider our students adults? A number of educationalists in the last forty years have seen adult learning as different to that of children. Since most students at university in the UK, US and Australia are legally adults, such a concept might be a significant feature affecting our practice in universities. However, we realise that notions of 'coming of age' are different throughout the world. For example, this can be particularly significant in some religions where adulthood can be understood to exist in those as young as 13 years old. Whether or not there are, or should be, distinctions in the way people learn – based on notions of adulthood and childhood – is therefore problematic internationally and cannot be our main concern here. Nonetheless, it is important to register that culturally (and intellectually) very many of our students are on the cusp of change – from lifestyles associated with parental control and lack of autonomy to legal adult status and more freedom. Others of our students will very clearly be 'adult' in years. Andragogy has been associated with a more student-centred approach to learning than traditional pedagogy. Malcolm Knowles has been a key figure in this debate, although the debate goes back to Victorian debates on Plato's educational ideas (Knowles, 1990).

Knowles argues that adult learners move from dependency to self-directedness and use their life experience to enhance learning. He also argues that they want to apply knowledge once it is learnt and want to learn when they meet new experiences. It is argued that adults should have a strong voice in their education and in the way that they learn. They are likely to be – or to wish to be – self-directed learners and usually need to be assured about the purpose of the learning. We will talk more about student self-direction in the discussion about small groups in Chapter 3. Different individuals will have varying views on the purpose of learning in any given situation and it is imperative that we engage with the diversity of students in any one group in order to help us address that. It is also stressed that adult groups are likely to have much to learn from their peers. The latter is even more reason to ensure that learning is fully inclusive of all the students in our groups. In a small group the students can be a rich resource for each other – often in terms of questioning, critiquing and evaluating and sometimes in terms of sharing knowledge.

What began as theories of adult learning have now become much more universally applied in the learning of students of all ages, but the extent to which less traditional pedagogical approaches to learning are employed in universities is very varied. In an increasing number of countries, and certainly in the West, the notion of student-centred learning and the aim of encouraging independent learning are now well-established. In the UK, the US and a considerable number of other countries this also links to the slow but clear democratisation of education.

Although we argue in this book for a globalised curriculum and sensitivity to different cultural points of view, it will be clear that the debates are rooted firmly in Western traditions and that we believe there is a well-researched evidence base for our stance. This does not mean to say we are not open to debates of other educational philosophies. Furthermore, the Western twentieth-century education systems have absorbed and appropriated certain aspects of Confucian and other Chinese approaches to education. These range from social and instrumental purposes of education to individual notions of moral good as an educative force. Confucius urged his students to take the initiative in learning (Palmer *et al.*, 2001).

If the above models underpin learning then the nurturing of the individual is critical, and inclusive practices should be an integral part of the whole. Ironically, increasing restraints on resources have meant that at the same time such modes of teaching have become more acceptable, pressures on staff time and on physical space are tending to drive class sizes upwards. This of course can make it more and more difficult for teaching staff to find time to prepare and deliver with such attention on the individual.

While these authors maintain that learning should be student-centred, and while knowledge transmission alone can never be a wholly satisfactory educational experience for university students, we also assert that there are times when transmission of knowledge from expert to learner is a key part of higher education. It is the level of expert knowledge that is discovered, and resides, in universities that makes higher education different from other sectors of education. But perhaps even so it would be better to think of students and staff exploring and pushing boundaries of knowledge together. The focus then is on the student experience and not on knowledge itself. For some academics this latter notion can be a source of tension. It can also cause anxiety for the academic who is caught between educational liberal principles and the commodification and managerialism found increasingly in higher education (de Groot, 1997; Shumar, 1997).

Even if we are not convinced by the above approaches to education then there are other extrinsic reasons for student-centred, individually focused education. The demand for increased accountability in all walks of life and the introduction of fees and loans mean students in the UK, US and many other countries pay significant amounts and build up

PAUSE FOR THOUGHT

- Do you see your students as adults emotionally/intellectually?
- How might your answer affect your approaches to facilitating their learning?
- Is drawing on life-experience relevant in your discipline?
- If yes do you use strategies to help exploit this?
- How does the notion of transformational learning apply to your subject?

considerable debts. This means that many are becoming more demanding about the type and quality of education they receive. We have already mentioned the increased tendency towards democracy, this means that students more frequently demand a voice in the processes of education (Butcher *et al.*, 2006).

HOW DO PSYCHOLOGISTS SUGGEST THAT STUDENTS LEARN?

Despite the frequent use of popular learning style models, such as Honey and Mumford (revised edition 2006), VARK (Fleming, 2001) and so on, there is an insufficient evidence base to advocate a single learning theory. In a recent literature review of work on 'learning styles' and pedagogy in post-16 learning, seventy-one different theories were considered (Coffield *et al.*, 2004). This review team claims that there is simply not the research base as yet to prove that any single approach is comprehensive or completely reliable. What more researchers are prepared to concede, however, is that the research that has been done suggests that students learn in different ways and have different preferences for how they learn. What is clear is that using variable approaches is a healthy approach in helping learners and teachers to increase self-awareness about strengths and weaknesses. Learners should be encouraged to seek out and use the strategies that work for them. Some of the tools offered by the learning style advocates can be useful to encourage this if used with great care.

Using variable approaches with students is also likely to be a more inclusive approach to learning than a single teaching method. Those who teach in higher education are likely to have been the successes in the system. By the time we teach we have perhaps settled in to our own preferred

33

approaches to learning, but these will not necessarily work for all our students. However, if the argument of offering flexible opportunities holds there is an inevitable irony: as we use a wider range of approaches so that all are fully engaged at some point or other in our teaching (and in their learning), the corollary is that there will always be points at which a number of students are not as completely engaged as others since that is not their preferred way of learning. In other words, we will still have to work hard to keep all the group with us at any one time! On the other hand, understanding about different learning preferences can sometimes help us cope with student evaluation of our courses, which appears to have contradictory expectations. A danger of using learning style models with students, if it is done badly, is that the 'results' the students obtain about themselves can become a self-fulfilling prophecy and a temptation for students not to bother to master other ways of learning. It is a delicate balance!

 PAUSE FOR THOUGHT

This is an authentic scenario. A mobile phone conversation overheard recently as a student appeared to give support to a friend: 'Well, just tell your supervisor it's not your preferred way of learning.'

What would you say to him/her if you were the supervisor?

One robust finding in research on how students learn is the difference between learning relating to conceptual disciplinary content (declarative knowledge) and learning relating to skills acquisition (procedural knowledge).

LEARNING DECLARATIVE KNOWLEDGE

Previous knowledge can help or hinder the learning of new knowledge. It has been demonstrated that students will retain new knowledge better when it links to previous knowledge. When new learning is not matched, or is contradictory to previous knowledge, learning may be hindered. The Stroop test is one test often used by psychologists to demonstrate this feature (www.adhd.org.nz/stroop1.html). Interestingly this test is also commonly used as part of the diagnosis of Attention Deficit Hyperactivity Disorder (ADHD), where the concern is how easy or hard the learner finds it to block out distracting features. You can also try this test at www. snre.umich.edu/eplab/demos/st0/stroopdesc.html.

LINKS TO PRIOR LEARNING

Psychologists suggest that because of the need to link to prior learning we should help students explicitly relate new ideas to what they know – wherever it is possible. It has sometimes been the practice in UK higher education to suggest to students that they forget whatever they have previously learnt of a subject because university approaches are very different to school ones. This has perhaps been done with the best intentions, in order to excite students about their new situation and to introduce them to a more critical approach to knowledge; however, it may be unhelpful to abandon prior knowledge for these reasons. It may be better to attempt to deal with the 'inappropriate' knowledge and use it more constructively. It could be that we should pay far more attention to transitions for students (e.g. school to university, course to course, year to year and so on) – especially in relation to inclusive practices (Jackson, 2003). Considerable ongoing international research into the first-year experience and retention may be one useful aspect of this (Yorke and Longden, 2004). For example, conferences on this topic are held annually (e.g. www.wlv. ac.uk/default.aspx?page=14007) and the Higher Education Academy has sponsored a research project into the first-year experience.

Where students are, for example, international students, the use of prior knowledge may need careful thinking through if we are not familiar with their background and culture and/or, for example, their school learning experiences. We said, in Chapter 1, that there are many UK 'home' students who have not approached university through the traditional school route. At least for them, many university programmes will have evolved over the years based on some consideration of what entry-level knowledge they have acquired from the UK school system. It becomes more and more complex for staff to understand the group's prior knowledge when the backgrounds are varied. There may be some necessity to discuss with the group what has been done previously and to discuss the different approaches. This can often be done in a positive way that would lead to constructive discussions about the different tensions and contradictions that exist in the academic understanding of the discipline at university level (see the History brainstorm exercise later in the chapter). However, approaches to this will vary hugely according to disciplinary traditions and content.

Engaging with prior knowledge admittedly takes time. Staff in the sciences who consider that there is a huge amount of content to cover – and especially where progress is based on cumulative acquisition – may need to rethink the content coverage or offer alternative ways of presenting supporting material, for example, in a virtual learning environment. Even with home students there is considerable debate, for example, about declining Maths entry-level standards, and Science departments are needing to find ways of upskilling many new arrivals. Concern in the sector, from time to time, means that this topic is one that reaches the national UK press periodically. See, for example, www.timesonline.co.uk/tol/news/uk/education/article1701561.ece.

 PAUSE FOR THOUGHT

- How do you ascertain the previous knowledge of your students?
- Think through what cultural previous knowledge might affect your students.
- The work by the Joseph Rowntree Foundation on educational disadvantage and poverty (www.jrf.org.uk/knowledge/findings/social policy/2123.asp), suggests areas in which some of our students from low socio-economic backgrounds may struggle. Does this/should this affect your work?
- How do you try to help your students negotiate their way through conflict and contradiction from previous sources of knowledge?

SETTING KNOWLEDGE IN A CONTEXT

Concepts consist of richly and highly interconnected networks of knowledge, and new knowledge will be remembered more easily if it is linked to existing or core concepts that are understood. Concepts also need to be presented within a context. Thus we are right to give examples to help understanding. Context setting is really about putting new concepts into the appropriate intellectual framework. Often to do this we resort to more commonly understood imagery; however, where we have international students we must take care that the metaphors and images we use to help set contexts are not so culturally specific that they are a hindrance rather than a help. Context setting can be counter-productive if an analogy is off-putting to students. For example, illustrations using popular culture such as football images – which are predominantly seen as masculine – have frequently made material seem less relevant to women. Very recently (2008) one of the authors was in a talk to medical professionals that exemplified the abilities of women by describing what excellent creatures they were because they were very adept at using washing machines. Thus the speaker's whole point was lost to a number of offended female doctors! There are still many examples of this crassness even in an age where sexism and racism are illegal. Appealing to popular culture to make our material more accessible can help many students but it needs to be done with sensitivity. One of the most difficult terrains has become humour. All we can do is to be aware and to remind ourselves to use it judiciously. Another example of ill-judged context setting can be the use of colloquial phrases and idioms that, while possibly making text more accessible for some locals, actually confuses rather than helps where the second language is not fluent. The suggestion here is not that we do not bother to try to make our material lively and appealing as appropriate, nor are we suggesting that all traces of our own cultures should disappear – international students have often chosen the institution in order to acquire knowledge of that culture – we just need to think carefully before we use phraseology and images that might exclude or divide. Most of us make mistakes from time to time in this and we should review our approaches occasionally. Nonetheless we should not let the fear of mistakes prevent us from context setting.

Research suggests that first-generation students are more likely than other students to leave university before they finish the course (Tym *et al.*, 2004), and we must ensure that our higher education discourses, often based on a different type of 'cultural capital', are not ones that exclude them from understanding. This is not to say we must abandon that which we hold dear – it may be this very thing that is being sought. But we must find a dialogue that enables them to access our world where that is appropriate. A poignant letter in the *Times Higher Educational Supplement* (*THES*), from a research assistant who attained her first class degree at 40 and speaks of herself as working class, highlights the contrasts in her different worlds:

> I am torn. On the one hand I am proud of my background – it has given me the strength to become an academic. . . . On the other hand there are parts of the academic world that appeal – the dialogue, the language, the debates.
>
> (*THES*, 24 June 2007)

Once the concepts have been introduced with due regard to the above features they should be revisited. Adding increasing complexity to them in a structured fashion has been shown to be effective in learning. This is often known as a spiral curriculum. Some institutions are designing new courses so that the overall degree programme ensures this (Hull York Medical School, for example), whereas others still revise individual degree modules in isolation. On a micro level it is helpful to think about how we do this in a semester or term and even in a seminar or lecture. The latter approach will clearly help the international students who are also grappling with mastery of a second language and will help those of the students with dyslexia who find sequencing arguments and concepts more difficult. Summary and consolidation, where appropriate, are especially important in inclusive education.

LEARNING PROCEDURAL KNOWLEDGE

There is some robust research on skills learning. It is suggested that there are three main stages: cognitive (e.g. descriptions of the rules); associative (e.g. tuning methods, pattern-recognition, etc.); and autonomous (skill becomes more rapid and automated). Practice is a critical factor in becoming proficient in skills learning. A number of studies of procedural knowledge are now being applied to the disciplines, for example, Maths and Molecular Biology (Sahdra and Thagard, 2003; Star, 2005). You may find similar articles on skills learning in your discipline.

Feedback is critical in skills acquisition; a learner also needs to know why, what and how they are doing a thing. More will be said about feedback in Chapter 9.

The point of any discussion about how students learn is probably most helpful where it, first, helps us to think through how we teach and, second, helps us as staff to help students improve their metacognitive skills. That is to say, we must help them to learn how to think about their learning and to *learn how to learn*. Knowing what works for them when learning something new will help them to learn more efficiently in the future. In an age of fast-changing knowledge this is an essential skill for our graduates. For example, this notion has particularly been informing medical school education in recent years, where it is recognised that the actual medical knowledge transmitted is relatively soon superseded. Once out of medical school doctors have constantly to acquire updated knowledge. Students must have the ability to reflect upon their own learning, to monitor their own progress and to learn efficiently.

PAUSE FOR THOUGHT

What might the different approaches to preparing for a seminar be if the work mainly relates to:

■ Procedural knowledge (carrying out actions appropriately and in a skilled manner)?
■ Declarative knowledge (complex, interconnected information and concepts)?
■ A mix of both of the above?

How might either one map on to issues relating to inclusion and diversity?

TOO MUCH COMFORT TO LEARN?

Much of this book will appear to be about reducing students' discomfort in order to create conducive learning environments, and indeed that is absolutely our case. Students cannot usually learn optimally when they are overly embarrassed and feel isolated or scorned and excluded from the group. However, and possibly paradoxically, this is not the whole picture. We are not assuming that students should never be taken to the edge of risk in order to make them learn. Some of our own key moments in the histories of our learning have been extremely uncomfortable moments. Graham Good, in a slightly different context – that of discussing academic freedom – says, 'Emotional comfort cannot be a valid goal for university education, which should challenge rather than reinforce existing assumptions and identities' (Good, 2000), and he goes on to say 'students should be told, "knowledge should change you. You should not demand that knowledge change to suit you by conforming to your current predilections"'. This means that there are times when, intellectually, students need to feel a little uncomfortable. But this must be handled sensitively and be part of the learning process. Discomfort must never be a result of attacks on aspects of students' backgrounds or lives over which they have no control.

One study of students in Malaysia found that the primary reason Malaysian students engaged in international education was to obtain jobs with multinational corporations. Non-Malaysian students in the same study wanted 'new ways of viewing the word, new habits of thinking and new skills and approaches'; they wished to 'procure new identities and to expunge provincial outlooks'; and they 'sought a personal meta-morphosis', the author writes (Pyvis, 2007: 236). They therefore typically made 'self-transformative investments in international education' and were more likely than the home Malaysian students to respond positively to challenging educational experiences. We must not underestimate the wishes and determination of students who have taken the significant step of attending a university that is away from their home country. Ensuring access and equity is not about making things so easy and comfortable that students will not be challenged to learn, nor is it about them being in such a state of fear that their learning ability is paralysed.

> In the best class I've ever been in . . . we always sat in a circle, and we were facing each other. In the beginning I was very, very uncomfortable, we were all staring at each other, and didn't really know each other . . . A lot of it was us giving presentations and breaking up into smaller groups and I think that is really what helps people to make their views known. . . . That's probably the best thing . . . it helps the students feel important, like what they have to say is important.
>
> (Student quote, University of North Carolina at Chapel Hill, 1997: 90)

SO WHAT ABOUT DESIGN PRINCIPLES FOR INCLUSIVE LEARNING?

The social model of disability, as already discussed, can be used as a basis for designing classes in an inclusive way that helps all students. However, there are times in small-group teaching when particular provision will need to be made for a student to assist their learning and integration; for example, for blind or deaf students. The Staff–Student Partnership for Assessment, Change and Evaluation (SPACE) Project refers to this as a 'contingent' or 'alternative' approach (Waterfield and West, 2006). The contingent approach is one, they say, where 'special arrangements' are made as the need arises, for example, extra time for assessment or special physical conditions arranged for assessment. An alternative approach is one where a repertoire of assessment arrangements is em-bedded into course design so that future disabled students can access these alternative arrangements. An inclusive approach is one, they argue, where outcomes are flexible and the same outcomes can be assessed in different ways for all students. We will discuss this in more detail in Chapter 9, but for now it exemplifies a possible model for all our practice. It will not always be totally practicable to take a fully inclusive path but wherever possible we should plan that way. Certainly, in our planning, we should think activities through to ensure that they are suitable for all students in order that we do not make individuals feel as though they are always 'special cases'. We are not suggesting that there should ever be any compromise of academic standards, but that we check our activities and see that they are as flexible as possible, while maintaining rigour.

Another model, similar in principle, is the Universal Design for Learning (UDL), as introduced in the USA. Its central principle is that the curriculum can be made accessible by adopting flexibility in learning outcomes, methods, material and assessment. In this context universal does not mean a single solution for all but multiple approaches as needed. UDL suggests that we enable learners to use different ways to acquire the same information and allow them to demonstrate what they know in different ways. The Open University is an example of an institution in the UK that has aimed to adopt this approach. For example, the 'Making Your Teaching Inclusive' website (www.open.ac.uk/inclusiveteaching/pages/inclusive-teaching/universal-design-for-learning.php) is a useful, practical site with tips for teaching inclusively.

Aligning content, learning outcomes, teaching and learning processes and assessment is critical; the *Promoting Access for Deaf and Hard-of-Hearing Students* website (www.rit.edu/~classact/side/universaldesign.html) gives a very good basic introduction to this method. Some institutions, such as the University of Tasmania and the University of South Australia, have attempted to extend UDL beyond disability, although there are limitations to it. Their sites offer useful practical information about

 PAUSE FOR THOUGHT

- How much control do you have over change?
- Are the approaches above practical in your context?
- Are there minor amendments you could make to your course to offer more flexibility?
- It is often heard said that more flexible approaches are 'dumbing down' university degrees. If this concerns us, how can we ensure that we maintain rigour and high-level academic content?

working in an inclusive way (www.utas.edu.au/tl/supporting/inclusive/
index.html, www.unisanet.unisa.edu.au/learningconnection/staff/
practice/inclusivity.asp).

 FURTHER READING

Reflective and Experiential Learning

Boud, D., Keogh, R. and Walker, D. (1985) *Reflection: Turning experience into learning*, London: Croom Helm.

Kolb, D.A. (1984) *Experiential Learning: Experience as the source of learning and development*, New Jersey: Prentice-Hall.

Moon, J. (1999) *Reflection in Learning and Professional Development: Theory and practice*, London; Kogan Page.

Schön, D.A. (1983) *The Reflective Practitioner: How professionals think in action*, London: Temple Smith.

Learning Styles

Coffield, F., Moseley, D., Hall, E. and Ecclestone, K. (2004) *Learning Styles and Pedagogy in Post-16 Learning: A systematic and critical review*, London: Learning and Skills Research Centre.

Entwistle, N. (1981) *Styles of Learning and Teaching: An integrated outline of educational psychology for students, teachers and lecturers*, Chichester: John Wiley.

Honey, P. and Mumford, A. (1982) *Manual of Learning Styles*, London: P. Honey.

Transformative/Andragogy/Adult Learning

Freire, P. (1972) *The Pedagogy of the Oppressed*, Harmondsworth: Penguin.

Jarvis, P. (1987) *Adult Education in the Social Context*, London: Croom Helm.

Knowles, M.S. (1990) *The Adult Learner: A neglected species*, 4th edn, Houston: Gulf Publishing.

Mezirow, J. (1991) *Transformative Dimensions of Adult Learning*, Jossey-Bass, San Francisco.

Rogers, C.R. (1980) *Freedom to learn for the 80s*, New York: Free Press.

Chapter 3

Including All Students in Our Small-Group Teaching

In the first part of this chapter we will discuss issues and ideas that may help enhance inclusive practice in small-group teaching, and in the second part we include a number of practical checklists for specific classroom situations. We will ask: What are 'small groups' in higher education teaching? Why do we espouse this as a beneficial way to teach? How do we ensure inclusion?

THE MAIN PURPOSES OF SMALL-GROUP TEACHING

The purpose and size of 'small' groups in higher education teaching vary widely according to institution and disciplines. Small-group teaching is described by David Jaques (2000) as having three main purposes:

1   encouraging students to organise their thinking by comparing ideas and interpretations with each other and giving expressions, and hence form, to their understanding of a subject;
2   providing extrinsic skill training opportunities such as team building, oral skills, eliciting information, persuading and so on);
3   presenting an opportunity for students to monitor their own learning and gain self-direction and independence from tutors in study.

For an amplification of this and for other useful information about small-group teaching see www.brookes.ac.uk/services/ocsd/2_learntch/small-group/.

At times, we may have other specific purposes for small-group teaching, such as reinforcing lecture material, testing knowledge, cross-linking subject matter, but these are perhaps less critical in terms of overall student learning than the larger overarching purposes mentioned above.

 PAUSE FOR THOUGHT

- Do you think there are other purposes? What is the balance of priorities in this for you?
- How does this relate to issues of inclusion for all students? Is the most likely area of difficulty regarding skills training or are there other difficult areas?
- How can you positively use differences in your groups to enrich the experience for all?

The main focus of this chapter is not on how to teach small groups – for that see the many existing guides. This chapter is rather about how to ensure our small-group teaching is inclusive. For a general background, however, Google searches bring up many practical tips on small-group teaching. One such is from the University of Alabama Medical School (www.uab.edu/uasomume/cdm/small.htm), but there are countless more.

It is also interesting to trawl the different exercises used in schools, commercial training and so on. One example of a useful site created by a publisher to accompany text books is the one on *Small Group Communication* (www.abacon.com/commstudies/groups/devgroup.html).

Many activities from such sites can be adapted for higher education with care. There is also considerable action research literature on small-group teaching. That is to say that many academics have interrogated their own teaching practices in small groups and written about their experiences. Information about the journal *Small Group Research* can be found at http://sgr.sagepub.com/.

For a good summary book on small-group teaching see Exley and Dennick's volume in this series (2004b) and see the classic work by Jaques (2000). Some of the earlier, more general material available was not written with particularly diverse groups in mind, and so this chapter is intended as a more focused reminder of the need to do that. Increasingly though there are a number of websites and projects that now inform this topic, and a sample selection is listed at the end of the chapter. The general principles from Chapter 1 apply to the preparation for small-group teaching, as do many of the suggestions in the subsequent chapters.

DOES THE GROUP SIZE MATTER?

Some claim that the optimal size for effective higher education small groups is between five and eight (Exley and Dennick, 2004b); others might find that a critical mass is ten or twelve. However, some staff may find that they are presented with a 'small group' that comprises twenty to thirty or even up to fifty students! We have previously commented on the irony that – just as we, as a sector in the UK, are attempting to focus more attention on inclusiveness in our groups and thus emphasising the vital need for smaller groups – many of us are actually faced with constraints that mean larger class sizes. We do not always have a choice. It is normally the case that we need to select activities accordingly. If assessed work is to be undertaken in the group then careful consideration of viable numbers is critical. Perhaps we need to consider the purpose of our small groups before we determine viable sizes.

WHY PROMOTE SMALL-GROUP TEACHING?

Ensuring that educational provision is for a diverse range of students is perhaps simply about appreciating and relating to the ways in which humans differ. It is in our small groups where we can explore the gamut of human experience more comprehensively and it is particularly in small groups that our students can learn from each other. It is in these groups that we can create more comfortable spaces for our students, but it is also in these environments that we can more safely, and in a more controlled fashion, push students to the limits of their comfort zones in order to enhance their learning. In such groups students learn to monitor their own learning effectively as they absorb feedback from the tutor and from other students and indeed as they hear themselves articulating their own ideas to others. All quite obvious, except that we know that working with groups of humans is actually never that simple! But it is in these small groups that we are likely to be able to assist our students to learn how to challenge and critique accepted knowledge and to advance the boundaries of their own learning. In small groups (as opposed to large ones) it is also easier to help students acquire many of the generic and transferable skills that are considered part of the 'employable' graduate's learning.

PAUSE FOR THOUGHT

- What is the optimal size for your groups? Why?
- If you do not have the ideal situation what do you do to try and make things better?
- What is the purpose of your small-group teaching?
- Do you spend time planning process as well as content (even for discussion)?
- What aspects of inclusive provision do you articulate as you plan, or do you tend to think you will deal with situations as they arise?
- Is an inclusive classroom the same as a diverse classroom? How might these two notions differ, if they do?
- Do you value small-group teaching and make the most of any autonomy you have to plan appropriately within a session, even if you cannot change numbers/timing/location easily?

If you are reading this in an institution where there is not the opportunity to teach small groups – or indeed, as increasingly happens, where the term 'small group' is mysteriously used for classes of over fifty – then read this for when you might one day be able to teach small groups, but more particularly to see what ideas, principles or activities might support and break down the larger groups you have to work with. In fact, most of the principles are very similar to those in the following chapter, it is simply that with large numbers the concern for, and involvement at, individual level is more difficult.

OTHER GENERAL CHALLENGES OF SMALL-GROUP TEACHING RELATING TO INCLUSIVENESS

Useful as it can be, we have already inferred that small-group teaching is not the panacea for all ills! High expectations in both students and staff often accompany small-group teaching and these may be unrealistic, or they may be thwarted for a myriad of reasons. While many students feel at their most secure in small groups, other students may well feel at their most vulnerable. In a well-run group they cannot hide in the crowd or be non-participatory. A survey of students at the University of North Carolina at Chapel Hill noted '[These] different learning styles explain why in most

PAUSE FOR THOUGHT

Think about the inclusive *content* of your syllabus for small-group teaching and not just the *process*.

In one discussion of gender and education in Science, Ruth Watts suggests that there has been a significant contribution of women to Science over the years. However, she claims, scientific knowledge has depended on the masculine determination of what forms of knowledge are appropriate. 'Others', she says, than the 'authoritative gatekeepers of the intellectual traditions' are capable of producing knowledge. It is especially in our small groups that we can encourage our students to question with us the perimeters of appropriate knowledge and help them learn how to begin to be the *producers of knowledge* and not merely the passive recipients (Watts, 2007: 283).

Are there areas in which we could usefully use small-group teaching to challenge and debate knowledge or conventions that have solidified in the syllabus simply because of history or convention – perhaps in material that implies the dominance of certain groups with regard to ethnicity, socio-economic roots, gender or age?

■ Look at your subject benchmarks (www.qaa.ac.uk/academic infrastructure/benchmark/default.asp) and see if there are areas where you could be more creative in addressing what is meant to be covered in your syllabus in a way that includes minority groups appropriately.

■ Are we helping our students to begin to be the producers and not merely the recipients of knowledge? In some disciplines this is clearer and easier to do than others – how does it work in your field of study?

■ Think back to Chapter 1 – do we ask the questions posed there when we meet new groups?

classes, the student evaluations show that some students see the group work as the most important part of their learning experience, while others from the same class complain that they dislike group work and find it unhelpful' (http://ctl.unc.edu/tfitoc.html).

For students who are 'non-traditional', a sense of exclusion may be even more keenly felt where they have to expose their thought to others.

ENSURING STUDENT INTEGRATION AND IDENTITY

Ultimately the small-group teaching context, together with a good relationship with a supervisor, may be one of the most important contexts for ensuring that students feel integrated into the university (more on the importance of this in Chapter 7). A study by Mary Fischer (2007) about how students settle into campus life suggested that having more academic ties (taken to mean, for example, connection with teaching staff) positively related to higher grades. It is also in the small group that we are likely to discover where students are struggling. Lindsay Neville in an article in the *THES* (1 June 2007), noted that 'some research highlights that it is likely to be front-line academic staff who spot a student in distress. Regular contact might allow them to detect changes in appearance or behaviour.' In the same article she comments that it 'also appears to be an unspoken expectation that we (academics) ensure our students are in a fit state to learn'. This is clearly more likely to take place in the small group than in the large lecture theatre. It is appreciated that not all countries expect this level of involvement from academic staff, but in the UK most institutions would aspire to this level of staff support of students.

ENCOURAGING INTER-CULTURAL COMPETENCE

In Chapter 7 we will speak more fully about the development of inter-cultural competence – both our own and that of our students. It is in the small group, for example, that we are likely to be more able to detect the difficult shifts involved in our students' acculturation processes. A study of migrant women higher education staff notes that, 'At any time the migrant can feel simultaneously "assimilated", "separated" and "marginalized"' (Lewis, 2005: 96). She says that many of the women in her study 'walked in two worlds and yet in none'. How much more might that be true of our students and where are we most likely to be able to help with this if not in the small group? It may also be in the small group that we are able to help our students feel they are not being stereotyped in terms of their learning; for example, Betty Leask comments that Asians are often stereotyped as surface learners (Leask, 2006), and various studies have claimed that negative stereotypes of minority groups about intellectual ability can affect performance (Steele, 1998). Many of these studies have implications for other variants of stereotyping – work in the US and the UK has shown the same effect of gender stereotyping on schoolchildren, for example, in Maths. A study from the University of Connecticut claims that gender stereotypes affect Maths performance (http://advance.uconn. edu/2001/010917/01091711.htm), and there are a number of other such studies.

In the small group we need to offer individuals additional support where they need it but not fall foul of unnecessary stereotyping – a difficult balancing act at times.

DEVELOPING STUDENT SELF-DIRECTION

Jaques points out that a purpose of small-group teaching is to help students become more self-directed learners (Jaques, 2000). Light and Cox (2001), in their worthwhile chapter on 'Facilitating Small Group Teaching', start with a useful Chinese quote: 'Of a good leader when his [sic] task is finished, his goal achieved, they say, we did that ourselves (Lao-tse, c.600 BC)'. The word 'facilitation' has lately received a bad press in some quarters because it became associated, for some, with trendy approaches and low-level or gimmicky teaching. But in its true sense it is what we should be doing when we 'lead' small groups. The *Oxford English Dictionary* says facilitation is to 'help forward', to 'promote' and to 'render easier'. This does not imply that we cannot input our 'expert' knowledge as appropriate, but the main aim of a seminar should be to direct students to finding their own material, to exploring concepts more fully, and to developing their own critical stance and learning.

Simon Cassidy says, in work on new students' ability (or lack thereof) to self-assess, 'this develops partly as a function of critical feedback from tutors'. Large numbers, he says, make this difficult. The corollary then is that it must be in small groups that we concentrate our efforts in helping students to develop their own ability to self-assess whether formally or informally. Cassidy says:

> The need for students to develop as independent learners is both fundamental to academic success in HE and essential to subsequent professional success . . . This involves a high level of self-awareness and the ability to monitor their own learning and performance.
>
> (2007: 314)

In the UK one of the weakest areas in the National Student Satisfaction Survey related to feedback (see, for example, www.hefce.ac.uk/learning/nss/).

It seems that students have not always perceived oral comments, for example, in seminars and tutorials, as 'feedback' and that we need to help them to recognise, and to use more effectively, our comments on their contributions offered in group work (see Chapter 9 for further discussion of feedback). Peer feedback is also a critical purpose of working in small groups.

Peer feedback, like self-directed learning in general, requires enough confidence to begin to fly from the metaphorical nest. This may take longer for students who lack confidence in, or knowledge of, the local systems and cultures of higher education, simply because unfamiliarity with accepted norms.

 PAUSE FOR THOUGHT

- Do your small-group sessions include opportunities for students to assess where they are in relation to the required learning at given points?
- Are all members of the group able to evaluate this in the same way or do some need more guidance?
- How do you check what they are learning during your seminars?

PREPARING TO USE SMALL-GROUP TEACHING IN AN INCLUSIVE WAY

It would be impossible to be able to predict or to outline all the varying situations where special attention may need to be paid to all students' potential needs. But, as we saw in Chapter 1, UK legislation demands that we give this some specific thought in relation to disabled students, ethnicity and age at the very least. We have argued for a holistic approach that means we should also think through potential issues for all in our small groups, and these might also include: younger or older than average students; international students; and students from a range of socio-economic and geographical backgrounds. We must also aim to include students who are experiencing short-term illness, adjustment problems, friendship problems, questions relating to sexuality and a host of other issues. At the end of this chapter we offer check lists that might aid the thinking through of appropriate actions for specific groups, but we have tried elsewhere to integrate our tips as suggestions for best practice with all students.

An irony is that small-group teaching is premised on philosophies that aim at active and inclusive learning but, as we have already stated, this very attempt can have moments that exclude some students. For example, if our students frequently change their seats as part of small-group interactivity, this may make things more complex for blind students. Group discussion can be very hard to follow for some hearing-impaired or second-language students, if not facilitated extremely carefully by the staff member. Background noise needs to be eliminated, and the group leader needs to ensure that only one person speaks at a time. It often helps to have some way of identifying who is speaking, for example, a gently raised hand.

When we first start out as academic teachers it is very tempting to spend every moment of preparation becoming more familiar with the academic content. We have probably all done this and been reading 'one last article' moments before we head to the class! It is critical in inclusive teaching to spend some preparation thinking about the process of how to run the class and not just about the academic content.

Having decided what we (i.e. also the discipline/department/university, etc.) want the students to learn (clear learning outcomes), we should think about how that will be 'taught' and how it will be assessed. When we are thinking about the actual activity for the sessions perhaps the first 'rule' is that in seeking new or supportive ideas for small-group teaching, and in determining optimal numbers for our groups, we should critique the 'advice' literature and the potential ideas of others (including normal departmental traditions and how the session has previously been taught) carefully and use them only as appropriate for inclusive teaching in our context – there is rarely a 'one size fits all' answer in these matters. We can only think through our own situation, aim to include all our students fully, and do our best having evaluated the guidance available.

Second, we may need to insert questions relating to inclusion as we read the general guidance material, or as we look at previous practice. Generally though, and despite the above caveats, of all the methods of teaching, small-group teaching, when used in an optimal situation, may be the key teaching technique to ensure we include all our students.

As Theresa Man Ling Lee has put it, 'When thinking through both content and process for small-group activity it should always seek to eliminate xenophobia and ethnocentrism' (Man Ling Lee, 2005: 203). If we are planning a series of sessions we should think through the calendar of events as we plan. Are there significant religious festivals or holy days that will affect our students and prevent them from attending or

SOME THOUGHTS ON AIDING PLANNING

1 What do I want my students to learn in this session?
2 What learning outcomes will I therefore write? (See Bloom's taxonomy for hierarchies of learning (Exley and Dennick, 2004b: 43).)
3 What activities will I use to achieve these ends?
4 How will this relate to assessment?
5 How does this session fit into the overall scheme of the programme
   for the students?
6 Who are the students?
7 How many?
8 How long will the session be?
9 Are there any unchangeable restrictions regarding physical environment?
10 Check equipment is ordered if needed and check that books/articles
   on any reading lists are available from the library/bookshop.
11 Are my plans suitable for all the students in the group – is it an
   'inclusive' plan?
12 Are there any 'contingency' or 'alternative' arrangements needed
   for any individual?
13 Check I understand what the students expect/need from the handbook information they have been given.
14 Check any formal requirements I need to adhere to – for example,
   practices for evaluation of the session.

Amend this list to make it suitable for your situation.

completing assignments? Are there submission dates that will be more difficult for carers of young children – such as school holidays? We cannot always cater for every contingency, and some of this will be about ensuring the students plan their own workloads appropriately. Often there is no one correct answer, for offering a solution to one student can potentially adversely affect the rights of another student. We will return to fair decision-making in Chapter 9.

PHYSICAL ENVIRONMENT

Check the room conditions before and during your teaching. Sometimes there are factors beyond our control, but it is nonetheless up to us to make these as optimal as possible. Consider temperature and lighting especially. Think about whether the layout of chairs assists or detracts from the dynamics you wish to create.

 PAUSE FOR THOUGHT

- What are likely to be the effects on conversation of the following room layouts: circle; horseshoe; rows of chairs; 'cabaret' style (i.e. separate tables); boardroom style (i.e. seated round the table)?
- Would you change the layout if you knew you had a student with a hearing impairment? If not, how would you ensure that all could participate?
- Think of your last seminar – draw circles to indicate people in the room. Draw arrows from circle to circle depicting the flow of conversation – do the arrows all come back and forth to you, or are there arrows crossing all over the diagram to indicate a flow of conversation from student to student?

Can all your students move around with ease in the activities you have organised? Think too of any hidden mobility issues. If you have more elderly students in your group you may need to be more aware of physical limitations. We have already discussed issues about hearing and clarity of speech, which can be more complex in groups with fluid seating arrangements, and you will need to strike a practical balance in all this. If you have opted for circles of chairs, can all students see any screen or board that will be used during the session? See the checklists at the end of the chapter for more details.

COMMUNICATION

In Chapter 1 we mentioned that perhaps the first essential to think through in respect of inclusion is communication. At the very least this means using inclusive language in our course material and in our oral communication. Small-group teaching depends by definition on communication, especially effective oral communication.

Exley and Dennick (2004a) consider the mechanics of good voice use, which cannot be underestimated. Self-evidently, if our students cannot hear then they will never understand. However obvious this may seem, we have all experienced seminars where the speaker's volume is a problem. For students with hearing or sight difficulties and for second-language speakers this is perhaps even more critical. Whilst the use of written material will probably be part of the learning material in groups, the main point of a seminar is, usually, discussion.

There may be disabilities, physical or mental, or second-language issues that make oral communication more complex. The UK veterinary medicine disability project, *Diverse* (Tynan, 2005), has identified some issues such as speech impairments, hearing impairments, autism, Asperger's or other autistic spectrum disorders and some mental health conditions or personality disorders that may act as barriers to effective social interaction. In small-group teaching we may need to think of support strategies if we have such students in the group.

For example:

1 Written summary notes might help – either distributed by us or, more efficiently for our time, notes done by the students (in turn) and checked by us.
2 Get students to summarise on the board.
3 Use some electronic pre-discussion if the facilities are there – all, including those who have more communication difficulties, can then come better prepared and orientated to sessions.
4 Likewise, electronic post-discussion material can help summarise and consolidate.
5 It is sometimes possible to distribute a printed plan of the session and the main points to be covered, which can help those who need more structure in their approach to learning and those for whom oral work is harder to follow.
6 A follow-up summary of, or links to, recommended reading can also help to ensure that the main points raised in discussion will be consolidated.

The *Diverse* project also highlights potential positive contributions from the groups of students mentioned in the list above, and they remind us that students who experience communication problems may actually offer increased communication where they focus more on listening in order to be able to understand. They may be more sympathetic to others, especially if they have disabilities, and may feel more empathy.

MEETING THE GROUP

Offer Your Name

Many students from other cultures are unsure of the tradition and courtesy regarding the use of names. For example, students in Bahrain tend to use Dr plus the first name (i.e. Dr Sue). Students from Japan or China, for example, may expect a formal mode of address. Even recent school-leavers from the UK may wonder how much more or less formal it will be than school. Mature students may have more confidence to use first names, but this may be alienating to some of the younger students in the group if they have not been encouraged to do so. Conversely, other older students, used to the workplace, may feel they should be more formal. It is even known to have students sitting in the wrong seminar for some time, and so it helps to check that the title of the seminar is clear! Such small and seemingly simple gestures can set an approachable tone.

Get Your Students to Introduce Themselves

Check against your class list – what you hear from them and what you have printed on the official list are frequently quite different things! There are other things to watch. For example, asking Muslims and Hindus for their 'Christian' name may not be very courteous! Other international students may wish, for various reasons, to use a name different to the one you have received on the registration form. For Sikhs, for example, the family name may indicate a caste and is often dropped. The use of Singh or Kaur for many Sikhs is a positive assertion of religious identity and a rejection of the inequality implicit in castes. Similarly, many Hindus have also dropped family names. To avoid embarrassment, it may be well to ask your students how they would like to be addressed (Clements and Spinks, 2000: 137).

Get Your Students to Learn Each Others' Names

Many group activities cannot work well unless the individuals can address each other positively, concisely and specifically. This may seem obvious, but one of the authors once taught a class that had, the previous term, with a different staff member, been expected to assess each other's oral contribution. They had not, even at the end of the term, been quite sure of each other's names and, since they were newcomers, had not wished to

SOME THOUGHTS ON STARTING GROUPS

1　Encourage everyone to say something at an early stage.
2　Get them to introduce themselves in pairs.
3　A more sophisticated version is to get them to introduce each other to the whole group – this is harder because they are not talking about themselves but it can also be easier because it is depersonalised for the shy ones. Processing and distilling key information about another person is a useful skill. A relaxed and light atmosphere for this enables them to speak for the first time.
4　Look at ideas for brainstorming.
5　If you have a few weeks with a student group, time spent on introductions is not wasted, however much content you feel you need to cover.

admit to this! So, they admitted the next term, their marking of each other had been a little haphazard! An extreme example, but even conversation cannot flow well where names are not known. If we have a blind student it is especially important for them to be able to have names articulated. Name cards could help for students with hearing difficulties and for students not familiar with the different cultural naming traditions.

SOME THOUGHTS ON USING GROUND RULES

1　Agree what general principles the group wishes to use for the running of the group. These may include respect for each other, arguing over ideas not personalities, one person speaking at a time, and so on.
2　Insert your own 'conditions'. For example, you may wish to insert requirements about necessary preparation ('a ticket to the seminar' is that they have done the required reading), or you may wish to ask for punctuality and say you will start on time regardless.
3　Make sure they are aware of course requirements. For example, there may be rules about attendances or reporting absences.

If group work is to be used, such ground rules are useful and can be referred back to if complications arise.

CASE STUDY TAKEN FROM A WOMEN'S HISTORY MASTERS LEVEL SEMINAR

Introductory Brainstorm[1] for a Course

Brainstorm onto an acetate, board, laptop or flip chart.

Ask what has:

1 worried students about the subject previously;
2 seemed less interesting to them (most subjects have areas that are less attractive or more difficult);
3 what is useful about the subject;
4 what has excited/interested them.

Adapt as appropriate to your discipline.

Explain exactly how the brainstorm will work, as students from some cultures may not be used to speaking freely or so personally, and others will be intimidated by the thought of your expertise. Tell them that the idea of a brainstorm is that they can say anything that comes to their mind about the topic. If you feel it is appropriate you can help the timid along by giving one of your own examples. Your approach will also depend on the stage/type of degree, and clearly we need to try to avoid the students being faced with the same warm-ups and ice-breakers too many times.

It is crucial to end with the positive aspects and try to answer the issues that have been raised in a summary, so as to end with enthusiasm for the subject. The discussion around the tension in the subject can usefully lead into a discussion of what the discipline/topic actually is in your/the department's eyes. This encourages all students to talk at an early stage as they are not being asked for high-level academic views but more informal personal ones. It also helps unpack some of the different gendered/cultural/socio-economic/political understandings of studying the discipline and introduces the notion that discussion and student critique are welcome. According to some authors, 'ice-breakers' have traditionally been expected to be neutral in content, but this purposeful using of the notion of the discipline can offer a meaningful and focused introduction to some of the intent and content of the course.

I find out names before this exercise and use them to help create a comfortable atmosphere and give all a chance to learn them. If there are students in the group who have never studied this discipline before, then questions will need to be amended; I extend the definition to include study at school and to other encounters such as television/social/hobby contacts with the subject. This may be harder in some disciplines, but using the widest and loosest definition of the discipline can then help add clarification to what study of this discipline at university – and at the specific level of the degree – means. The ensuing discussion about the meaning and purpose of the discipline/topic can be pitched at whatever level is suitable. It is interesting to observe the different entry levels of understanding: after 12–15 years of using this exercise on a Masters course it is clear that some years the level of understanding is far higher than others, and this exercise helps me to know how to pitch further work. Each year I have felt it must be time to replace the exercise, but its value still remains very clear in the context of this programme.

This session also gives you the opportunity to observe group dynamics, cultural understandings and differences and to check that all can hear and see clearly if you operate group discussion in this way.

Some universities suggest that staff could ask students to e-mail them or let them know some other way if they feel that anything adversely affects their interaction with the group.

Leading Discussion

There has sometimes been a misapprehension that seminar discussion needs no planning and that conversation will simply flow. The introduction of learning outcomes then took this to the other extreme, where it was often expected that staff plan to such a high degree that there was little space for spontaneity or for unintended or unexpected outcomes. In running discussion groups a midway compromise is often needed. We cannot always predict where our students will want to go in discussion, and yet we must ensure that our aims for their learning through discussion are clear. Unfocused and rambling seminars are seldom optimally effective.

Murdoch University in Australia suggests the following quick checklist for leading class discussion in an inclusive manner:

1 emphasise the importance of considering different approaches and viewpoints;
2 make it clear you value all comments;
3 encourage all students to participate in class discussion;
4 monitor your own behaviour in responding to students;
5 re-evaluate your pedagogical methods for teaching in a diverse setting;
6 speak up promptly if a student makes a distasteful remark even if jokingly;
7 avoid singling out students as spokespersons.

Types of Questions in Discussion

The survey at The University of North Carolina mentioned previously (http://ctl.unc.edu/tfitoc.html) was based on a large-scale consultation with their students. One of the points made repeatedly by members of the minority groups consulted was the resentment when students are asked for the view of the group they are seen to represent, without any apparent understanding of the hugely diverse views there may be in such a group. Thus a student from Costa Rica cannot be seen to speak on behalf of other Hispanic groups such as students from Mexico or Argentina or for third-generation Hispanic Americans. The same might be true of a 'woman's view' or a student with a learning disability. Thus, a primary rule is not to assume that any one student should be asked questions as a representative of a whole group.

When we ask questions do we want to:

1 clarify information;
2 test knowledge;
3 stimulate idea and knowledge creation;
4 aid the construction of argument;
5 other?

The type of question we use will depend on our purpose. We may need to avoid closed questions (i.e. those with yes/no answers) if we wish to encourage answers that are not monosyllabic. More specific 'checking' questions may be helpful to second-language students in their early stages. For example, if we seek synthesis we can ask, 'How does that connect with . . . ?' or 'Could you summarise?'. We may wish to ask questions that seek elaboration or that lead students into developing an idea or argument. We should give students time to answer and must be honest and probing but encouraging in our responses. Careful use of questioning will help not only those students unfamiliar with our conventions of learning and discussion, or those with poorer language skills, but also strong students who need to hone argumentation and critical thinking skills. In other words, it is helpful to all students.

Light and Cox (2001) remind us that, even for strong students, seminars can be threatening as well as effective. In group situations there are challenges from those who wish to dominate, from those who do not trust, from others with hidden agendas, those who seek to scapegoat and so on. As Light and Cox point out, simply reading good advice does not always help us manage group dynamics since often what is needed is behaviour change in the students concerned. This rarely happens overnight!

Furthermore, there may be students from cultures that place different emphasis on oral culture. Until recently, many Japanese students, for example, had principally experienced written English in school, with few oral opportunities. Conversely, there are students (some African ones, for example) who are more used to a dominant oral culture.

An addition might also be to monitor our own language. A glossary relating to racial and ethnic expressions can be found on the Ryerson (Toronto) School of Journalism's 'Diversity Watch' website (www. diversitywatch.ryerson.ca/glossary/). It offers a quick and useful way for the contextualising of appropriate and inappropriate terms based on various journalist association style guides. (Note that it is designed for Canadian use but is still extremely relevant elsewhere.) We would need to adapt such glossaries for local use. Incidentally, Toronto has, for many years, appeared to be one of North America's most multicultural cities, and so the story of the birth of this site – where unrest arose from inappropriate use of language – is a particularly salutary reminder of the need for all of us to update and monitor our approaches.

Culture and Body Language

Jaques (2000) reminds us that communication is not simply a matter of expressing ideas clearly. He says:

It is often suffused with unintended effects, fears and dislikes, and unconscious motives. Often the non-verbal part of communication is the most eloquent. A great deal is revealed about what a person is really thinking and feeling by their facial expression, posture and gestures.

This can be especially difficult for international students. Eastern, Latin American and some Caribbean cultures, for example, can deem it rude to make firm eye contact; while in the UK it is often thought rude not to. There are different comfort zones regarding physical proximity and there are varying approaches to challenging questions or teacher authority. All of this also has implications if we see verbally aggressive students as brighter. We should be sensitive to this as far as we can. A number of online sites exist to offer quick advice to travellers on local customs such as the above, although the information should be treated with caution. Glancing at them can help us think through areas that may need consideration for enhancing our cross-cultural competence; see, for example, www.kwintessential. co.uk/resources/global-etiquette/india-country-profile.html.

However, we should not become inhibited and unnecessarily or falsely limit our own personalities. If we are good and caring teachers, single accidental slip-ups should not damage our relationships beyond repair.

Student Embarrassment

We have already talked about the optimal comfort zone for students to learn in. It is, of course, in the small group that sensitive issues may come to a head. Beatrice Quarshie Smith quotes an African student who says,

> the ever present issue of accent and the tendency for the professors and peers to ask for repetition of anything I say created embarrassing moments for me. It is demoralizing to realise that people around you will always prick up their ears to catch what they consider as an accent that they find difficult to cope with.
>
> (Quarshie Smith, 2007: 63)

In large groups students with such feelings will not be 'forced' to speak, but in small groups they are unlikely to avoid having to participate if staff are managing the group well and ensuring participation. We must always seek to minimise embarrassment. And yet it is important that all in the group can hear and understand all comments; our job as facilitators is tactfully to ensure this.

61

SETTING TASKS

Having planned and thought through activities as above, there are a number of ways in which the group can be subdivided. More detailed suggestions can be found in Jacques (2000), Exley and Dennick (2004b) and other guides. A few are briefly listed at the end of the chapter. The key interest as far as this text is concerned is to ensure that all are included, whatever approach is chosen.

Subdividing Groups

When we subdivide groups we should think carefully about how we will manage this. Different academics have different ways of doing this, and our own decisions will vary from situation to situation. Frequently staff allow students to self-select their groups, and there may be occasions for this but it is not always the best way. Physical impairments may make it essential that we, and not the students, manage the subdivision of groups in order to ensure access, hearing or sight lines. Careful managing of this can help all students. The *Teaching for Inclusion: diversity in the college classroom* website (http://ctl.unc.edu/tfitoc.html) suggests that students typically sit next to those who resemble them and that seating arrangements can end up divided on gender or racial lines. Self-segregation may not be harmful to learning, they claim, but it may 'limit the new perspectives gained'. Friends sitting together may often mean those of like views sitting together. Mix those from the back with those from the front and so on if you think a mix will benefit all. Where we direct the subdivision we should never appear to single out particular groups. For example, where we have two students of the same race we should take care not to appear to keep them segregated all the time. A variety of ways of approaching group divisions is likely to be the most practical answer. More detailed suggestions for this can also be found in Professor Barabara Glesner Fines' *Peer Teaching* manual for the Law School at University of Missouri Kansas City (www.law.umkc.edu/faculty/profiles/glesnerfines/bgf-home.htm).

Concluding and Following Up Seminars

Seminars should finish on time and not run over. The conclusion should offer a summary of critical points and the opportunity for questions and clarification. It should be made clear at the end of the session what the

SOME THOUGHTS ON SUBDIVIDING GROUPS

(Decide what the point is for your group and explain your rules very carefully; confusion is counter-productive!)

1 Number/letter individuals a, b, c, d, and then put those with each letter together – all 'a's, all 'b's and so on.
2 Mix more-experienced students with those who are less so.
3 Pairing.
4 'Crossovers' (e.g. give each group a label such as A1 – first they work together; then the As can work together, then the 1s, etc.).
5 'Snowballing'/pyramiding (e.g. groups of two move to work in groups of four then eight, etc.).
6 Goldfish bowl (e.g. one group observes another group in action and then comments).
7 Brainstorm (explain your rules, especially if students from other countries not used to such 'free for all' discussion).

Get the students to report back where useful – choose carefully how this will happen to avoid boredom and too much repetition (e.g. one to three major points from each group is often enough). Write results on flip charts, overhead projector or laptop.

requirements are for the following session and for any work that needs to be done in the interim. Submission details and contact information also should be clear at this point. It is wise to try to leave yourself a little free time at the end of seminars to follow up on individual queries. It is at this point that you are most likely to be able to talk to those who require any special provision or those who are unsure of the system.

CHECKLISTS AND TIPS FOR PARTICULAR SITUATIONS

The Open University in the UK has a useful website for aiding inclusive teaching: www.open.ac.uk/inclusiveteaching/pages/inclusive-teaching/.

Some of its very practical suggestions are amended below and amplified by suggestions from Clements and Spinks (2000).

63

Good Practice for All Might Include . . .

General preparation – issues to consider for an inclusive approach:

1   Think about thorough preparation of process as well as content.
2   Understand why you have designed your syllabus in the way that you have – *don't overpack it, so that you can leave time for process as well as content.*
3   Reflect diverse backgrounds on your syllabus, in your readings and in other materials such as visual aids – is the course material genuinely appropriate for a global world?
4   Have you checked the physical environment?
5   Ensure arrangements are made ahead of time with appropriate staff (e.g. room bookings, porters, audio-visual and so on).
6   Ensure you have made appropriate arrangements if you have been informed about anyone who needs particular conditions.
7   Are you familiar with the course requirements as the students' handbook outlines them?
8   Is your group is likely to be affected by absences from religious holidays, school holiday periods, and so on? Think how this might affect activities and planning.

The First Meeting

1   Make sure course-work requirements and deadlines are clear.
2   Make your course goals clear to all students and give continual feedback on how students are meeting them on it.
3   Are contingency or alternative approaches needed? Ensure you have spoken with everyone who has specific requirements regarding disability and that these are being followed up.
4   Make sure that anyone unfamiliar with the UK system is not left unclear because of assumptions of a knowledge of the system.
5   Create ground rules with the group if you think these will help.
6   Make sure arrangements for future meetings are clear.
7   Ensure the students know how and when they can contact you.

Your Delivery

1   Speak clearly; at an appropriate volume; at an appropriate pitch (e.g. lighter female voices can get more easily lost in some spaces); at an appropriate pace.
2   If you or your group members turn away, stop talking so that what you say is not missed.
3   Do not cover your mouth (e.g. by chewing on a pencil or holding a piece of paper in front of your mouth).
4   Lip reading may actually help second language students as well as students with a hearing impairment; psychologists of speech perception tell us that, to aid understanding, most of us lip-read more than we would imagine.
5   However, don't exaggerate lip movements.
6   Men with beards should keep them trimmed well back from the lips.
7   Aid emotion/feeling by (sensible!) gestures or facial expression if appropriate.

Your Relationship with the Students

1   Get to know your students – be approachable.
2   Try to learn names and how to pronounce them correctly – ask all the students for their preferred options and for pronunciation if you are unsure and write it down as an aide-memoire if you are likely to forget.
3   Get to know your students as individuals rather than as representatives of particular groups.
4   Learn to be a good listener.

Handling Discussion and Questions

Possible Techniques for General Understanding and Discussion 'Etiquette'

1   Keep what you are saying as straightforward as the topic allows.
2   Summarise key points and repeat key phrases and write notes on the board; this will clarify the learning for all the class.
3   Read aloud/talk through text, calculations, graphs and so on, as appropriate to aid clarification.

4   Spell out new or unusual vocabulary.
5   Allow silent time for students to look at visual aids/handouts of new information to be discussed.
6   Count to ten before you speak if there is silence after your questions; this allows time for considered responses.
7   Repeat other students' questions if unclear (do this routinely for all students!).
8   Ask their views, don't just give yours.
9   Present different sides of issues.
10 Allow students to disagree with you or others, but within guidelines that promote a safe learning atmosphere in the classroom.
11 Depersonalise controversial topics and structure assignments, when appropriate, to let your students choose topics with which they are comfortable.

Possible Ways of Avoiding Discriminatory Handling of Discussion

1   If you are using material with outdated language (or, for example, all male pronouns) point this out and slip in preferred current options so they do not assume you concur.
2   Are you giving male/female students the same level of attention?
3   Use gender-neutral terms if you are referring to both genders.
4   Take care with the use of idioms or with illustrations that depend on cultural knowledge that students may not possess.
5   Try not to reinforce stereotypes; for example, using male pronouns when referring to engineers or female pronouns when speaking of nurses.
6   Do not ask students to speak on behalf of whole groups that you assume they belong to, but do ask them for their own views and experiences.
7   Try not to speak in culturally specific assumptions; for example, religious worship 'is on Sunday' — it is not for Muslims or Jews.

Avoiding Unpleasant Strife

1   Do not let hurtful comments go undealt with; decide how serious it is as to how much time should be spent resolving issues.

2   Remind students to focus on the argument not the person (and do not let this mask any personal cruelty).

3   If things do get heated, ask students to step back from the argument and, as appropriate, analyse what went on and learn from it (it may not always be appropriate to highlight it or it may be better to deal with appropriate individuals).

4   If argumentative tension relates to academic content and yet becomes overly personal or hurtful it may be appropriate to stop and set different tasks; for example, getting students to research the issue to debate in a different way at a later date.

5   If a situation looks like escalating into something more serious discuss with your appropriate colleagues (Chair of Department/ teaching committee/equal opportunities staff, etc.).

Other Aspects of Group Organisation

1   Try breaking the larger 'small' groups into pairs or threes.

2   Try using written text instructions or discussion notes some of the time.

3   Accommodate different learning styles and promote collaboration between students.

4   Ensure students are carefully and sensitively pushed out of their comfort zone where it helps learning.

5   Monitor classroom dynamics to ensure some are not over-dominant.

Relationship with the Environment and the Group

1   Check and monitor temperature and air freshness where possible.

2   Is the lighting appropriate for students with a vision impairment?

3   Is the sound level good?

4   Eliminate background noise as far as possible (but this often means a decision between better temperature control and quietness!).

5 Do not stand with backs to the window or in dark shadow. Lighting is important to those who cannot see well or who may be lip-reading.

6 Sit at the same level as the students – at times and if possible – but stand if you feel you cannot be heard.

7 Allow the use of equipment that supports communication such as tape recorders, laptops, Braille note-takers and so on. (Our own view is that it is a courtesy to ask the group if they mind their comments being taped and respect any sensitivities there might be.)

 PAUSE FOR THOUGHT

■ Do you consciously monitor the above from time to time?

■ Have you had/should you consider voice training? Many academics would not see this as a priority but if you do not have a naturally strong voice you need to ensure you can be heard. Furthermore, voice problems can be an occupational hazard for us all, training can help you to use your voice properly and reduce chances of damage to your vocal chords (see Exley and Dennick, 2004a).

Other institutional guidelines include http://mathstore.gla.ac.uk/ headocs/34dyslexia.pdf. This provides a useful and practical list of strategies for staff working with students who are studying Maths and have dyslexia.

The Oxford Brookes University *Supporting Students with Dyslexia* website (www.brookes.ac.uk/services/hr/eod/guides/dyslexia.html) is one of a range of excellent guides on working inclusively.

GENDER AND DISCUSSION

A number of researchers have investigated the effects of gender in the classroom and on conversation generally (Pearson *et al.*, 1991; Tannen, 1996). In the UK, an awareness of this has brought some changes in habits, but there are likely to still be areas where we need to watch the gender

SOME THOUGHTS FOR STUDENTS WITH VISION IMPAIRMENTS

In addition to the above general good-practice suggestions:

1 You will need to be especially aware of the physical layout of the room. Normally it would be easier for blind students if room layout was predictable and kept the same.

2 Notify the student if seating arrangements are changed or the furniture is moved.

3 Warn the student before the session if there is going to be significant movement or if you have introduced a projector into the middle of the room, for example.

4 Ensure any student with a guide dog has an appropriate space to accommodate the dog comfortably.

5 The suggestions above for students with hearing difficulties regarding noise are also particularly relevant to ensure that all discussion can be clearly heard.

6 Describe any visual information clearly.

7 Provide alternative formats (Braille/electronic) as appropriate.

8 Find a way to help students record sessions if helpful.

9 If there is a note-taker, accommodate them appropriately – talk to the student using their name.

10 You may have to organise reading longer in advance so that recorded versions can be available.

11 Mark the difference between essential reading and that which is of interest.

dynamics of a group to ensure equity. It has been shown that teachers tend to:

1 call on male students more frequently;

2 wait longer for males to respond to questions;

3 give male students more eye contact following questions;

4 remember the names of male students;

5 use these names when calling on them;

6 attribute their comments in class discussion ('Michael said . . .');

7 interrupt female students before the end of their response;

SOME THOUGHTS FOR STUDENTS WITH DYSLEXIA

In addition to the above general good-practice suggestions:

1   Adopt a structured, multisensory teaching style (useful for all students!).
2   Present material in a structured way.
3   Provide a clear, concise framework – give an overview of the topic at the beginning of areas that you will cover and aims.
4   Present information in small chunks – break down processes into steps, with opportunity for feedback to check understanding and develop language skills.
5   Present material in different ways – from particular examples to general concepts and from general concepts to particular examples.
6   Build in repetition and reinforcement – when introducing new concepts, give concrete examples and explain points in different ways before moving on to a new topic, sum up what you've covered so far, encourage questions, stress importance of practice.
7   Present information in a visual form – design a 'mind map' or 'pattern plan' to give an overview of a topic/identify links, draw a flow chart to illustrate a process, show a video clip in which a process can be observed/discussed.
8   Encourage students to make their own meaningful connections to what they are learning.
9   Suggest memory tricks.
10 When introducing new subject-specific vocabulary give a brief definition and examples.
11 Speak directly to the class and avoid ambiguous language.
12 Minimise the amount of information to be transcribed during a lecture – use handouts.
13 Limit information on presentations to key points – elaborate on separate handouts.
14 Use board for illustration/elaboration, not note-taking; give notes on separate handouts.
15 For handouts, do not put too much information on one sheet. Do not justify right-hand margins as this leads to uneven spaces between words and makes the text hard to follow.

16 Make handouts and presentation slides available in advance. Check whether the student requires the handouts on coloured paper and/or in electronic form.

17 Provide concrete tasks, such as cloze-type exercises to complete/ check in class, paired/small-group activities.

18 Avoid activities such as written group work that could embarrass the student.

19 Minimise background noise.

(Adapted from Anglia University)

8 ask males more questions that call for 'higher-order' critical thinking as opposed to 'lower-order' recounting of facts.

(University of North Carolina at Chapel Hill)

Others have shown that female students:

1 give their statements less loudly and at less length;
2 present their statement in a more hesitant, indirect or 'polite' manner;
3 use 'I' statements – 'I was wondering . . .';
4 qualify their statements more – 'possibly';
5 add tag questions – 'isn't it?', 'don't you think?';
6 ask questions rather than give statements;
7 accompany their statement with smiles or averted eyes rather than more assertive gestures such as pointing;
8 apologize for their statements – 'I may be wrong but'.

(Amended from Georgia Tech, US)

Regionalism

Regionalism can be a hidden discriminator in discussion; most countries have accents or areas about which there are stereotypical jokes. A north–south distinction is not uncommon, for example. Regionalism can be an asset or a source of discomfort. This is often associated with a kind of class consciousness. Students can be uncomfortable about regional accents but would seldom say so.

SOME THOUGHTS FOR STUDENTS WITH HEARING DIFFICULTIES

In addition to the above general good-practice suggestions:

1   Control background noise.
2   Allow only one person to talk at a time.
3   Try not to feel embarrassed if you do not understand a deaf student. It is better to ask them to repeat their comments than to pretend you have heard.
4   Try not to alter your normal speech pattern, but also not to obscure your mouth with your hands, not to sit/stand with your back to a window (which places you in silhouette), but not in shadow either.
5   Attempt always to face the front when lecturing, and not to move about too much, which can interfere with microphones. Try not to talk when your back is turned.
6   Gain the deaf student's attention (subtly) by flicking lights on/off or indicating with your hands.
7   It is easier for deaf students to follow a lecture if they have 'head-line' notes, handouts and so on. This is even more useful if provided well before the lecture.
8   Allow some pauses for interpreters/note-takers to catch up.
9   Speak directly to the deaf student, not to their support worker (unless asked a direct question by the worker).
10   Repeat questions from the group, in case the deaf student misses them.
11   Be aware that the hum from a projector can adversely affect hearing equipment. Turn it off where possible.
12   Write important announcements or unfamiliar words/technical terms on a board.
13   If using a video, inform the student well in advance, as some firms offer transcription or subtitling.
14   In small groups, try to arrange seating so that everyone can be seen.
15   Make sure that where a loop system is useful it is available.

(Amended from University of Birmingham)

PAUSE FOR THOUGHT

- Do you recognise these gendered aspects of the classroom? Or have things 'moved on'?
- Do you monitor to ensure you do not accidentally slip into any of the above habits that do not allow women to participate fully?
- Some men have an awareness of the above and that can make it harder for them. How do you check all feel at ease with this?

SOME THOUGHTS ON SEXUALITY

Gender issues may be about deeper issues of sexuality. A number of institutions recommend that to set a comfortable tone you should:

1. assume that not all students in the class are heterosexual;
2. react firmly to homophobic remarks (laughing them off is not an option);
3. give assignments that will not force gay people, lesbians or bisexuals to 'come out';
4. speak of 'bisexual men' or 'bisexual women' rather than simply 'bisexuals';
5. use acceptable terms when speaking about gay/lesbian issues; for example, do not assume that partner equals husband or wife of the opposite sex;
6. use the term sexual orientation not sexual preference; many gay and lesbian people do not feel they have chosen their sexuality;
7. not assume that HIV positive people are gay or that only gay people engage in activities that put themselves and others at risk;
8. be aware that the word 'queer' has been re-adopted by some members of the lesbian, gay, bisexual and transgendered community but not by others, so it may be better to avoid this term unless you know precisely why you are using it and it is in a positive way.

(Amended from: The University of North Carolina at Chapel Hill and University of Waterloo, Ontario)

Students with Chronic Medical Conditions

Students may not wish to tell you about chronic medical conditions, but you may notice a marked change in performance – be aware that it may be illness related. Be sensitive where discussion addresses such topics – there may be someone in the room closely affected, either themselves or their family members – and be sensitive to frequent absences if illness-related – check progress and access to course material.

Short-Term Illness

Ensure that any students with short-term illness have appropriate provision to help them keep up with the work. Virtually all institutions have special arrangements for assessment in such cases, but you will need to ensure that such students have access to material from your seminars too. Frequently they will enlist the help of friends in this process, but that may not be a comprehensive enough mechanism. Check that they have access to course materials and so on. Such students may not be fully focused when they are present in seminars and may need more patience from you than usual if they are to stay on track.

SOME THOUGHTS ON STUDENTS WITH LIMITED MOBILITY

In addition to the above general good-practice suggestions:

1 Remember the impairment is only a part of the individual.
2 Ask privately about what is needed.
3 Plan activities ahead with access in mind.
4 Try to ensure a comfortable seat.
5 Clear obstacles.
6 Check if surface needed for writing.
7 Contact portering staff if you need to maintain access conditions or particular furniture for the whole term/semester.
8 Do not expect them, for example, to raise hands to speak if that is too painful.

PAUSE FOR THOUGHT

You have a student in your group who has an unfortunate and aggressive manner. Do you do anything?

It would depend. Has this been a problem over a number of weeks? Does it appear to adversely affect the group? If yes, it may be that there is an opportunity to discuss this with the student if you think it would help both him/her and the group. Try to determine the future action that is best for *the whole group*.

There may be an oral skills exercise that you could integrate to help all members, but it must never appear aimed at one person.

 PAUSE FOR THOUGHT

You have a student with a hearing impairment for whom English is not the first language and it is making communication difficult in the group, and the other students are clearly frustrated. What do you do?

Look at ways of producing more written aids. Discuss ways the students can include and help the student but also find ways they can progress their own knowledge. Discuss online aids with the disability unit and see if there are ways you can produce material that would help. See if more online discussion would help. If there is content to get to grips with offer an extra session for that student. With the individual's permission you could talk with the group about what strategies could be used.

 PAUSE FOR THOUGHT

Group discussion is difficult.

Have you tried a 'tutorless group'? Set them specific tasks and leave the room and then come back and discuss answers. This sometimes gets discussion started.

Break them up into pairs; set specific tasks; ensure they are preparing – try having a 'passport to the seminar' (i.e. they must do half a page of written preparation).

PAUSE FOR THOUGHT

How do you react if a student from a particularly strong religious or ethnic background is adamant that women are not equal?

How do you handle discussion where there are two students from opposing ethnic groups and both are adamant their position is right?

Ensuring inclusion and appropriate learning for diverse students often means there is no one correct answer. See Chapter 9 for a discussion of decision-making and ensuring fairness and justice.

Encourage the groups to discuss the issues without attacking the individual. Remind them of the relevant ground rules the group has set. You may be able to advise on reading matter that handles these issues; invite speakers who are used to handling the issues (e.g. in the second case you may have politics members of staff used to handling ethnicity in post-war reconstruction or similar). Ask the students to research the opposite position and come prepared to articulate it. Talk through the learning outcomes and make it very clear why you are having this discussion – in this context it is for them to learn about particular knowledge or skills and not for them to put the world to rights or to win an argument; agree to differ.

 PAUSE FOR THOUGHT

You have a blind student in your group. Do you announce this publicly and ask others to regard them as a full member of the group in all respects?

The best solution is to check with your student what they want. In the University of North Carolina student survey referred to previously, one student was adamant that this was the right approach for him while another student did not want this.

See Chapter 7 and discussion of 'empathy'.

CONCLUSION

Light and Cox (2001) conclude their chapter on small groups by suggesting that our behaviour in small groups may often be counter to normal social conventions, that is to say that we do not ask dinner party guests to spilt into small groups, nor do we stop them when they do! But they also suggest that we try to assure some of the positive experiences of our social groups when we run small groups. Of course, the purpose of our sessions is learning, but also for it to happen in a context of positive emotional reaction within the group; a party that has gone well! However, we must also remember that parties can actually be extremely uncomfortable occasions for those whose hearing or sight is limited or whose language is different to that of the majority; we would wish all our guests to leave feeling included in the good will. We need to be good hosts in our seminars as a part of being good educators. Some academics may balk at this image, but this approach need not diminish our ability to further our disciplines, indeed we are far more likely to enthuse our students if we appear to be interested in them as individuals. As Light and Cox (2001) suggest, we need consciously to integrate content and process in group work, and ensuring integration is probably mostly about human kindness. UK discrimination legislation is based on comparing the treatment of one person with another and treating no one less favourably – this we must aim to achieve.

As we will repeatedly say in this book, there is rarely a right or wrong answer. At the end of the day we can only (a) check that there is no absolute correct answer (i.e. university policy or legislation that says we must react in a particular way); (b) check that there is no clear evidence from experts that a particular way is the only way or the best way to proceed; or (c) make our own carefully considered decision in the light of the information available, in the good faith that we are acting in the best interests of the student, the university and other interested parties.

Despite all the tips and suggestions above, one student offers the following advice:

> Tell the young [sic] teachers not to get hung up on majority or minority – just act themselves, you know. Most of the time that helps a lot more than getting hung up on the minority and the difference and worrying about, you know, trying not to offend some body. You end up doing that anyway, because you're nervous, and you're trying hard!
>
> (University of North Carolina at Chapel Hill)

NOTE

1   You may be told that you cannot use the term brainstorming because it is offensive to people with mental health difficulties. This is not the case, and there is nothing wrong with using the term in the context of collecting ideas from a group of students. See National Society for Epilepsy (2005) for a discussion on this topic.

 FURTHER READING

Baume, C. and Baume, D. (1996) *Learning to Teach: Running tutorials and seminars*, Oxford Brookes University: Oxford Centre for Staff and Learning Development.

Chalmers, D. and Fuller, R. (1996) *Teaching for Learning at University*, London: Kogan Page.

Dennick, R. and Exley, K. (2004) *Small Group Teaching Tutorials: Seminars and beyond*, Abingdon: Taylor & Francis.

Fry, H., Ketteridge, S. and Marshall, S. (2003) *A Handbook for Teaching and Learning in Higher Education: Enhancing academic practice*, London: Kogan Page.

Habeshaw, S., Habeshaw, T. and Gibbs, G. (1992) *53 Interesting Things to do in your Seminars and Tutorials*, 4th edn, Bristol: Technical and Educational Services.

Jaques, D. (2000) *Learning in Groups: A handbook for improving group work*, 3rd edn, London: Kogan Page.

Light, G. and Cox, R. (2001) *Learning to Teach in Higher Education*, London: PCP Publishing.

 USEFUL WEB RESOURCES

www.bmj.com/cgi/content/full/326/7387/492
A webpage by David Jaques on teaching small groups in medicine.

http://ctl.unc.edu/tfitoc.html
University of North Carolina at Chapel Hill provides an excellent site and possibly one of the most comprehensive sites on the topic of inclusive teaching.

www.uchsc.edu/CIS/SmGpChkList.html

www.nottingham.ac.uk/teaching/resources/methods/smallgroup/
Both these sites provide a range of checklists for you to monitor your small-group teaching preparation.

www.diversityweb.org/diversity_innovations/institutional_leadership/campus_climate_culture/index.cfm
This US site has helpful links on diversity in higher education.

Chapter 4

Working with Students in Large Groups

Chapter 3 discussed the issue of inclusion and diversity in relation to small-group teaching. It will not be surprising to learn that much of the information presented in that chapter is also relevant to large-group teaching; in particular, many of the suggestions noted in the checklists at the end of the previous chapter apply equally to large-group teaching.

Chapter 3 noted that it was not really possible to determine what constitutes a 'small group', and the same applies to large-group teaching. One of the main differences between the two methods of teaching is the role of the lecturer: in small-group teaching the lecturer will often be acting as a facilitator of discussions, whereas in large-group teaching there is likely to be more focus on the lecturer initiating and providing discussions about a particular theme. This is not to say that the role of the lecturer in large-group teaching is to 'deliver' material, nor that the students should be passive recipients of information, and we would encourage the use of interactive lectures.

Agnew and Elton (1998) provided the following list of reasons why large group sessions are used in higher education:

1 They are a very cost effective means of teaching large classes.
2 They are useful when bodies of factual information need to be presented to students.
3 They enable teachers and students to organise their time effectively.
4 They enhance control over class content, facilitating curriculum and study-programme planning.
5 They are an efficient use of lecturer time as once prepared they are quickly updated and reusable.
6 They can lead to personal satisfaction.

7 They introduce students to the language of the discipline.

8 They can impart enthusiasm for the subject.

9 They allow key concepts and principles to be promoted.

(Agnew and Elton, 1998: 1)

DESIGNING LARGE GROUP SESSIONS

Information in this chapter reiterates and builds on the advice provided by Exley and Dennick (2004a), and we would advise anyone new to lecturing to look at this resource.

Core Requirements

The first question when designing our curriculum as a whole, regardless of whether it will focus on the use of large group sessions, is 'What are the core requirements of my course/module?' (Teachability, 2000). Determining the core requirements of a course may not be as easy as we might first anticipate, but it is a useful exercise to think about what we really want our students to have achieved once they have finished the course. Once the core requirements have been determined, then they can feed into the development of a constructively aligned curriculum (Biggs, 2003) (see also Chapter 9) by forming a basis for the construction of learning outcomes and consideration of appropriate teaching, learning and assessment strategies/activities that will allow the students to demonstrate that they have met the identified core requirements.

One of the best ways to start considering the amount of 'content' to include in a large group session is to consider what the students *must know*, *should know* or *could know*. The *must know* relates to the core requirements, whereas the *should know* and *could know* relate to topics that, depending upon time, can either be delivered by other approaches such as independent learning (should know) or probably dropped completely (could know). This is a useful approach to ensure that we are not delivering too much content in our sessions, and is particularly useful when trying to develop a student-centred curriculum that involves active learning techniques.

Teaching and Learning Strategies

In considering appropriate teaching and learning strategies, we need to address the fact that our students may have different learning styles. Exley and Dennick (2004a) make reference to a number of learning-style inventories, and although there is some debate about the validity of some of these inventories (see discussion in Chapter 2 and Coffield *et al.* (2004)), it is generally acknowledged that different students will learn best from different teaching and learning approaches. It is also worth considering the fact that within a large group session our own preferred learning style is likely to be in the minority compared with the group as a whole. It is therefore important that we do not simply teach in a way that we learn best, but to include a variety of approaches. This variation will not only address a range of learning styles, but should make our sessions more interesting for our students. One way in which we can introduce more variety into our teaching is to incorporate more active learning techniques in our sessions, and we would recommend Exley and Dennick (2004a) for a discussion on the use of active learning in lectures as well the resources provided by the Centre for Active Learning at the University of Gloucestershire (www.glos.ac.uk/ceal/).

While we are developing our teaching and learning methods, we will need to consider how accessible our course is and how we can ensure that an international perspective is embedded throughout the curriculum. In terms of accessibility, what are we asking students to do in a lecture and how might this impact on some students? For example, a student with a hearing impairment might find it hard to participate in small buzz group discussions within a large group, owing to the high level of background noise.

Although we will not always know the location of the room in which we are teaching when we are designing our sessions, it would be useful to consider how this might impact on what we are asking our students to do. For example, is there provision for wheelchair users and, if so, how flexible is this? (It is desirable for a wheelchair user to be incorporated into the student group where possible, rather than having to be in a set position at the front or back of the room. This is often more important in a small-group teaching situation; see Chapter 3.)

Diversifying the Curriculum

There are several aspects of diversity that we should consider when developing our curriculum, for example, internationalisation, gender, age and disability. It is worth noting here the difference between internationalisation and globalisation, which are often used interchangeably. In this book we are taking the term *internationalisation* to mean the integration of international and intercultural dimensions into the curriculum and *globalisation* to refer to the increased interconnection of, for example, technology, values, ideas and people across a global market, and the subsequent development of cross-cultural skills to assist students to work in such a market. (See also Chapter 10.)

To be truly inclusive, diversity issues should be integrated and embedded within our curriculum rather than being considered as an add-on. An example of the latter approach would be to devote some specific time to, for example, the role of women in chemistry. Making specific reference to a particular area of diversity can sometimes imply that the topic is something that is considered by the lecturer to be 'not normal'. Highlighting particular issues can also be viewed as tokenistic and a quick-fix method of addressing the diversity agenda. Using the same example as above, a more inclusive approach would be to make reference to female chemists and their work in the same way as references are made to male chemists.

The same issues apply when considering other aspects of diversity. Owing to the fact that the majority of the research papers and text books that we read will be written in our first language, it is often the case that we will develop a view of the discipline that is centred on our own cultural beliefs. Unless we encounter academics from other cultures at international conferences, it can be difficult to find alternative views of our discipline from other cultures. However, if we do introduce other cultural perspectives of our discipline then we should ensure any such references do not come across as odd or inferior, and that alternative views and cultures are respected (Ryan, 2000).

 PAUSE FOR THOUGHT

- How do you currently deal with diversity issues in your curriculum, if at all?
- Are you aware of other international perspectives relating to your discipline? If so, how are these incorporated into your curriculum?
- Would you say that your references to experts in your discipline reflect an appropriate balance in terms of gender and internationalisation?
- Have you considered whether, and how, disability issues have impacted upon the development of your discipline?

Establishing an Appropriate Atmosphere

Although, as noted in Chapter 1, we should not make assumptions about our students' experiences or attitudes towards teaching and learning based on stereotypical views of other cultures, it is important to understand that there will be differences between our own philosophies of teaching and learning and those of our students. This could apply equally to home students as to international students. It may therefore be useful to be very explicit about our own view of the role of lecturer and student. This may take the form of a group discussion about students' expectations of higher education teaching and learning. You may find that some students have been more used to a tutor-centred culture, where there is respect for the tutor and where students tend not to be critical of what is said or what has been written in the research literature, and where there is an expectation of a 'correct' answer (Ryan, 2000). While we may be trying to develop a more student-centred curriculum, where we expect the students to be more independent and critically to analyse and challenge the research literature and our own views and opinions, some students may resent the fact that we are asking them to do the work of finding out the answers and may consider that we are not fulfilling our obligations to them. Our philosophy and expectations therefore need to be made clear, in order to ensure that all the students know what we are requiring from them. It is unfair to assume that the students will be used to our approach, or will be able to determine our expectations through subtle hints and clues.

To further develop an appropriate atmosphere in our sessions, and for the students to be clear about what they should and should not be doing, we may find it helpful to develop some ground rules, either form-ally or informally (see Chapter 2). It is important that the students have some ownership of these ground rules, either by developing them themselves or by discussing and editing some draft ground rules that we may provide. These ground rules may include a description of our responsibilities and our students' responsibilities, in addition to statements regarding the use of appropriate language; for example: 'The use of lan-guage that discriminates against students on the basis of ethnicity, gender, sexual orientation, age, religion or disability will not be tolerated.' We may also find that the development of such ground rules will help to increase all students' knowledge and awareness of diversity issues.

Resources

Resources associated with large-group teaching include handouts and audio-visual materials such as presentation software and video/DVD/ sound recordings. This can also include general course-specific material, such as information about the course and reading lists (see Chapter 6 for a discussion about reading lists).

Handouts

More detailed information about handouts and their uses is presented in Exley and Dennick (2004a). What we would like to do here is to emphasise some of the important points about making handouts inclusive.

Regardless of whether your handouts are a summary of your presentation, or are providing additional information, it is sensible to ensure that whatever information you include in the handouts makes sense, particularly if the handouts are also intended to assist students' revision for assessment purposes. Although it is tempting to put as much information as possible on a handout, owing to the costs associated with reproduction for large groups, it is important to make sure that they are clear and uncluttered. The handouts should be written in clear English, and should use an appropriate font and point size (generally 12 point text in a sans serif font such as Verdana, Helvetica or Arial).

Some students will benefit from handouts printed on coloured paper. Often the advice provided is to print all handouts on buff or pale coloured paper, as this will assist some students (e.g. students with dyslexia); however, the cost of providing handouts can be increased substantially if coloured paper is involved. Also, students who use a colour overlay (see, for example, www.essex.ac.uk/psychology/overlays/overlaysM1.htm) or spectacles with tinted lenses to help read printed text may find that the effect of the overlay is negated by the use of coloured paper. A different, and yet still inclusive, approach would be to make an announcement at the start of the course asking whether there is anything that you can do to assist the students' learning, such as providing handouts on coloured paper. It is possible that only a small number of students will request handouts on coloured paper, and it may be appropriate to make separate arrangements for the students to collect these handouts outside the session as they may not want their peers to know that they have a learning difficulty. In this way, we will be addressing the requirements of our group in a manner that does not make assumptions about what they will need.

84

Presentation Software

It used to be considered poor practice to read out the content of presentation slides on the basis that 'we are all able to read'. Although it is true that our students will be able to read, it is not necessarily true that they will be able to read quickly or accurately. We may find that students with dyslexia, students with a vision impairment and students who are not studying in their first language will appreciate the fact that we are reading the text from our presentation. (See Chapter 5 for a discussion about preparing accessible presentations.)

It is also useful to know how to hide a presentation slide when you want to; this has the benefit of bringing the focus, and the students' attention, back to you; for example, we may find that students are copying information from a slide when we actually want them to listen to an important point that we are discussing. To hide a slide within Microsoft PowerPoint®, press the 'b' button on the keyboard during an on-screen slideshow to make the screen go black, or the 'w' button to make it go white (depending on the brightness of the room and the nature of your presentation). Pressing the 'b' or 'w' button again will return to the presentation.

Another point to note is that presentations created using specific software such as Microsoft PowerPoint® do not have to be linear. Unlike old-fashioned slide projectors, where the slides had to be placed in a set order in a carousel, most presentation software will allow you to jump to a particular slide at any point during the presentation. This saves the problem of scrolling back or forward through slides to get to the one you want, perhaps because a student has asked a particular question that relates to an earlier slide. This scrolling back and forth can sometimes be very confusing for the students who are watching you. In order to go to a particular slide in Microsoft PowerPoint®, you will need to know the slide number. This is achieved most easily by printing out your presentation and either marking the slide numbers on the handout yourself, or using the slide number feature available within the software. To go directly to the slide of interest, type in the slide number and press 'Enter' on the keyboard. The added advantage of this technique is that you can add additional slides at the end of the presentation, which may be helpful to expand on, or clarify, specific points if required. If the students are having difficulty in understanding a specific aspect of the presentation, then it would be possible to jump directly to one of these slides and then to return seamlessly to the presentation when finished.

WORKING WITH LARGE GROUPS

Audio-Visual Materials

The images that we show in our sessions may provide an important, but perhaps unconscious, impression about our attitude towards diversity issues. Are they biased towards particular identities? If so, how can we modify our use of images in future courses in a way that is not tokenistic?

If we are showing audio-visual materials, then it is important that these are accessible to all users. Providing a transcript of video/DVD clips is essential for students with hearing impairment, and will also prove to be beneficial to students who are not studying in their first language. In terms of students with a vision impairment, we must also consider whether the commentary makes sense without the images. If this is not the case, then we may have to provide a detailed description of the images to supplement the commentary (see Chapter 5 for a discussion about describing images).

DELIVERING LARGE GROUP SESSIONS

Having considered some of the issues relating to the design and development of a large group session, the next stage is to focus on the delivery of the session itself.

Recognising Inclusive Practice

If you have not already done so, try videoing some of your teaching sessions. It may take a short while to overcome the embarrassment of watching yourself during the playback, but it can be worth it. When viewing the video, try to answer the following questions (note: even if you do not intend to video yourself, you could always consider these questions while you are delivering a session).

1 Is my speaking voice clear?

This may relate to a number of factors including:

(a) the projection of your voice;
(b) use of a microphone (if appropriate);
(c) accent;
(d) pace of the session.

It may be necessary for you to use a microphone if you are in a large room or lecture theatre, or if you have students with hearing impairments who require the use of an induction loop system that transmits the sound

86

directly to a hearing aid. One problem that you may have encountered if you have been in an audience when someone is using a fixed microphone is that if the speaker turns around to look at the screen then the projection of their voice is lost. This highlights the general good practice of making sure that we only talk while looking at the audience. This good practice should also be remembered if using a radio microphone that allows us to move around; although it will be possible for most students to hear us if we are using a radio microphone and looking away from the student group, we will be disadvantaging those students who are trying to lip-read.

If a microphone is not present then it is important that we resist the urge to shout, as this will put a strain on our throat and vocal chords. Your institution may run staff development workshops on voice projection, and if you find yourself with several sessions in large rooms with poor acoustic properties then it may be worth attending one of these workshops. (See also Exley and Dennick (2004a).)

There is not much that you can do if you have an accent, but you can try to ensure that you speak as clearly as possible. In particular, we can improve our diction by pronouncing the ends of words. This will also tend to reduce the pace of the session slightly, which may help a number of students. What we should try to avoid is slowing down the pace of our delivery for the benefit of international students, or exaggerate words because we know that we have some students with hearing impairments. Clarity can be enhanced through a controlled pace, rather than a slow one. Exaggerating words and slowing the pace unnaturally have the effect of distorting our mouth so that it is harder to understand and to lip-read.

2 Do I repeat students' questions so that everyone can hear what was asked?

Depending on the acoustic properties of the room it may be necessary to repeat, or paraphrase, questions and comments from students. Not only does this have the advantage of allowing us to clarify and check what is being asked, but it also means that our response will be in context for those students who were not able to hear the original question. This is a particularly useful technique in tiered lecture rooms, where the fact that students are in rows facing the front means that a student towards the back of the room – regardless of whether they have a hearing impairment or they are not studying in their first language – is unlikely to hear anything that is said by students towards the front of the room.

3 Is my use of language clear and appropriate?

This is one area that it would be good for us to scrutinise in some detail. How clear are we when we talk? Do we use overly complicated sentences and jargon in order to put a point across to our students? In particular, we need to consider our use of metaphors and analogies that may make perfect sense to us, and probably to home-based students, but may not make as much sense to international students. If we use metaphors and analogies then it is useful to explain how these were derived, rather than simply describing what they mean; an international student is more likely to remember the meaning if they understand the context in which the expression was first derived (Carroll, 2005).

Similar warnings also need to be applied to anecdotes and the use of humour. Anecdotes can be a very useful method of making a particular point, but it is important to ensure that they do not contain cultural references that would not make much sense to international students. Our use of humour can potentially be open to misinterpretation by some groups of students. Many jokes are made at the expense of particular groups of people, and, although we would not wish for students to take offence at any jokes that we make, our use of humour needs to be handled carefully and with consideration to all our students.

It is worth analysing the terminology that we use in our classes. What we are aiming for is to use language that will not cause offence to our students, and that should be viewed as a common courtesy rather than addressing a particular political correctness agenda.

It is worth noting that the correct use of language will vary from country to country, and it would be useful to make a note of language that is considered to be appropriate for the area where you teach. For example, 'people of color' is a term used in the USA, but is rarely heard in the UK. The 'Diversity Watch' glossary noted in Chapter 2 (www.diversitywatch. ryerson.ca/glossary/) is a good place to start for issues relating to language.

It is also worth considering whether the questions that we ask students within a session are clear and appropriate. Many of us use this technique as a way of determining declarative knowledge within the group, and to use the students' own experiences to enrich our discussions. It might be useful to reflect upon how clear we are being with the questions that we ask, as it might be difficult for a student who is not studying in their first language to be able to interpret what is required from quite broad, or open-ended, questions. When asking questions we should be careful not to expect individual students to act as representatives for particular groups, for example, expecting a wheelchair user to represent the views of disabled students or an international student to represent the views of their country or culture. We must remember that within any particular group there will be a range of opinions, and it is not fair to ask individual students to represent the views of a culture as a whole.

Not only should we consider the language that we are using, it is also important that we take note of the language, terminology and jokes made by other students. If students are using language that could be considered inappropriate or discriminatory against a particular group of students, then we will need to address this issue. If we do nothing to stop such practice then we will be sending mixed messages to our students regarding the inclusive nature of our sessions; on the one hand we will be trying to demonstrate inclusive practice, but on the other we will not be putting a stop to discriminatory practices from other students. How this is dealt with in the session will depend on the context in which the discriminatory practice occurs, but it may be appropriate to have a group discussion about discrimination and to bring in comments from all students. There will, however, be occasions where this type of action is not appropriate, and it may be necessary to deal more directly with the issue. Whichever approach is taken, it is important to explain the rationale behind the action and to emphasise the atmosphere that we are trying to cultivate in our sessions.

4 Do I respond to a range of students?

It is worth checking to see whether we – probably unconsciously – respond to particular students, or groups of students, during our sessions. For example, do we have a tendency to look to female or male students, or students from particular ethnicities, for the answer to our questions? There may be some students who tend to provide the answers to our questions, but it is important to ensure that all students are given the opportunity to respond and to participate in the session. The use of active learning techniques, such as asking students to discuss a question or an issue in pairs or small groups before responding, will help to ensure that all your students are engaged with the topic of discussion. Many students will find it less intimidating to provide a group response to a question, rather than their own ideas, particularly in the early stages of their higher education experience. Increased use of such techniques may start to develop an atmosphere where students feel more comfortable in responding to questions on an individual basis. In this respect, it is very important to ensure that the way in which we respond to students' responses is appropriate. Even if a response is 'wrong', then it is likely that this could be discussed in terms of why it may not be the most appropriate answer, and might perhaps be because the student had not fully understood the question in the first place. What we must not do is to make the student feel embarrassed by the fact that they had provided an incorrect answer; it may have taken a lot of courage for the student to respond, and a negative response may mean that they will be unlikely to provide answers to future questions. The same outcome can also occur if we heavily praise some students' responses and not others. Imagine how it might feel to a student if we have overly praised the previous student's comment but not theirs. There may have been nothing wrong with their comment, and our aim might have been to provide encouragement for the first student, but this can appear as a negative response in relation to our reaction to the other student.

5 Do I 'signpost' my session?

Students can get a lot more from your session if you indicate clearly what you intend to do. The old adage 'say what you're going to say; say it; say what you've said' is useful to remember. We will discuss in Chapter 5 about making lecture notes available in advance of a session, as an aid to signposting, but there are techniques that can be implemented within the session itself. For example, briefly outlining the structure at the start of a session and making it clear when you are discussing issues that should be noted can help students to move from *taking notes* (i.e. writing down everything that is said without really thinking about the topic) to *making notes* (i.e. making choices in what is recorded, while also listening to, and trying to understand, the topic in more depth). Appropriate pauses, repetition and changes in pace can also be helpful as a way of signposting important information; for example, slowing down the pace of the session could be used as a method of emphasising particular points.

6 Do I provide instructions for activities visually as well as aurally?

With an emphasis on incorporating active learning techniques into our sessions, it is important to explain to our students exactly what we want them to do in the activities. This may be clear to us but it is not always clear to the students, unless they know what the outcome is meant to be. To assist with this understanding, it can be useful for all students to have a back-up for the instructions given to the group; for example, announce the instructions to the group but also have them displayed on a screen. Keeping the instructions on the screen throughout the activity will be helpful to the students as they work through the different steps of the activity, and to ensure that they remain focused throughout the task.

7 Do I demonstrate examples of disability etiquette?

Although we are trying to highlight an inclusive curriculum that does not focus on particular groups of students, it is useful to be aware of a couple of issues relating to disability etiquette in large-group teaching. In particular, these could include the following:

- If we have a student in our session who requires a sign language interpreter, it is important that we build some breaks into the session as it can be very tiring for both the student and the interpreter. Also, if the student asks us a question, we must make sure that we respond to the student and not to the interpreter. (This can be difficult at first, as we will not be responding to the person who is talking to us.)

- We may also have support workers in our sessions who are making notes for disabled students. We must not assume that the person that the support worker is sitting with is the disabled student. Some students do not wish their peers to know about their impairment or learning difficulty and may ask the support worker to sit in another part of the room. It is therefore important that we do not make specific reference to individuals that we may know have an impairment, as this fact may not be known to others.

- Facing students while talking will not only be useful for students who might be lip-reading, but it can also be helpful for students whose first language is not the language of study. We must ensure that we do not continue talking when turning to write something on a board or when we are looking at a projection screen, as anything that we say at this time could be lost to a number of students. However, the fact that we face the students when we talk will not be very helpful if the lighting is such that they cannot see our face. It may be necessary to dim the lights in order for the students to read a presentation projected onto a screen, but the quality of many projectors nowadays means that it is not necessary to plunge the students into complete darkness.

How do we Know if the Students have Learnt Anything?

It can be difficult in any large group session to determine whether our students have actually learnt anything, but this is becoming increasingly important with the increasing diversity of our groups. It is helpful if we have some methods of making an initial evaluation of our students' knowledge, when they have participated in one of our sessions. Some suggestions as to how this could be achieved are as follows:

1   Active learning activities not only provide the students with a break from listening to us, but can also provide an opportunity for them – and us – to check their understanding of a particular issue by discussing it with peers. For example, the use of techniques such as paired discussions, small-group discussions and brainstorming, can give you a reasonable, and quick, indication of the knowledge level within your group.

2   Asking students to indicate the 'muddiest point' of a session (Angelo and Cross, 1993) can be a very useful and quick way of finding out if there is a topic that may not have been explained clearly. This method works by asking students to write down on a piece of paper one aspect of the session that did not make complete sense to them. The students then leave these, anonymous, pieces of paper on the way out. Depending on the number of issues raised, the muddiest point(s) can either be addressed at the start of the following session or this method could be used if there is a break in the session, and the relevant topic(s) can be addressed when the students return.

3   Informal in-class tests can be used as a way of gauging knowledge. There is an increasing use of *classroom response systems* that allow questions to be projected via a computer and the students to respond using handsets. Most software packages will present a visual image of the responses, and this can be a very effective way of determining knowledge. It is worth noting, however, that overuse of this kind of technology can result in student fatigue –

to the extent that you may not be getting an accurate picture of our students' knowledge – and it is important to ensure that this is one of a range of methods of collecting information about our students' progress.

 FURTHER READING

The following publications discuss the issue of large groups in a general way, rather than specifically in relation to inclusion and diversity issues, but many of the points made are complementary to the advice given in this chapter.

Bligh, D. (1971) *What's the Use of Lectures?* Exeter: Donald Bligh.

Cryer, P. and Elton, L. (1992) *Active Learning in Large Classes and with Increasing Student Numbers*, Sheffield: CVCP Staff Development Unit.

Exley, K. and Dennick, R. (2004) *Giving a Lecture: From presenting to teaching*, Abingdon: Routledge Falmer.

Gibbs, G. and Jenkins, A. (eds) (1992) *Teaching Large Classes in Higher Education*, London: Kogan Page.

 USEFUL WEB RESOURCES

Creating Accessible Lectures for Disabled Students (Teachability Project, University of Strathclyde)
> One of the guides in the Teachability series, focusing on creating an accessible curriculum for disabled students: www.teachability.strath.ac.uk/chapter_3/tableofcontents3.html.

Diversity and Complexity in the Classroom: Considerations of race, ethnicity, and gender (Barbara Gross Davis, University of California, Berkeley)
> Strategies and tactics for dealing with diverse classrooms: http:// teaching.berkeley.edu/bgd/diversity.html.

Inclusive Teaching (Center for Instructional Development and Research, Washington)
> Resources covering issues such as: perspectives on what excludes students; strategies for inclusive teaching; resources for inclusive teaching: http://depts.washington.edu/cidrweb/inclusive/index.html.

Making your Teaching Inclusive (Open University)
> Focusing on disabled students, these webpages provide practical advice and include video clips detailing students' experiences: www.open.ac.uk/inclusiveteaching/index.php.

Race and Pedagogy Project (University of California, Santa Barbara)
> An interactive site exploring issues about 'race' in the classroom: http://rpp.english.ucsb.edu/.

Teaching for Inclusion: Diversity in the college classroom (University of North Carolina at Chapel Hill)
> Online version of the 1997 publication, providing information about several aspects of diversity in the classroom, focused around specific groups of students: http://ctl.unc.edu/tfitoc.html.

Teaching International Students Guides (University of Leicester)
> A series of short guides focusing on different aspects of the student life cycle: www.le.ac.uk/eltu/abouteltuweb/TeachingISGuides/index.html.

Teaching in Racially Diverse College Classroom (Centre for Teaching and Learning, Harvard University)
> A series of tips, prompts and questions for staff to consider: http://isites.harvard.edu/fs/html/icb.topic58474/TFTrace.html.

Chapter 5

Inclusive e-Learning

WHO ARE THE BENEFICIARIES OF E-LEARNING?

For certain groups of students, the use of e-learning (also known as: technology-enhanced learning; learning technology; communication and information technology (C&IT); information and communication technology (ICT)) has the potential to significantly improve access to, and ability to participate in, higher education. However, in direct contrast to this, incorrect or inappropriate use of the technologies can generate potentially insurmountable barriers against participation. In this chapter we will consider the use of some of the more common e-learning technologies and how we can ensure that their implementation facilitates participation and learning.

Chin (2004) noted that e-learning has the potential to:

1 save time;
2 enhance learning;
3 accommodate more students;
4 be cheaper;
5 be innovative;
6 be easy to use;
7 be interesting for students to use.

(Chin, 2004: 5)

It should be noted, however, that poorly designed e-learning can actually have the opposite effect to some of the points listed above; for example, an online course consisting mainly of large amounts of text for students to read on the screen will hardly be particularly interesting or innovative and is unlikely to enhance learning.

PAUSE FOR THOUGHT

Given the topic of this chapter, it is interesting to reflect upon how we feel about e-learning. Is this something that you are interested in? Are you an early-adopter in terms of e-learning initiatives, or are you someone who tends to hold back until they are fully convinced about the usefulness of the technology? Either way, reflect on what it is like when you try a new electronic experience. For example, this could be your first participation in an online discussion forum, creating a profile in a social networking site such as Facebook, or perhaps entering an immersive virtual world − such as Second Life − for the first time.

For some of us these experiences can be quite daunting; there may be different rules of etiquette to consider, and the use of language may be different from what we are used to. What we are suggesting is that the uneasiness that we might feel with regard to e-learning situations could mirror the uneasiness that some of our students feel in other higher education environments (see also Chapter 1); for example:

- mature students returning to education;
- students studying in a language that is not their first language;
- students participating in a course where they are part of the minority group within a substantial gender imbalance, for example, a male student in a subject allied to Medicine or a female student in Engineering (see Table 1.2);
- students who have recently left school or college, who are unfamiliar with the terminology used in higher education.

Bearing some of these points in mind, what groups of students do we feel would benefit from the use of e-learning? The most obvious answers to this question would probably be:

1   students who are not able to attend face-to-face sessions on a regular basis (i.e. distance learners); and
2   disabled students.

Although it is undoubtedly true that both groups of students could benefit from the use of e-learning, we would like to move away from the idea that this is only really suitable for these two groups of students. One of the main advantages of this form of learning is its *flexibility* of use. e-learning does not just have to be of benefit to students at a distance, it can also be of benefit to on-campus students, for example, through:

1 fitting learning around other commitments (e.g. work or family);
2 promoting independent learning;
3 providing feedback through formative assessments and quizzes;
4 suiting particular learning styles;
5 promoting time management skills;
6 providing a back-up of learning materials and resources (e.g. for revision purposes);
7 promoting ownership of the course, materials and students' own learning;
8 providing electronic, searchable copies of documents that can be adapted for other purposes (e.g. translation software).

Although these points emphasise some of the advantages of using e-learning in our teaching, we are well aware that there are a number of disadvantages such as:

1 Lack of access to the technology. This could include issues such as not being able to access a home computer because of competition from a partner or from children; speed of a home computer connection to the Internet; and compatibility issues relating to software. It has been noted that there is an important gender issue relating to the use of computers at home, in that women are often disadvantaged when it comes to accessing home-based equipment. It is not the case that women are reluctant to use computers, simply the fact that they may not be able to access relevant equipment as easily at home as they can at work (Talbot, 2004).
2 Copyright and intellectual property right issues. It is important that the material that we are providing for students is legal and that we educate students with respect to copyright and encourage this practice in assignments.
3 Solitary learning. Some forms of technology-enhanced learning can be a very solitary experience, and students may find that this highlights feelings of isolation.

4   Not addressing students' preferred styles of learning. This style of learning may not be suited to all students, and it should therefore be used in conjunction with other teaching and learning strategies.

These disadvantages need to be acknowledged and considered when we design and develop e-learning opportunities.

 PAUSE FOR THOUGHT

We have introduced some of the advantages and disadvantages of e-learning for students, but what do you consider are the advantages and disadvantages for us as lecturers?

DISABLED STUDENTS AND E-LEARNING

Although it was noted above that we should not just be considering disabled and distance learners when discussing e-learning, it is important to consider the requirements of some disabled students when implementing e-learning opportunities.

A few of the issues facing disabled students are as follows:

1   Students with a vision impairment may need to use a screen reader in order to access information.
2   Deaf students or students with a hearing impairment may need captioning of audio material.
3   Students with dyslexia may have problems participating in synchronous and asynchronous discussion forums.
4   Students with autistic spectrum disorders may have problems with screen flicker.
5   Mobility impairments may prevent students from using a mouse or keyboard, or from sitting at a computer for any length of time.

By addressing some of these issues, we might also be helping other students who encounter similar issues but for very different reasons. For example, students whose first language is not the language of study may

encounter similar problems to students with dyslexia when participating in online discussion forums, such as reading and responding to text
messages while trying to interpret any emotions that might be conveyed
in the messages.

TechDis (www.techdis.ac.uk/resources/sites/2/simdis/index.htm)
and WebAIM (www.webaim.org/simulations) have provided some excellent online activities that simulate the effect that a student's impairment
may have on their use of technology. These activities do not simulate the
impairment itself, but give a useful indication of some of the issues and
difficulties that can be faced by some disabled students when engaging with
e-learning.

Assistive Technologies

Assistive technology is a term used to refer to products that can help
disabled students to undertake aspects of their work. Assistive technologies
can refer to a number of products, some of which may be computer-based
technologies such as screen readers or speech-recognition software, but
which can also include non computer-based hardware products such as
coloured overlays. We have included reference to assistive technologies
in this chapter not because they are sometimes computer-based, but
because it is important to realise that we cannot make assumptions about
how our students will be accessing online material. For example, we may
have students with upper-body mobility difficulties who are not able to
use a hand-operated computer mouse and who might be using technologies
such as a head pointer (e.g. www.aidis.org/support/smartnav_3.php or
www.cameramouse.org/), a foot-operated mouse (e.g. www.footmouse.
com/) or the arrow keys on a standard keyboard (Cooper, 2003).
Therefore, when we are designing courses that include some form of e-
learning, we should bear in mind that it may take some students longer
to complete certain tasks.

If you would like to know more about assistive technologies, or are
aware that you have students who may benefit from such technologies,
we would recommend the TechDis Technology Database (www.techdis.
ac.uk/index.php?p=3_1) and the Emptech database (www.emptech.
info/about_us.php). These databases provide a useful starting point when
considering some of the assistive technologies that some of your students
could use, but it should be noted that it is advisable to discuss potential
choices with the students themselves and to obtain professional advice
before purchasing and implementing any of the identified technologies.

COMMON SOFTWARE PACKAGES

We thought it would be useful to consider some of the issues relating to the accessibility of materials produced by two commonly used software packages: Microsoft PowerPoint® and Microsoft Word. Although some of the points mentioned in the following sections apply specifically to these products, it would be useful to ensure that the accessibility issues considered here are addressed by other, similar, software packages that you may be using.

Microsoft PowerPoint®

PowerPoint® is one of the most commonly used software packages for presentation purposes, and there are a number of ways in which such presentations can be made more accessible to disabled students, particularly students with vision impairments.

General accessibility points to consider are as follows:

1 Do not be afraid of white space; there is no need to include too much information on a single slide.
2 Consider the '666 rule' (e.g. Westland, no date), that is to say, no more than: 6 words per line; 6 lines per slide; 6 continuous slides of text (text-heavy presentations should be broken up with student-centred activities and/or the use of images, animations, video or audio clips, etc.).
3 Use an appropriate point size (e.g. 28 minimum for standard slide text).
4 Use bulleted lists.
5 Sans serif fonts are generally easier to read on a screen.
6 Use left alignment of paragraphs (i.e. text with a straight left edge, but not a straight right edge), as this maintains a regular spacing between words. Justified text distorts the lengths of words and spaces.
7 Ensure a good contrast between the colour of the background and the text and make sure that the text is clear (i.e. avoid using green or red text, as this may be hard to read for students with a colour-blindness).
8 Avoid patterned backgrounds and the use of text overlying graphics.
9 Restrict the number of different text colours, font types and animated transitions used within a single presentation.

10 Use the 'slide colour scheme' so that your presentation is suitable for the teaching room that you are using: a dark background and light text are better for dark rooms, and vice versa.

11 Slides in handouts can be made larger by using landscape orientation (this can be altered in *Page Setup*) and four slides per page. Although the pictorial representation of each individual slide is larger, the disadvantage of this method is that it does not include lines for making notes adjacent to each slide, although there is room for students to write in the margins if they wish to do so. It will depend on how you want your students to use the handout as to whether this method is appropriate.

(After Gravestock, 2006b: 26; Gravestock, 2006a: 36)

The use of the set templates within PowerPoint® is the first requirement for an accessible presentation. Any text added to the 'Slide Layout' template boxes can be read by a screen reader and can be saved in a different format (for example, rich text format) by using the 'File, Save as . . .' function. It is possible to check what information will be available to a screen reader, or for saving to an alternative format, by viewing the Outline tab (Figure 5.1).

Information that is included within additional text boxes that are not part of the template cannot be read by a screen reader and will therefore be ignored (Figure 5.2).

A similar problem occurs when an image is added to the presentation, that is to say the image cannot be read by a screen reader and any information contained within the image will not be accessible to some students. One way to rectify this is to 'hide' a description of the image behind the image itself, making sure that this is done with one of the text boxes from the Slide Layout templates (Figures 5.3 and 5.4).

Figure 5.5 shows how this presentation would look if it was saved as a rich text format file at this point.

Of course, it is important that the description of the image is detailed enough so that anyone who is not able to view it will be able to determine why it is being used and what information it is conveying. For the sake of clarity, the image in Figures 5.3 and 5.4 was simply labelled as 'Photograph of Mount Etna'; however, depending upon the reason why this image was incorporated in the presentation, this may not adequately describe the photograph to a student with a vision impairment.

101

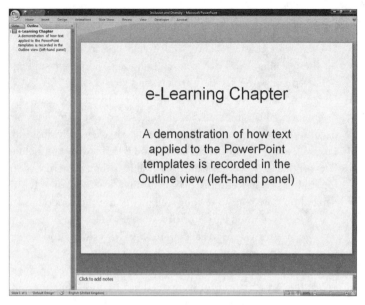

FIGURE 5.1 Illustration of how text entered into one of the standard slide layout templates is recorded in the Outline view panel (left-hand side of the screen). Any text shown here can be read by a screen reader, or saved in an alternative format.

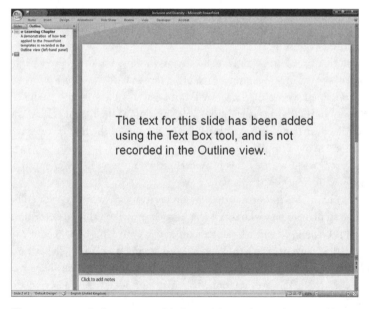

FIGURE 5.2 Information added to additional text boxes will not be recorded in the Outline view.

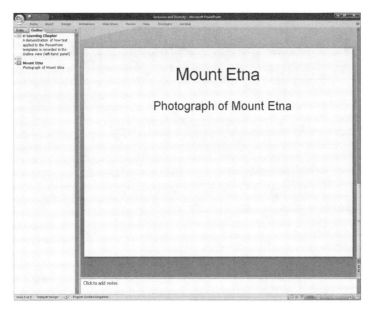

FIGURE 5.3 Text describing the image is added to one of the Slide Layout templates.

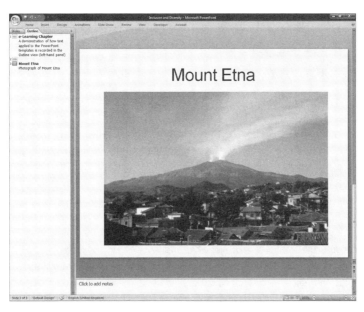

FIGURE 5.4 The image is imported and enlarged so that it covers and hides the text box behind it. Note that the text is still visible in 'Outline' view.

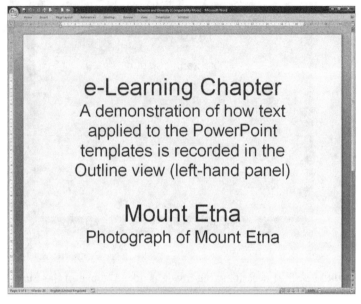

FIGURE 5.5 Rich text format version of the presentation. Note that the information from the second slide – which used an additional text box – has not been transferred to the document.

 ACTIVITY

The following activity is an excellent way to practise describing images. For this activity you will need two people, a pen or pencil, some paper and a suitable image to describe. If you have not had much experience of describing images before, then it is suggested that you start with a simple line drawing like the one shown in Figure 5.6.

The object of the activity is to describe the image to your partner in as much detail as possible so that they are able to reproduce what you are describing.

You should sit back-to-back with your partner, so that the person drawing the image cannot see what you are describing. Only you are allowed to talk; the person who is doing the drawing must not ask any questions nor seek any clarification, and you are not allowed to ask questions to see if they have understood what you have said. The person drawing the image should take your instructions as literally as possible and should draw exactly what you tell them without making any assumptions. For example, if you were describing the inside of an electric plug, you might start by giving the detail of the shape of the plug itself and then move on to the fuse, wires and screws. What you might not have mentioned is that the wires and fuses have to be inside the plug. If the drawer were being mischievous – and we would encourage this – then they would be within their rights to draw the fuse and wires somewhere else on the page.

After completing the description have a look to see how successful you have been.

What have you learnt from this? What would you do differently if you were to repeat the activity?

The main conclusion that often results from this activity is the importance of giving a quick overview of the image first, before describing the detail. It is very common for the person drawing the image to run out of paper, because they were not given an overview of what the image looked like and may have started their drawing too close to one of the sides of the page.

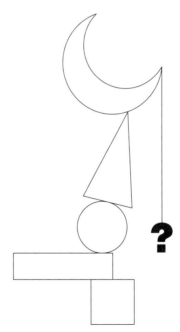

FIGURE 5.6
Simple line drawing for
a description activity.

The fact that text boxes do not record information in the Outline view also has implications for presentations that take advantage of the animation features present within the software, as these animated sequences can be based on information or images that are added to separate text boxes. However, it is important to realise that this does not mean that presentations have to become dull or boring in order to be accessible. One way to maintain appropriate animation sequences is to describe what is happening – typing your text into one of the Slide Layout templates as before – and to cover this using a rectangular box with the line and fill colour the same as the background. The animation can then be placed on top of this box. Depending upon the sequence in which you add material to your slide, it may be necessary to use the 'Order' feature to ensure that the description of the animation is sent to the back of the slide. (You can think of this layering as a pile of transparent acetate sheets: the acetate at the very bottom of the pile represents the master information for the slide, e.g. background colour; directly above this is the description of the animation; and above this is a filled box that will hide the description and that is the same colour as the background. The acetate at the very top of the pile will contain the animation.)

Microsoft Word

Some of the general points noted above relating to Microsoft PowerPoint® will also apply to Microsoft Word documents, for example:

1　Ensure that text is a suitable size. This is generally considered to be Times New Roman 12 point, or equivalent.
2　Restrict your use of different font types within a single document.
3　Use left alignment of paragraphs.
4　Allow wide margins and spaces between paragraphs.
5　Use numbered/bulleted lists to reduce the density of text on a page.
6　Avoid large numbers of continuous upper text characters, as this can be difficult to read.
7　Use bold formatting for emphasising words or sentences in preference to italics or underlining, as the latter can make the words appear to 'flow' together.
　　(After Gravestock, 2006a: 33–34; Gravestock, 2006b: 25–26)

One specific aspect of Microsoft Word that will assist with accessibility is the use of styles within documents. There are a number of *styles* that can be applied to paragraphs of text: for example, Heading 1, Heading 2 and Normal. These styles can be changed to suit your document, and any updates made to one part of the document can be applied to all paragraphs that have been allocated to a specific style if required. Apart from the ease of changing the formatting of several paragraphs simultaneously, the real benefit of using styles is that they will structure a document. Conversely, if you simply alter the formatting of text to indicate a change in heading, for example, by enlarging and/or emboldening the text, this will have no impact on the structure of a document. Using styles means that if a document is converted to another format – for example, hypertext mark-up language (html) or portable document format (pdf) or through the use of more specialist software such as Wimba Create (www.wimba. com/products/wimbacreate/), which creates accessible webpages from Microsoft Word documents – then the structure of the document is taken through into the new format and will assist accessibility.

Figures 5.7–5.10 demonstrate the difference in structure between a document that uses styles and one that does not.

VIRTUAL LEARNING ENVIRONMENTS

A virtual learning environment (VLE) is a web-based course management system 'that integrates tools for content delivery, communication, assessment, and student management' (Littlejohn and Higgison, 2003: 5). VLEs include products such as the BlackBoard Academic Suite (www. blackboard.com/products) and Moodle (moodle.com/).

The use of VLEs can vary from an online repository of information relating to a particular course at one end of the spectrum, through to highly interactive and participative courses at the other. Although the notion of using a VLE simply as a repository of information will not be utilising the technology to its full extent, it has been pointed out that such information can be very useful for students, and placing it in one central area means that the students know where to go if they have any questions or issues relating to the course (Bostock, 2007). Such information could include a course handbook, reading lists and details about the assessment activities for the course. In addition, a lecturer may also publish information relating to forthcoming lectures, for example, Microsoft PowerPoint® slides. This latter point is often cited as an example of good practice, as it provides useful information about the structure of the session and any new terminology that will be introduced. Such information would be of specific benefit to:

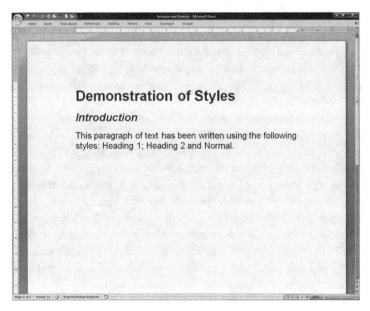

FIGURE 5.7 A document that has been written using styles.

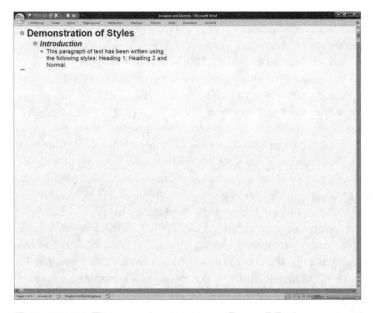

FIGURE 5.8 The same document as in Figure 5.7, shown using the Outline view option to demonstrate the structured nature of the document.

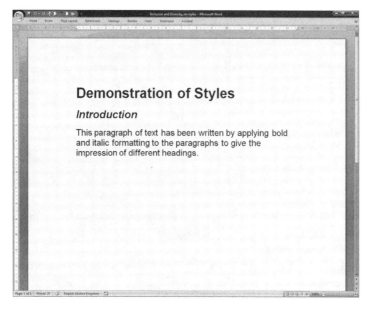

FIGURE 5.9 A document that has been written without styles and that uses formatting to give the impression of headings.

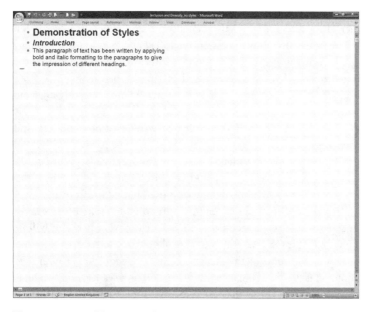

FIGURE 5.10 The same document as in Figure 5.9, shown using the Outline view option to demonstrate the unstructured nature of the document.

1   deaf students who use a sign language interpreter, particularly if agreement is required about the signing of new terminology;
2   international students;
3   students with dexterity problems, who are unable to take notes quickly during face-to-face sessions;
4   students with dyslexia;
5   students with slow reading speeds; and
6   students with social anxiety.

(Gravestock, 2006b; Newland *et al.*, 2006; Ryan, 2005)

If the session is particularly interactive, then this approach would be a good way of providing the students with information that you may wish them to prepare in advance.

The benefit to these students is that they will be aware of the relevant disciplinary discourse in advance. Also, with a basic idea of the structure of the session they may be able to concentrate more on developing their knowledge of a topic rather than trying to understand new concepts as they are being introduced while simultaneously trying to make suitable notes, something that can be particularly difficult for the groups of students identified above. An interesting point to consider here, however, is whether other students could also benefit from knowing this information in advance, either for similar reasons identified above or because we may have students in our groups who would be interested in undertaking some additional reading and research around the topic, so that they get more from the face-to-face session itself and can engage more actively in group discussions.

What is not being proposed here is that we should be publishing full lecture notes in advance of sessions. This would not be particularly helpful to some of the groups of students mentioned above, as a large amount of text to digest prior to a session could be quite intimidating. Also, if this information is being provided, then what is the value added from attending the face-to-face session? On this point, it is important to note the relevance of managing students' expectations. Be very clear what it is you will be providing and the reasons why students should still attend face-to-face sessions. An indication of the structure of the session, along with new terminology, is hardly a replacement for attending a session, and students need to be clear that this is the case. However, it is worth noting that, in a study undertaken in 2003 at Durham University, it was found that less than 1 per cent of students stated that they would not attend lectures because the notes were available in advance (Newland *et al.*, 2004).

110

Some general points of good practice in relation to virtual learning environments, which should assist with the accessibility of your online course for all students, are as follows:

1   Allow students time to become familiar with the layout and navigation of the virtual learning environment, prior to undertaking the online activities. Try to maintain consistent navigation, to aid students with a vision impairment (Newland et al., 2005). A hard-copy or electronic handout distributed outside the VLE that provides information and tips about the structure of the course will help to orientate students. Consider whether an online site map would be helpful.

2   Ensure good colour contrast between the text and the background (Pearson and Koppi, 2006). If possible, let students change the background colour and the colour of the text. If this is not possible, consider recommending that the students download the TechDis user preferences toolbar (www.techdis.ac.uk/index.php?p=1_20051905100544), and determine whether its use is compatible with the VLE.

3   Provide contact information on the front page, with a helpdesk number and email if appropriate (Pearson and Koppi, 2006).

4   Use clear and concise language throughout the course. Try to 'chunk' information, so that students do not have to scroll excessively to read online material. Try to keep the amount of online reading to a minimum.

5   Indicate if a link opens a new browser window.

6   If you are directing students to external websites, be as specific as possible about what you want them to do. Many students will be able to skim-read and browse the sites quickly, but some students with vision impairments may find this difficult, and it may take them a while to determine why you are asking them to visit a particular site.

7   Try to ensure that there is a mixture of interactive activities within the course that require individual and group-based responses. This means that, if a student is waiting for responses to a message posted within an asynchronous discussion forum, they are able to engage with an independent activity that does not rely on interaction with other students or staff. Individual activities may include reading research articles from electronic journals, watching or listening to a video or audio clip (assuming

that appropriate transcription or captioning is available for students with vision or hearing impairments), or undertaking formative quizzes and surveys.

8   Provide electronic documentation in a variety of formats (e.g. documents in Microsoft Word format, rich text format – rtf, or portable document format – pdf). Name files in an obvious and meaningful way that will make sense to students (Newland *et al.*, 2005).

9   Indicate approximate times for how long you would expect students to spend working on a particular activity (it may be useful to indicate online and offline time, depending upon the nature of the activity).

10 If appropriate, provide an explicit link from your online activities to specific learning outcomes, or course aims.

The design of specific content-based webpages within VLEs is beyond the scope of this book; however, anyone responsible for designing such pages should follow the guidelines set out by the World Wide Web Consortium as part of its Web Accessibility Initiative (WAI) (www.w3.org/WAI/).

Discussion Forums

Synchronous and asynchronous discussion forums provide students with the opportunity to discuss course-related, and other, issues online. The former discussions occur in real time, the latter allow students to post messages that can then be read and responded to at a later time or date. Such discussion forums are generally moderated by a tutor, who could be considered to be an online facilitator and whose role is to:

1   encourage participation from all students;
2   make sure discussions are relevant and appropriate to a particular topic thread;
3   summarise discussions;
4   prompt additional responses, or deeper thoughts, through the use of open-ended questions.

Synchronous discussion forums may be a problem for students who are not able to type or read quickly. Some students may have coping strategies to deal with such situations, such as using speech-to-text recognition software, but be aware that some students, including international students, may find this form of communication difficult to engage with. There may be appropriate times when such tools are used, for example, if a quick decision is required, but it may be advisable to keep the use of synchronous chats to a minimum.

Examples of good practice in relation to asynchronous discussions are as follows:

1   Ease your students into asynchronous discussions with a simple and non-controversial topic (often this is not course-related). This will allow all students to practise, and feel comfortable about, sending messages to a forum (Salmon, 2000).

2   Provide clear guidelines as to what you expect from the students, and what they can expect from you as a moderator (Newland *et al.*, 2005). These guidelines could also indicate whether you are expecting the students to write in a formal or informal manner. For many discussion forums, the latter may be more appropriate as a method of encouraging a dialogue. Although the messages need to make sense, you might indicate that errors in relation to spelling and grammar will be acceptable.

3   Encourage students to write obvious, relevant and meaningful titles for discussion topics and threads.

4   If you are acting as a moderator, monitor the messages to ensure that cultural differences are being respected and are not being misunderstood. Although informal language may be encouraged in asynchronous discussions, it will be necessary to be firm and to stop any inappropriate use of language in relation to inclusivity and diversity issues. Depending upon the nature of the comments made, it may be more appropriate to address the issue and perhaps open it to the online group as a whole for a separate discussion, rather than deleting the message completely.

IMMERSIVE VIRTUAL WORLDS

Finally in this chapter, we thought it would be appropriate to mention the popularity of immersive virtual worlds (IVWs), also known as multi-user virtual environments (MUVEs), such as *Second Life* (www.secondlife.com/), *Active Worlds* (www.activeworlds.com/) and *There* (www.there.

com/). IVWs can simulate activities and environments that it would not normally be possible for students to experience, and because of such potential benefits a number of educational institutions have developed virtual campuses in IVWs, where students and other users can visit and participate in educational activities.

One of the benefits of IVWs includes the fact that their popularity is worldwide, and it is therefore possible to interact with users from many other cultures. Such interactions can enhance the possibility of increased awareness of globalisation issues. The creation of avatars (a virtual representation of the user) also allows the user the chance to develop their own online persona, and some disabled users with visible impairments may use the opportunity to create a non-disabled avatar; however, it should be noted that it is possible to create a wheelchair-using avatar in some IVWs, which can appeal to students who do not wish to hide their impairment.

Some of the disadvantages to consider with IVWs include the fact that it will be harder for students with vision impairments to access such environments. Although the accessibility of IVWs is likely to improve as their popularity increases, we should still consider what activities we are asking students to undertake in the virtual worlds and how accessible these might be. One of the main issues is the time that it can take to get accustomed to such environments. The setting up of an avatar and learning about the online culture of IVWs can be time-consuming. This is an important issue to consider with respect to students who may be accessing such environments from their home computer, and where there might be some competition from other family members for computer use. A possible consequence of participating in such environments is that some students may get addicted to the environment itself, and they may have to develop time management skills in order to continue to participate in their educational online activities as well as their social ones.

FURTHER READING

Newland, B., Pavey, J. and Boyd, V. (2005) 'Accessibility in Learning Environments and Related Technologies (ALERT)', Durham University and Bournemouth University. Available at www.bournemouth.ac.uk/alert/.

Newland, B., Boyd, V. and Pavey, J. (2006) Enhancing disabled students' learning through virtual learning environments, in: Adams, M. and Brown, S. (eds) *Towards Inclusive Learning in Higher Education: Developing curricula for disabled students*, London: Routledge, pp. 143–153.

Seale, J.K. (2006) *E-Learning and Disability in Higher Education: Accessibility research and practice*, Abingdon: Routledge.

 USEFUL WEB RESOURCES

Additional information about creating accessible Microsoft PowerPoint® presentations is provided by:

- WebAIM: www.webaim.org/techniques/powerpoint/.
- TechDis publication Creating Accessible Presentations: www.techdis. ac.uk/resources/sites/accessibilityessentials3/index.html.

Additional information about creating accessible Microsoft Word documents is provided by:

- WebAIM: www.webaim.org/techniques/word/.
- TechDis publication *Writing Accessible Electronic Documents with Microsoft Word*: www.techdis.ac.uk/resources/sites/accessibilityessentials2/index.html.

In addition to the above, TechDis have published a range of *Accessibility Essentials* documents: www.techdis.ac.uk/index.php?p=3_20.

Creating Accessible e-Learning Resources for Disabled Students (Teachability Project, University of Strathclyde)
This is one of the guides in the Teachability series, focusing on creating an accessible curriculum for disabled students: www.teachability.strath. ac.uk/chapter_7/tableofcontents7.html.

Chapter 6

Students' Academic Experiences Outside the Classroom

Not all learning takes place within a higher education institution. Some of this learning may be facilitated by a lecturer, for example, through directed fieldwork, but it should be recognised that the students themselves will have a large degree of control over many aspects of their own learning, for example, through conducting research using academic texts and journals (see below). Also, the direction of the learning could be facilitated by other agencies, such as during work-based or placement learning. Whatever form this learning takes, we must acknowledge that it is an important aspect of the students' overall experience of higher education.

This chapter will focus predominantly on fieldwork, as it is during such out-of-classroom experiences that students' problems and issues can often be magnified, but the issues raised through the discussion of fieldwork will also be relevant to other aspects of learning outside the classroom. By careful planning and development we can ensure that such experiences are as inclusive as possible.

FIELDWORK

Many disciplines view fieldwork, which can be considered either as a day trip or a residential trip, as an activity that is core to their work. Fieldwork provides students with the opportunity to put theory into practice and to experience real-life situations that are not possible to replicate fully in the classroom.

Skills and processes that can be developed through fieldwork include:

1   observation and recording skills;
2   analytical and problem-solving skills;

3   data collection;
4   leadership and responsibility;
5   application of research methods;
6   independent learning;
7   group work.

Fieldwork is therefore an important way for students to learn outside the classroom environment. In particular, fieldwork to foreign locations can provide an excellent way of introducing diversity and inclusion issues into the curriculum. This chapter will be structured to provide some general information that will assist with starting to develop inclusive fieldwork for all students, and will be followed with some more specific issues relating to particular groups of students.

General Issues

The key question to ask in relation to fieldwork is 'Why are we visiting a particular location?'. To answer this it will also be necessary to consider the question posed by the *Teachability* project (see Chapter 4): 'What is the core requirement of the module or course?'. What are we trying to achieve from this fieldwork, and how does a particular locality fit in with this overarching aim? It can sometimes be the case that field trips to particular localities change over the years depending upon the personal preferences of the staff who are leading the trip, and it is often useful to return to these fundamental questions to ensure that the sites visited are still addressing the main academic rationale for the trip.

It is good practice to provide opportunities in preparatory fieldwork sessions for students to disclose any particular requirements that they may have. This may include specific dietary requirements, details of medication and times at which this must be taken, or timings for prayer. It is also possible that some students who have not previously disclosed an impairment, because it does not have an impact on their normal day-to-day activities, may do so because this may be exacerbated by fieldwork; for example, a student with asthma may not have disclosed this information previously because they may not have thought that it was important, but in relation to fieldwork, possibly in a remote location, this could be an important health and safety consideration.

One example of good practice, proposed by Birnie and Grant (2001) to help to reduce anxiety for students with mental health difficulties but which can actually benefit all students, is to provide very clear and detailed

117

information prior to engaging in fieldwork. Many students are likely to be anxious about an activity such as fieldwork if they are unsure about what they will be doing, or if they do not have full details regarding the accommodation, eating and social arrangements. Providing this information in advance of the trip will ensure that the students are more relaxed and more prepared to undertake the work required of them.

When providing information in advance we need to be as comprehensive as possible and should not assume that the students have any prior knowledge of what we will be asking them to do. Photographs and video footage of the field locations will be beneficial, if it is available, and can be hosted on a VLE or perhaps used in a video podcast or digital story related to the trip (see the section on Mobile Learning at the end of this chapter).

General logistical information could include the following:

- *Transport and travel.* Give clear information about all aspects of the travel arrangements. How often will you be stopping? Will the students need food for the journey, or will this be provided? Will lunch be somewhere where students can buy food? Will cashpoints be available? Will there be opportunities for students to pray?

- *Weather.* Although we cannot predict the weather for fieldwork, it is useful to give an indication as to what it might be like and the most suitable clothes that the students should bring, both for fieldwork and for socialising. Rather than saying 'It will be cold', it would be more helpful to give an indication of the temperatures, including any possible wind chill.

> I once took two students from Oman on a field trip to Snowdon, N. Wales, where it snowed throughout the trip. Although I had mentioned that this was a possibility, the students had never seen snow before and had not realised how cold it could be. Their understanding of cold was in relation to temperatures that they were used to in Oman.
>
> (Quote from a Geology lecturer)

- *Luggage.* Is there a limit to the amount of luggage that the students can bring?

- *Money and documentation.* What will the students need to bring money for? What documentation is required, for example, passports and visas? Are cashpoints available nearby?

■ *Communication*. What methods of communication will be available at the location(s)? Is there a wireless network? Is the location in an area with a poor mobile phone signal (sometimes the case in some more remote fieldwork locations)?

■ *Personal health and fitness*. Approximately how much walking is required on each day, and what is the nature of the terrain?

■ *Medical facilities*. What are the arrangements for first aid and where is the nearest medical facility? What medication will students need to bring themselves?

■ *Living and sleeping arrangements*. This topic can cause a lot of anxiety for some students. We should be clear about the number of beds in a room and details of other information such as shared bathroom facilities. It is advisable that sleeping arrangements are sorted out before arriving at the final destination. Also, what bedding will be provided? Are students expected to bring towels?

■ *Food and drink*. What will the students need to bring, or buy, during the trip and how much is this likely to cost? What will be provided and how frequently will this be? If there is to be a limit on some aspects of food provision, for example, the number of sandwiches available for lunch, what are these limits? (If students know this information in advance then they are able to supplement their meals if they wish.) What cooking facilities will be present?

(List based on Birnie and Grant, 2001: 5–6)

The same amount of detail will also be required for the daily activities to be undertaken on the trip. Information, such as the risk assessment for the location, length of time that the students are going to be at a particular site, and whether they need to take their lunches, is often presented verbally at the time, but it is also useful to have this written down and given to the students in advance so that they can organise themselves. For example, some students may need to take medication at a particular time of the day, perhaps with some food, and having knowledge of the locations, timings and activities in advance will help them to plan the times of their medication. The same is also true for students who may have to take time away from their activities for prayer. Information about the task that students will be expected to undertake at the location should be detailed. (It would be useful to refer to the activity in Chapter 5 about describing images for students with vision impairments to get an idea about how much information may be required, and how much we might take for granted.)

119

Owing to the nature of fieldwork, it can often be very difficult for all students to hear what we are saying when we are trying to introduce an activity in the field, therefore a written backup of this information on a handout or in a fieldwork guide is very beneficial. In addition to the fact that providing this information in advance will allow the students to prepare for the activity, it also allows time for students with dyslexia or students who are not studying in their first language to read, interpret and understand what will be required of them.

SOME THOUGHTS ON INCLUSIVE FIELDWORK: INTERNATIONAL STUDENTS

It is useful to be aware of religious festivals that may be taking place while you are on fieldwork and the implications of these festivals for students, for example, periods of fasting. There are a number of calendars on the Internet that provide information about religious festivals, such as the BBC Multifaith Calendar (www.bbc.co.uk/religion/tools/calendar/).

Some students will wish to pray at specific points during the day and may need a quiet place where this can be achieved, possibly with facilities that allow the students to cleanse themselves. Most prayer timings are based on the position of the sun and are therefore likely to vary depending upon the location of the fieldwork. Calculators on the Internet provide information about prayer timings for different locations (for example, www.bbc.co.uk/religion/tools/calculator/).

Depending upon the nature of the fieldwork, it is also useful to consider whether the type of site to be visited will impose restrictions on students; for example, because of religious beliefs some students may have problems visiting some types of farm.

All international students should be able to participate in social activities. Some students will not wish to socialise in pubs or other locations where alcohol is being served, and so it is important to ensure that a range of locations and social activities is available to the students.

If going abroad for fieldwork, it is worth checking with the students that there are no problems with regard to visas or access to the country of destination.

Disabled Students

The Geography Discipline Network has produced a series of six guides aimed at supporting staff in the development of fieldwork for disabled students. The guides address specific impairments and are available online from www2.glos.ac.uk/gdn/disabil/. Although the following summaries are largely based on information from these guides, we would recommend that you look at the relevant guide if you are developing fieldwork and know that you will have students in your group with specific impairments. All the general information noted above will also apply.

SOME THOUGHTS ON INCLUSIVE FIELDWORK: STUDENTS WITH VISION IMPAIRMENTS

As for students with mobility impairments, it is important to ensure that students with vision impairments are able to access all aspects of fieldwork, including accommodation, eating and socialising areas. It is possible that some students with vision impairments will need to bring a support worker with them, and their needs and requirements will also have to be taken into account when planning fieldwork. It may also be necessary to include provision for a guide dog, and to educate other students with regard to guide dog etiquette (see Guide Dogs for the Blind Association, www.guidedogs.org.uk/) (Shepherd, 2001).

Some students may need to bring particular items of equipment, such as a Braille typewriter or voice recorder, that they use for their normal on-campus study. However, there may also be additional items of assistive technology (see Chapter 5) that may benefit the student, depending upon the tasks to be undertaken on the field trip; for example, equipment for producing tactile maps of field locations (see National Centre for Tactile Diagrams, www.nctd.org.uk/). It may also be useful to check the TechDis Technology Database (www.techdis.ac.uk/index.php?p=3_1) and the Emptech database (emptech.info/about_us.php) to determine whether there are any other assistive technologies that would be of use to the student during the field trip.

For other vision impairments, such as colour-blindness, it is important to ensure that colour is not the sole means of conveying specific information to the students (Shepherd, 2001); for example, graphs or other illustrations where the symbols are the same but presented in a different colour to distinguish between different sets of data.

SOME THOUGHTS ON INCLUSIVE FIELDWORK: STUDENTS WITH MOBILITY IMPAIRMENTS

When considering the needs of students with mobility impairments on fieldwork, many of us will start to think about the nature of the terrain that will need to be negotiated. However, it is also important to consider the accessibility of all aspects of the fieldwork locations including: accommodation; washing and toilet facilities; study/lecture rooms; eating areas; and social spaces. It is also important to remember that many students with mobility impairments will tire easily, and it will be necessary to consider the timings of all activities throughout the day. This may also include the necessity to load or unload a wheelchair from a bus or coach. Mobility issues may arise unexpectedly through other conditions, such as vertigo; for example, a student with vertigo may find it very difficult, or impossible, to walk along a cliff path (Gardiner and Anwar, 2001).

In terms of the nature of the terrain, is it accessible to a student with mobility impairments? If not, are there alternative sites that might be suitable for addressing the learning outcomes that would be covered by the other site? If a suitable location is available then it would be inclusive to insist that all students visit this site, rather than simply getting the student with a mobility impairment to visit the accessible site while the other students visit another site somewhere else (Gardiner and Anwar, 2001). Depending upon the nature of the trip, the situation may arise where there are no other suitable locations. In such a situation, it may be necessary for the student to miss visiting particular sites, but they will need to understand what the sites are demonstrating and what tasks the other students undertook. This could be done through some form of virtual fieldwork (see p. 126), but other strategies include: having a debrief of the site with the disabled student present, preferably with some visual material to demonstrate what was observed, or for the other students to take appropriate photo/video footage and to present a summary of the site to the disabled student, perhaps after returning to the fieldwork accommodation.

SOME THOUGHTS ON INCLUSIVE FIELDWORK: STUDENTS WITH HEARING IMPAIRMENTS

Students with hearing impairments should be provided with appropriate written information; however, it is worth remembering that if a student has been deaf since birth then their sign language will be their first language, and they may need additional time to read material. Ensuring that written information is provided in advance will assist these students. When in the field we should try to do as much of the briefing as possible before entering the field site, as traffic noise, wind and the wearing of hats or hoods will make it more difficult to hear what is being said. Having this information written down will help all students who may not be able to hear everything that is said (Wareham *et al.*, 2001).

If a student uses a sign language interpreter, then it is likely that the interpreter will accompany them on the field trip; this has to be considered in terms of logistics for travel and accommodation. In the UK, the student's Disabled Students' Allowances should help to provide financial support towards the cost of the interpreter. If the student is using an interpreter then we should:

1 make sure that the interpreter can hear us and can see any relevant visual aids;
2 look at, and talk to, the student, not the interpreter;
3 remember that there is a lag between what is said and the interpreter being able to communicate this;
4 not ask the interpreter to participate in discussions.

(Wareham *et al.*, 2001)

If a student is lip-reading, then we must ensure that our face is not obscured, for example, by clothing nor silhouetted by a strong light behind us. A student who is lip-reading will not be able to make notes at the same time, and so it will be necessary to have a note-taker available. As above, for UK students, the Disabled Students' Allowances may be able to contribute towards this cost.

As a precaution, if you have a student who uses sign language then it may be appropriate to learn some emergency warning signs. Examples of warnings using British Sign Language (BSL) are available at www2. glos.ac.uk/gdn/disabil/deaf/ch10.htm (Wareham *et al.*, 2001).

123

SOME THOUGHTS ON INCLUSIVE FIELDWORK: STUDENTS WITH MENTAL HEALTH DIFFICULTIES

We have already discussed the importance of providing detailed information in advance to help to alleviate anxiety, but Birnie and Grant (2001) have noted some additional arrangements that may have to be considered for, and discussed with, students with mental health difficulties on fieldwork:

1 ensuring that the student does not work alone;
2 monitoring and checking that medication is taken;
3 offering single room accommodation;
4 providing additional staff or a helper to support the student;
5 providing alternative locations for exercises if a student is anxious about, for example, heights or enclosed spaces.

(Birnie and Grant, 2001: 9)

Residential fieldwork may bring to light student behaviours that have not been observed before, such as eating disorders or self-harming. Birnie and Grant (2001) note that, although tolerance of some behaviours should be encouraged, there is a point at which some of these behaviours become unacceptable, and the interests of the other students have to be taken into account. Sometimes a student will be unaware that their behaviour is causing distress to others, and a simple discussion with the student may alleviate any further problems.

SOME THOUGHTS ON INCLUSIVE FIELDWORK: STUDENTS WITH DYSLEXIA

Chalkley and Waterfield (2001) note the following problems that students with dyslexia might experience while on fieldwork, depending upon the severity of their dyslexia:

1 taking accurate notes in non-classroom environments;
2 multi-sensory tasking, for example, listening, observing, recording and reading;

3   speed of handwriting and legibility;

4   organisation of time;

5   orientation, reading maps;

6   slow reading speed for accurate comprehension;

7   visual perceptual difficulties with poorly photocopied material, particularly black print on white background;

8   remembering field trip arrangements;

9   group work;

10 recording data and making mathematical calculations.

(Chalkley and Waterfield, 2001: 5)

Clear and detailed instructions in advance will assist students with the arrangements of the trip, particularly if these are presented in different formats (e.g. written, verbal and electronic). A 'buddy' system or other peer support process will also assist the student, particularly in making sure that their notes are clear and comprehensive. Sharing tasks with peers will also spread the responsibility, so that it may be easier for a student with dyslexia to concentrate on a particular aspect of a group task. Choosing tasks that play to the strengths of a student with dyslexia may also be beneficial to the group work as a whole. Chalkley and Waterfield (2001) note the following strengths demonstrated by some students with dyslexia:

1   good powers of visualisation;

2   creative thinking skills;

3   visuo-spatial skills;

4   holistic, rather than analytical, approach;

5   good applied and problem-solving skills.

(Chalkley and Waterfield, 2001: 4)

When producing handouts to be used in the field, we should be aware that white paper can produce excessive glare for some students and they may find it hard to read text on such paper. This will be exacerbated if the weather is bright and sunny. It may be necessary, after discussion with the student(s), to provide some handouts on coloured paper in order to reduce glare. We should also ensure that the handouts reflect good practice in terms of layout: for example, 12 point, sans serif text (such as Arial, Helvetica, Verdana), wide margins, bulleted/numbered lists, left-justification, and sparing use of underlining and capital letters.

125

Virtual Fieldwork

Virtual fieldwork is a term given to computer-based representations of a field location, from a webcam at one end of the spectrum to interactive simulations at the other. The use of virtual fieldwork is generally considered to be as an additional activity to real fieldwork, rather than as a replacement. In particular, virtual fieldwork can be used very effectively for pre-trip familiarisation purposes. Videos or aerial photographs of a field location can give a good indication to students about the nature of the terrain that they will be encountering. The increase in worldwide aerial photographs, for example, through Google Earth, has made it easier to provide detailed information of this type for the benefit of students undertaking fieldwork.

WORK-BASED OR PLACEMENT LEARNING

Work-based or placement learning (WBL) provides students with an excellent opportunity to develop skills relevant to their future employ-ability. WBL can also provide an opportunity for all students to increase their own diversity awareness, by being placed with providers who have a diverse workforce (Arshad, 2006). It is therefore important that all students who wish to undertake some form of WBL as part of their higher education course are given appropriate encouragement and support to participate in such an opportunity.

While acknowledging the difficulties in defining the terms work-based learning and placement learning, the Quality Assurance Agency for Higher Education (QAA) uses the following definitions for the purposes of Section 9 of the Code of Practice:

> Work-based learning is regarded as learning that is integral to a higher education programme and is usually achieved and demonstrated through engagement with a workplace environment, the assessment of reflective practice and the designation of appropriate learning outcomes. [. . .] Work-based learning is often accredited, ranging from a single module within a programme to an entire programme that includes, at its core, activities and learning outcomes designed around the individual's occupation, whether paid or unpaid.
>
> (QAA, 2007: 4–5)

> Placement learning is regarded [. . .] as the learning achieved during an agreed and negotiated period of learning that takes place outside the

institution at which the full or part-time student is enrolled or engaged in learning. As with work-based learning, the learning outcomes are intended as integral parts of a programme of study. It is important that each student is supported by the institution throughout his/her placement experience, to ensure that specific learning related to the programme can be achieved.

(QAA, 2007: 5)

Students should be encouraged to think about WBL at an early stage. One way in which this can be achieved is by allowing students who have already completed a placement to be provided with an opportunity to discuss their experiences. This could be a face-to-face discussion with potential WBL students, or it could be done through a poster or video presentation. Whatever method is chosen, it is important to ensure that the students providing feedback on their experiences represent a range of identities.

In terms of UK legislation, both the higher education institution and the WBL provider have a responsibility for students' welfare and well-being. It is the responsibility of the higher education institution to ensure that any provider abides by the relevant legislation. In addition to health and safety, this could be ensuring that the provider has appropriate equal opportunities and disability strategies, and that staff in the provider institution are aware of, and abide by, these strategies. With regard to disabled students, it would also be worth discussing with the student the potential advantages and disadvantages of disclosing an impairment to the provider and, if disclosure is to take place, which specific employees within the provider organisation should be made aware of this information (Fell and Wray, 2006). Further information regarding disabled students and placement is provided in the Disability Rights Commission's (DRC) *Code of Practice: Employment and occupation*, which suggests the following:

It would be reasonable to expect the sending organisation and the placement provider to co-operate to ensure that appropriate adjustments are identified and made. It is good practice for a placement provider to ask a disabled person about reasonable adjustments before the placement begins, and to allow him [*sic*] to visit the workplace in advance to see how his needs can be addressed. Once a particular adjustment has been identified, it would be reasonable for the sending organisation and the placement provider to discuss its implementation in the light of their respective obligations under the [Disability Discrimination] Act.

(DRC, 2004: 153)

127

It would be useful to consider whether the good practice identified above, with regard to allowing a disabled student to visit the provider prior to the start of a WBL opportunity, could be extended to all other students, in order to provide an initial orientation and to reduce anxiety at the start of the placement.

Wray *et al.* (2005) have highlighted the need for early planning when allocating WBL opportunities for disabled students, as there needs to be enough time for the provider to be able to implement any necessary adjustments. It is also considered good practice to have a written agreement between the educational institution and the provider that details the following (Wray *et al.*, 2005: 36):

- the nature of the disability;
- what adjustments will be made;
- how adjustments will be funded;
- what action will be taken if adjustments are not provided;
- who is to be informed of the student's disability at the placement;
- systems for maintaining communication between the practice assessor/teacher, the student, the placement staff in the university and the disability adviser.

Once a student has started working for a provider, clear guidelines need to be made available to students so that they are aware of the correct university procedures to follow should any problems arise, for example, in relation to any issues of discrimination.

It is important for students on WBL opportunities to be provided with appropriate communication mechanisms, both with the university itself and also with other students. Communication is vital for the ongoing monitoring of the students' placements, as there could be unforeseen situations that may arise during the placement. Some of the communication is likely to be via face-to-face meetings between the university tutors and the placement students, but these are likely to be relatively infrequent owing to the time constraints on both staff and students. Additional communication mechanisms that could be used might include: an asynchronous discussion forum within the institution's VLE (see Chapter 5); email; short message service (SMS); or the setting up of student groups within social networking sites such as Facebook or within IVWs such as Second Life. All of these will provide support for students, should they require it, with the host educational institution and with their peers.

128

DIRECTED LIBRARY WORK

One way in which we would expect our students to undertake additional learning outside of the classroom is through the use of learning resources such as books, journals, newspapers and appropriate Internet sites. Although we would anticipate that the students would be able to develop their own skills in researching a particular topic, it is usual to provide a starting point for students' research via a reading list.

Some students can feel bewildered when presented with long reading lists, as this may be very different from what they have been used to prior to entering higher education. We may feel that we are providing a comprehensive resource that will allow students to read around a particular topic, but without specific signposting some students may struggle to identify the relevant aspects of the resources that we are providing. In particular, international students and disabled students – for example, students with dyslexia or students with a vision impairment – may find it hard to skim-read texts, and may therefore take much longer to identify and assimilate information of interest. They may also assume that they have to read all the identified resources, when we may have intended them to be used as starting points for specific aspects of research. It has been suggested that students who are not studying in their first language can take up to twice as long to read a text, compared with students studying in their first language, and, in addition, may have to read the text repeatedly before fully understanding it (McLean and Ransom, 2005). Such students are therefore likely to read fewer texts, and it would therefore be beneficial to such students if we can assist them in getting the most out of the resources that they are able to read.

Structuring our reading lists is one way in which we can help our students, and can be achieved by providing:

1   prompts highlighting important aspects of the resources that the students may wish to concentrate on; for example, specific chapters, sections or excerpts within a publication;
2   incremental lists that indicate primary texts that must be consulted, followed by other resources that may be of interest;
3   questions for the students to consider as they are reading;
4   annotated bibliographies;
5   links to electronic versions, if available, as this may assist with searching for particular words, screen readers and translation software.

129

Also, providing opportunities for students to discuss key resources, for example, within a seminar (see Chapter 3), will help all students to feel more confident in understanding the readings that they have been given.

MOBILE LEARNING

Mobile learning, often abbreviated to m-learning, is the use of mobile technologies to access learning resources away from the location of study and at a time that is convenient to the student. Mobile technologies can include: mobile phones; smart phones; personal digital assistants (PDAs); digital media players, games consoles; and pocket personal computers or laptops.

One of the increasing uses of m-learning relates to the development of educational podcasts. Podcasts are short audio presentations that can be downloaded onto a personal digital media player, including some mobile phones, or accessed from a computer. The benefits of podcasts are the fact that they can be listened to at a time that is convenient to the student, and that it is easy to replay specific sections of the podcast. Students have reported that podcasts have helped them to:

1 organise weekly learning activities;
2 stay focused;
3 develop positive attitudes towards lecturers;
4 make formal sessions more fun and informal;
5 support independent learning;
6 enable deeper engagement with the course.

(Edirisingha and Salmon, 2007)

Uses of podcasts include the following:

1 Summaries of lectures, perhaps with an introduction to the structure of the following session. This could also include information on the topics to be discussed and any new terminology (see also Chapter 4).
2 Support for activities that the students will need to undertake as part of the course. This could include instructions for the students to follow, or information about additional resources.
3 Discussion about topical issues relating to a particular course; for example, summaries of relevant news reports and details about where to find additional information.

4   Distribution of information relating to health and safety issues, for example, relating to fieldwork, placements or laboratory work.

5   Hints and tips. These may relate to procedures, such as laboratory work, or updates to rapidly changing information such as developments in the legal profession or information about newly released software.

6   Interviews with other colleagues and external experts in the discipline.

In terms of inclusion and diversity issues, the use of podcasts could form part of an institutional strategy aimed at informing students about academic procedures and to assist with their cultural acclimatisation, particularly when they first arrive in higher education. Podcasts can also provide a useful backup for important information given to students, and the use of images through video podcasts or digital storytelling, in addition to the narrative, can assist in increasing the accessibility of this method of communication. The use of podcasts made by existing students within an institution, outlining their own experiences in higher education, could also assist towards the inclusion and diversity agenda, provided that a range of students' views are represented.

 FURTHER READING

Fell, B. and Wray, J. (2006) 'Supporting disabled students on placement', in Adams, M. and Brown, S. (eds) *Towards Inclusive Learning in Higher Education: Developing curricula for disabled students*, London: Routledge, pp. 164–175.

Kukulska-Hulme, A. and Traxler, J. (eds) (2005) *Mobile Learning: A handbook for educators and trainers*, London: Routledge.

 USEFUL WEB RESOURCES

Creating accessible placements, study abroad and field trips for disabled students (Teachability Project, University of Strathclyde)
    One of the guides in the Teachability series, focusing on creating an accessible curriculum for disabled students: www.teachability.strath.ac.uk/chapter_5/tableofcontents5.html.

Learning Support for Disabled Students Undertaking Fieldwork and Related Activities (Geography Discipline Network)

A series of six guides aimed at supporting disabled students undertaking fieldwork: www2.glos.ac.uk/gdn/disabil/.

m-Learning

Website dedicated to mobile learning: www.m-learning.org/.

Placements and Students with Additional Learning Needs (Bournemouth University)

A handbook for staff, developed by Bournemouth University for the 2001–02 academic year. Although there have been some changes to the legislation, this guide still contains some useful advice: www.bournemouth.ac.uk/academicsupport/documents/SpecificNeeds/PlacementsDisabilityHbook01–02.pdf.

Providing Work Placements for Disabled Students: a good practice guide for further and higher education institutions (Department for Education and Skills)

Guide published in 2002 that details the responsibilities of institutions in developing placements. As above, although there have been some changes to the legislation, this guide still contains some useful advice: www.lifelonglearning.co.uk/placements/front.htm.

The National Council for Work Experience

This site has guidelines for international students and work placements: www.work-experience.org/ncwe.rd/news_282.jsp.

Chapter 7

Students' Lives Out of the Classroom

WHAT IS THE ROLE OF THE ACADEMIC IN SUPPORTING STUDENTS 'OUT OF THE CLASSROOM'?

So far most of what we have said in this book has either related to situations in the classroom or, as in the previous chapter, to more formal educational aspects of life at university. This chapter will look at a range of topics related to the broader lives of our students as they occur in tandem with the overtly educational activity. Our own experiences as students are likely to have a profound influence on our attitudes to this. If we have experienced close interaction with academic staff we are likely to assume that this is normal in most universities. If we have experienced larger, more impersonal institutions we may be shocked at the increasing expectations of many universities that academic staff are involved in students' 'welfare' matters. Globally, institutions vary enormously. Some UK universities, for example, have systems whereby students see a personal supervisor/tutor at the beginning and end of term, or even more frequently, to discuss overall progress (and, as a part of this, any aspect of the students' lives that are affecting academic progress). At the other extreme some institutions have 'Directors of Study', where students only tend to approach staff where there are more serious issues relating to the course. Thomas and Hixenbaugh in *Personal Tutoring in Higher Education* (2006) suggest there are three main models to personal tutoring in the UK. The third, as yet less common, model centres around full-time professional counsellors and advisers.

We argue in Chapter 3 that it is front-line staff – that is to say academics during teaching or supervisions – who are most likely to spot, or be approached about, issues affecting students that need more specialist levels of support. Given the theme of this book you might expect us to argue that a range of circumstances extraneous to academic ability affect student performance and the learning experience. We also suggest that there are students for whom living at university can be more of a challenge simply because they are away from home and from their usual support systems, or because some feature of their lives means that they are in a minority. Whatever you decide your position on welfare/pastoral support is, and whatever your university's expectations are, the fact is that students will come to you for support when they encounter personal problems.

 PAUSE FOR THOUGHT

- What 'welfare' support do your students have?
- Find your institution's guidelines for personal supervisors/tutors if you have not been given them.

However, while the expectation of academic involvement seems to increase, so too does the level of expertise that is needed to deal with certain issues. The most important decision for academics in this respect is to decide where our role ends and where the specialist role (dyslexia, immigration, counselling support/advice, to name but three) begins. This is critical in regard to all our students, but is likely to be even more so in relation to aspects of inclusion and diversity. For example:

Research with working class and first generation entrants suggests that these students are especially likely to benefit from a proactive, integrated and structured approach that prioritises relationships rather than the onus being on students to know how to access services when they need them from staff they do not know.

(Thomas and Hixenbaugh, 2006: 31)

 PAUSE FOR THOUGHT

- Find your university student support office webpages or handbook.
- Familiarise yourself with the broad outline of provision and the specialist services available on your campus.
- Do not ignore welfare issues but do not be tempted to overstep your role – point your students towards expert help wherever appropriate.

In an article in June 2007, in the *THES*, a senior lecturer summarised how a number of studies had identified the substantially increased burden upon UK academics in terms of supporting students in a welfare role. However, it is still clear that academics are generally seen to be the ones who are most likely to identify problems in students because of their regular contact. Whatever your official function, or your personal stance, if you are reading this you are likely to be one of these 'front line' staff. What does this mean for us?

1   Efficient recording of information about students, since we cannot be expected to keep all the personal details in our heads. The paper trail is a boring chore for most but absolutely essential if things go wrong. It may, in the long run, reduce our time spent chasing loose ends.

2   Talking to our students.

3   Empathising with our students where appropriate.

4   Being careful to follow through where we promise action.

5   Informing those responsible if we do suspect problems (personal tutors, director of studies – whoever in our institutions is meant to be 'in charge' of this. Cover your back with an e-mail if you sense your concern is being dismissed.

6   Who might help? Welfare experts, other academics and departmental administrators can be very helpful, along with porters and cleaners/staff in residences if matters are residence-related.

In Chapter 3 we referred to Neville in the above article who says there appears to be 'an unspoken expectation that we ensure our students are in a fit emotional state to learn' (*THES*, 1 June 2007). As we said in the context of small-group teaching, most UK (and many other) universities assume this is a part of the academic's role to a greater or lesser extent. It certainly appears to be the expectation of the Higher Education Funding Council for England (HEFCE) that higher education institution staff ensure the welfare of our students – and for this reason questions about student welfare were an integral part of the subject review (audit) process on the quality of teaching. What might be more pertinent to ask is how we determine the balance of dependency and the creation of independent learners.

PAUSE FOR THOUGHT

■ What is the attitude in your own institution to students leaving before completion?

■ What efforts are made to keep students?

■ What do you see as your part in this?

■ Think through your personal limits as to what you will, and will not, get involved in, in terms of supporting your students beyond the overtly academic?

THE AGE OF MAJORITY, THE PAPER TRAIL AND CONFIDENTIALITY

The historical tradition of UK students living away from home before they were legally adults, in part explains the development of a system where universities were *in loco parentis* for their students and legally obliged to look after their welfare. Now, in the UK and elsewhere, the legal age has been lowered, and this has left a complex and rather muddy situation. In fact, although the age of majority is 18 in general, there are lower limits for certain things. For example, over-16-year-olds in the UK can sign consent forms for surgery.

The confidentiality of over-18s must be respected, yet parents often expect some involvement – as the financial backers and loving parents if nothing else! Talking to concerned parents may not be simple. In very rare cases, such as abusive relationships, even seemingly innocent requests about a student's whereabouts can contain hidden agendas. Tell parents you must have the student's permission to disclose information to them. However, you need not be heartless, and there are usually ways of addressing their worries, such as asking the students to make contact with them. Where students are from strongly hierarchical family cultures, it may be even more important to explain carefully the reasons why we cannot divulge information to them.

We must respect the confidentiality of those over the legal age of majority and seek permission before disclosing any confidential information to other staff and students. But there will be exceptions to this: in cases of criminal behaviour, for example. We should always seek advice from our institutions about such serious issues. Furthermore, we will need to be circumspect if we e-mail other academic staff about our students.

In the UK, confidentiality of information is also related to legislation such as the Data Protection Act – we must seek advice before releasing sensitive information if we are at all unsure. We should take care always to leave a clear paper trail demonstrating our support of students, but we should also be careful that this record does not include anything personally defamatory, lest students ask to see their disclosable records. (See Chapter 10 for more detail on this.) Aim to record facts about the situation rather than personal judgments about an individual's character. Your institution will have information on what must legally be shown to individuals about themselves should they request it. At the same time, the notion of the 'duty of care' of universities is legally complex and unclear. Seek advice, especially, for example, if you are involved in off-campus activities, such as residential study visits, with the students.

 PAUSE FOR THOUGHT

- Find out who is responsible for data protection in your institution.
- What guidelines are there to help you know which information may be disclosed and which not?

THE IMPORTANCE OF STUDENT INTEGRATION AND OF POSITIVE IDENTITY WITH THE INSTITUTION

There is a huge body of literature that suggests that student integration and student identity are extremely important for student success. This literature is not uncontentious, and not all agree that ensuring integration is the business of the academic (Laöhteenoja and Pirttilaö-Backman, 2005). However, much of the research demonstrates that good retention rates are linked to a strong sense of positive student identity and a clear feeling of belonging to, and integration with, the institution. This positive integration is frequently linked with what might be termed welfare support and also with 'out-of-class' student social activity. The UK system (and indeed many others) is premised on an assumption that universities will offer a good 'all round' experience to their students. The infrastructure must be appropriate and academic staff must be aware of what the expectations are regarding their contribution in all of this.

137

In the UK, Australia, North America and elsewhere, there is considerable discussion about 'retention figures'. Low rates of student withdrawal have been seen as one of the hallmarks of success in good universities. (There is clearly a different presumption in some other European countries.) Good student integration has also been strongly linked to high levels of retention in Australia and North America. If, therefore, you are teaching in a UK university or similar, it will be assumed that, to a greater or lesser extent, you will play a part in the university's mission to integrate and to keep its students. We indicated in Chapter 3 that certain groups of students are more likely to withdraw than others (see also Quinn *et al.*, 2005).

Withdrawal is not a one-off event, 'it is a process' (Basit, 2006: 406). It is crucial therefore that supervisors, tutors and other staff intervene to help with students' difficulties before they become too great. One study, for example, found that most of the withdrawals happened because problems were not ameliorated early enough. Major concerns of those who left were personal and health reasons, but discrimination and finance were also reported concerns. Other students left because they had chosen the wrong course.

Over the last twenty years, a number of the many studies focusing on student integration have been based on the model provided by Tinto in 1975. This suggests that a student enters university with unique personal and academic characteristics and skills and each has their specific desires and aims. The student then encounters the university structures and social groups. Tinto claims that the level of the student's commitment will be strengthened or weakened depending on the fit between the student and this environment, both social and academic. Tinto argues that those who fit well will persevere more. The interplay between the academic and the social is important in this model. Clearly this model is not uncontentious, and academics argue about the balance and extent of the critical factors. It is evident from studies that minority student groups find it harder to make the fit than other, more traditional students. Identifying 'at risk' students has become a strategy at some institutions to try to reduce withdrawals. The *Star* project at the University of Ulster, for example, produced an induction audit tool to help staff interested in identifying those who may potentially be at more risk of withdrawing. Whatever we feel about the importance of integration and the strength of the research on it, common sense dictates that, usually, a happy student who is positively involved with peers and with staff is more likely to stay the course and is more likely to do well!

THE STUDENTS' FIRST-YEAR EXPERIENCE

A number of recent studies have focused upon the first year experience and on the lack of preparedness of many for university life. This lack of readiness is not only about the compatibility of student and course, but also about the quality of relationships between academics and students and the students' processes of establishing friends and networks. Suggestions for enhancing these features have especially included extended induction periods, but also the use of interactive and collaborative learning methods to facilitate the development of peer groups, and staff-students relationships have also been key.

 PAUSE FOR THOUGHT

Consider how you (personally and institutionally) welcome your new students:

■ Do they have a formal induction from the department/school? Is it sufficient?

■ If no, what could you do additionally to set the scene for them as they commence your course?

■ To what extent do you wish to encourage their participation in wider university activities – academic and social?

■ What cultural/physical factors may affect such involvement? Do they have part-time jobs? Families? Are there language issues? Mobility issues? Health issues?

■ Is there ongoing awareness/support in these areas beyond the induction period?

Refer back to Chapter 1.

A UK study of students who left one university stressed the need for tutors to consider social reasons why students leave university. It found that academic integration took secondary place to social integration. Friendships and accommodation-related reasons were common. No one is suggesting that it is the academic's duty completely to sort out such problems – indeed that would probably be impossible even if it were appropriate. However, the academic is located in a position that may contribute to providing a 'safe space' until the student sorts out such problems. Furthermore, studies have clearly shown that a crucial factor to aid retention is the quality of relationships between academic staff and students. We maintain that support from academics is essential in underpinning integration into the course. Practical difficulties for students with sight, hearing and mobility impairments can be numerous with regard to integrating into the social life of the university. So it can also be for students from religious or social backgrounds that discourage the alcohol-fuelled activities in which many students engage.

- Do you have a check list of things to discuss with your first years in early meetings?
- What would you do if one of your new students said they were lonely?

WHAT ARE THE VARYING ROLES OF THE ACADEMIC?

As an academic there are three broad divisions in terms of our 'out-of-classroom' involvement with students:

1 general welfare support for those we teach;
2 those we supervise as a personal tutor or supervisor (i.e. welfare as opposed to academic tutor);
3 our collegial role as part of the world of academia.

GENERAL SUPPORT FOR THOSE WE TEACH

Universities vary in their expectations of us in this. In the universities in which the authors teach there is a high expectation that staff who teach, and not merely the personal tutors, will pay considerable attention to student welfare. However, common assumptions would be that, although you may talk through difficult issues with the students you teach, or they may approach you for advice, you are not responsible for any involved or detailed sorting out of problems or issues. Students whom you teach should normally be directed to their personal supervisor/tutor to sort out non-academic issues. Of course life is never so simple, and it would obviously be inappropriate to decline to talk through an issue with a student who bursts into tears in teaching contact time! Furthermore, it may well be you who notices changed behaviour in a student whom you see each week or in their responses (or lack of) to feedback on work. Having broached the issue in such cases and where immediate suggestions are insufficient, the problem should normally be pursued by the personal supervisor/tutor. At all times you should alert such staff to serious concerns about academic progress. How much else you tell them about the reasons for this might be about negotiating confidential areas with the student concerned and preferably persuading them to go and discuss the issues themselves. Research for Universities UK has highlighted the universities' moral duty to minimise potential risks to students, and the same research highlighted that it is likely to be front-line academic staff who spot a student in distress (*THES*, 1 June 2007).

Where our contact is only with huge groups, then perhaps our part can mostly be in pressure groups (e.g. committees) to persuade such institutions to set up systems to ensure student welfare is paramount and to ensure manageable workloads for staff.

PERSONAL TUTORING

Many universities expect staff to supervise a number of students in a role that involves some oversight for their welfare as well as their academic work. In some places this is called personal tutoring or personal supervision. In other institutions staff may have a more academic-related title such as 'Director of Studies' where it nonetheless relates, not to directing the programme, but to offering personal support to underpin students' studies. Increasingly, institutions are explicit in the guidelines they give to such staff (e.g. University of Bath, www.bath.ac.uk/internal/tutors/index.html) but many more are not. Personal tutors (or whatever they are called in your institution) are very likely to be the first port of call for assistance where students are disabled or where they need to request special help. Where students have disclosed a disability, institutions should ensure that this is notified to personal tutors. If a student discloses a disability to you then you should contact your disability office or relevant departmental/faculty link for the appropriate course of action. Your institution should offer you guidelines about your minimum role. How many times a term or a semester should you meet with your personal supervisees? Are you expected to be proactive or reactive? To whom do you report incidents? To whom do you turn for specialist help?

One common theme in personal tutoring is continuity – so we may well have oversight of a student for all of their time as, for example, an undergraduate. Research has shown that students are more likely to turn first to their tutor for advice than to the specialist services (Thomas and

Hixenbaugh, 2006). In the UK, the introduction of mandatory Personal Development Plan (PDP) schemes (see also Chapter 8) is also going to hook tutors more tightly into discussion of student aspirations and long-term goals.

 PAUSE FOR THOUGHT

Find out what your institutional requirements are regarding student Personal Development Plans.

See *Personal Tutoring in Higher Education* (Thomas and Hixenbough 2006) for a selection of evidence to demonstrate the effectiveness of personal tutoring and a range of models for personal tutoring.

 PAUSE FOR THOUGHT

There are suggestions about, and experiments into, the idea that more full-time counsellors should be appointed (rather than using academic tutors). However, research tends to demonstrate that increased retention occurs when tutor relationships are more personal. What is your view? Where do you feel the limits of your expertise lie in terms of giving advice?

Staffordshire University lists the following as possible students' issues for its staff who are personal tutors:

1 student has disclosed a disability;
2 student is struggling with academic work;
3 visa problem;
4 language support;
5 careers-related issue;
6 financial difficulty;
7 change of course/uncertain about course;
8 accommodation problems;
9 wishing to appeal assessment result;
10 general complaint;

TABLE 7.1 Possible action plans for approaching welfare problems

Role	Initial action	Secondary action	Follow-up
Personal (pastoral/welfare) supervisor	Discuss with student in depth Keep written record	Refer to Programme Director/Chair of Board Studies/Director of Studies or appropriate in your institution; discuss with and/or refer student to specialist advisers such as disability or international offices	Discuss again with student – check progress/action, etc.; maintain contact with relevant staff; update written record
Postgraduates who teach (GTAs)	Approach your mentor/course leader or similar for advice; refer student to personal tutor; mention concern as appropriate to personal tutor; keep written record	Check with those concerned that issue is being dealt with	Monitor student as appropriate; update written record; approach relevant staff again if issue remains; keep the programme leader informed lest there are serious consequences, e.g. for assessment
Lecturer – teaching role	As in row above; you may find you become more involved than a GTA in the appropriate action for helping the student	As in row above; discuss ongoing actions with appropriate colleagues	As in row above; you may be involved in examination boards or other committees where cases are discussed – keep thorough notes

11   student has disappeared;
12   emotional problems;
13   parent seeking information about a student;
14   social issues (e.g. lack of contacts in university).

All students are vulnerable to life's difficulties: bereavement – for example, if a parent dies; lack of funds; divorcing parents; illness; falling out with friends; loneliness; accommodation problems; homesickness; drink; drugs; depression, to name but a few. An inclusive approach means ensuring that none of these students suffers unreasonably, and support is likely to include guidance where they have made mistakes and brought on their own problems. But our particular concern in this book is to ensure equity where factors outside the student's control are making life more difficult than that of other students. Even where we are experts (for example, psychiatrists in medical school teaching), it is not our designated role to act as the expert in these situations, although our expertise may inform those who act in the official role. The hardest decision is often when to pass the student on for more specialist help. A maxim of sooner rather than later is probably best. The specialist can then decide who is best placed to help. Universities employ a vast raft of support staff for precisely this job. Sometimes services – for example, counselling services – are stretched, however, and it may seem like help is too slow in coming. In some instances, such as immigration advice, only trained and accredited staff are allowed to give advice. All the more reason to encourage the students to seek help at an early date.

Advice relating to academic matters will need to be handled following institutional procedures. Never be tempted to rush into offering solutions to students in distress that are ill-thought out or beyond your remit. For example, it is highly unlikely that, however serious a situation our student is in, we will have the power to waive summative assessment without approval from others. General complaints or complaints about other members of staff should be directed to a senior member of the department or school, often the Head.

PROTECTING YOURSELF

Student welfare problems can be extremely time consuming. It is important that we protect ourselves. Keep a professional distance and do not get over-involved. We should think carefully about student access to our mobile and home numbers. It may not be wise to release the latter, but it is our decision and views vary. It is sensible to set earliest and latest contact times if there may be a problem. If we are particularly worried about students we should make sure that they know appropriate university contact numbers such as residence staff, counselling, health centre and so on (see Table 7.1). It is important that higher education institutions allow sufficient time for staff to deal with student welfare issues if that is the expectation. Since this can be hard to negotiate, it is best to be aware of how this is accommodated in any work load allocation system that might exist.

EMPATHY

One of the most critical abilities for a personal tutor is that of empathy. Increasingly, medical students are being told that enhancing communi-cation with patients is extremely dependent on their empathic approach. In order to treat their patients well, they are told, they need to under-stand the situation from the patient's point of view – they need to 'put themselves in the patient's shoes' as far as is possible. Empathy is not the same as sympathy; it goes one step further. For personal tutors empathy is critical for two reasons. First, as with doctors, any advice will be more effective if it is grounded in an understanding of where the student is situated and therefore how the realities and the perceptions might be realistically addressed together. Second, empathy is a key skill (or more appropriately ability) in helping to combat discrimination. It is only as we try to understand how others think and feel that we can begin to find solutions to situations that do not cause offence. 'In order to develop intercultural competence one has to meet someone who differs from oneself . . . one also has to do something together on an equal footing' (Heidemann, 2000).

TUTORING MINORITY GROUPS

As personal tutors we may need to spend more time assisting students from minority groups. By this we do not only mean racial or ethnic groups but any student who is not in the dominant and major group in your institution. Throughout this book our message is that good practice for international students, disabled students and so on is good practice for all. We have aimed to use a social model that does not make any particular group or 'type' of student a 'problem.' We firmly believe in the richness of diverse student groups. Teaching in the Centre for Women's Studies, University of York, is firmly based on this premise, for example, and the rich international mix genuinely adds to the student experience. Many of the dissertations are based on knowledge and experience from students' home countries, intertwined with the particular approach to academic content and critique that is based on research in the discipline. Having said this, it is the reality that students such as international students may well be deserving of more time from us because of the increased number of hurdles they can experience, and because of the greater number of adjustments (both cultural and material) that they often have to make. Where the students' backgrounds are more different from our own it can be more difficult to behave empathically. We do not want to add to erroneous stereotypes, nonetheless there are some issues that occur quite frequently. One of the critical caveats is to remind ourselves that students never fit into one group or category. We must always deal with individuals as human beings not members of a group. Furthermore, there is always, in any one person, a mix of race, class, gender, age, sexuality and health. Thus seeing a particular issue as the result of only one of life's features is almost always unhelpful. However, in these respects we cannot be 'difference blind'. It is practical and helpful to be alert to the fact that all these areas can be the root of study problems, and where difficulties occur for any one student they may well need our help to redress the inequities for them in their academic lives.

TALKING TO THE STUDENTS

When we first meet students for whom we are personal tutors we should have an open conversation – asking the types of general question that will elicit information to help us guide them in settling in, in study and in prioritising tasks. We should find out about their lives and establish good communication as it is critical at an early stage. We should not imply that we are only available if they have problems, as they may feel they have to have a serious problem to come and see us – and, of course, what students see as serious will vary hugely. We should always make sure that we, and our supervisees, are in possession of the student services handbook or webpages. Direct all the students to the appropriate support services as relevant. We should make ourselves aware of what specialised support is on offer as the need arises. We need to ensure that we have their essential details and that they have followed whatever the university requires in terms of registering with doctors and so on. We should make sure that they are aware of the various possibilities for social networking as well as for academic progress. Where we say we will find out something for students we should always follow it up, but wherever possible try to put the onus on them to pursue things. It may be efficient in the long term to create a short checklist for ourselves to ensure we do not miss covering essential issues – this sounds tedious but after similar discussions with ten students it is easy to become confused!

In our first critical meetings we may need to pay more attention to the following points; these suggestions are not comprehensive but are offered as a starting point:

Older Students

1 Life cycle issues – responsibilities of carers (children or other relatives), health.
2 May be nervous about meeting the demands of domestic and study requirements.
3 May be anxious about returning to study after years.
4 May find it hard to readjust after being in charge of work teams, etc.
5 Mid-life issues can be complex.
6 Bereavement may be more likely to impact on study.
7 Significant financial strain can arise from keeping mortgage payments going, etc.

Younger Students

1 May be unusual in the UK if they are under 18 and not old enough to take part in certain activities (e.g. alcohol purchase) – a possible problem for socialising.
2 Parents may be kept informed and are still legally responsible; institution has particular duties of care in these cases.
3 You should be informed by your institution about any under 18s you supervise.

International Students

1 May face a major transition in terms of adapting to a new culture.
2 May encounter some hostility or even racism from others (this need not only be related to colour – in the UK, American and German students, for example, can be subject to taunts).

147

3   May face an entirely different approach to study and assessment.
4   May face heavy pressures from high expectations at home (for example, from parents or funding employers).
5   May face language concerns.
6   May face financial pressures.
7   Religious observances may be different to the host country's major religion(s).
8   Approaches to gender may be different to host institutional cultures.
9   Important family links may be difficult to maintain.
10 Comprehensive records (for example, regarding health, may not have accompanied students).
11 Possible homesickness.
12 Possible different emphasis on written and oral culture to host nation.
13 War, civil unrest and so on in home country – there are areas of the world where this is a significant factor for some of our students.
14 Disappointment with the new country – failure to live up to the expectations of student life in the host country.
15 Cultural differences between supervisor and student.

Acculturation is not a linear process – our students may appear to be handling a transition in their lives well one term and be unsettled by their sense of fragmented identity the next. We need to 'authenticate hybrid identities that are under construction' (Quarshie Smith, 2007: 65).

In an article on conflict between graduate students and their supervisors, Adrian-Taylor *et al.* stress the importance of social interaction for a good student experience. This is highly likely to apply to all types of student, but specifically they find that 'the number and quality of relationships an international student has with the host country nationals is positively related to his or her adjustment' (Adrian-Taylor, 2007: 92). They say that supervisors are important to all students but may be the 'central figure of the lives of these [international students]'. They suggest that it is likely that international students will have fewer social supports than home students. Research suggests that host nation students approach supervisors for advice on academic matters and friends for emotional/personal problems, but that international students go to supervisors for help with both (Leong and Sedlicek, 1986).

148

There are a number of frameworks that can act as checklists for meetings with our international students; in fact they may act as a useful guide for all our students. One such taxonomy is Pelletier's, cited by Bartram and based on a meta-analysis of related UK studies (Bartram, 2007: 206). She suggests we look to:

1 practical needs;
2 emotional needs;
3 cultural and integrational needs;
4 language;
5 pedagogy;
6 needs relating to curriculum and assessment;
7 needs associated with performance outcomes.

Part-Time Students

1 May be carers – what are their commitments?
2 May be earning to pay their way or support others – what are their job commitments?
3 Are often older students (see above).
4 Are they more isolated?
5 Do they need help prioritising time (many will be experts at juggling, but do not assume this to be the case!).
6 May have unexpected work deadlines.
7 May have many competing priorities.
8 Travel distances can be troublesome.

Part-time students have given lack of time as the most common issue for study problems. This can mean that even the mechanisms put into place to support students are not used by part-timers as they feel too busy. They commonly do not go through the same integration process as full-time students and often keep their pre-existing support networks. They can sometimes, therefore, suffer less of an identity crisis than younger, full-time students. Conversely, these same support systems can be a source of tension for many, and it may make it more difficult for them to build strong ties to the new life. Family, work and non-student friends can cause a significant pull away from study. Kember, amongst others, has suggested that class time dedicated to discussion can help lessen isolation for such students. He suggests that some tasks be group tasks and that even on distance courses teleconferencing (or use of a VLE, see Chapter 5) can promote interaction (Kember, 1999: 123).

Flexible, modular programmes are, at one level, advantageous to older, part-time students, but they can also mean increased isolation and anonymity as it is harder to identify with a cohort of students. Kember's main proposal is better provision for child care since this is a main source of anxiety for part-time students.

 PAUSE FOR THOUGHT

- How does part-time work affect your students?
- Do you know if there are regulations about how many hours students are allowed to work if full-time students?
- Is the assessment cycle more problematic for carers of young children?

Home Students From a Minority Ethnic Background

1   Danger of host institution's staff and students not differentiating between different black, mixed and ethnic cultures and/or international students.
2   Some cultures expect females to agree to arranged marriages – this may cause internal conflict for such students as they socialise with more independent peers.
3   Some may face extremely high expectations from families.
4   Some may experience racism.

A withdrawal survey amongst students from initial teacher training programmes showed similar reasons for withdrawal among all types of student – and there were usually a number of reasons not a single one. However, there were often additional factors for minority ethnic students; for example, racism experienced in the school placements could compound the feeling that a wrong choice had been made. Racism was not usually a reason for leaving but it 'doubtless strengthened resolve to leave' (Basit *et al.*, 2006: 407). Eighteen per cent of the group interviewed for this survey believed they were victims of deliberate racism in their institution. Only a third said they had reported it. One reported that a number of trainees had left her course because of a particular tutor and that three years later this tutor was still in place despite the complaints.

PAUSE FOR THOUGHT

■ Do any of your students experience racism in the institution?
■ From students/staff/others?
■ What support do you offer your students who feel they have suffered from racist treatment?
■ Who in the institution can you go to for support on this?

A number of minority ethnic students feel they experience unwitting consequences of belonging to an ethnic minority. Withdrawers in the above survey often felt isolated: 'I was placed in a group where out of 20, I was the only non-white student' or 'I felt subtly excluded by the majority white middle-class trainees. My support group consisted of a practising Jew, a Muslim, an Asian Christian, an epileptic and myself (black Caribbean), which I think is very telling' (Basit *et al.*, 2006: 402).

 PAUSE FOR THOUGHT

■ How do you ensure equity in your approach?
■ How do you talk to students who feel that you are victimising them because of their ethnicity when you feel you are actually treating them the same as others?
■ How do you ensure students on placements get a fair deal?

Over one-quarter of the minority ethnic students in the above study perceived the need for more support from higher education institutions. They often wanted moral support, encouragement and information about progress. 'There appeared to be a need for the . . . institutions to be proactive in the support given.' Many of them felt the need for more support from the higher education institutions when their placements proved problematic. There was a clear need for the institution to monitor the help from the workplace mentors. A number of similar projects demonstrate the usefulness of good orientation and of good mentoring.

Modood's work has warned us against some mistaken conflations sometimes found in reports about the experiences of minority ethnic students – for example, in general, the experiences of Pakistani and

Bangladeshi origin students are very different to those of black Caribbean origin students. We must be wary of very broad assumptions in this area (Modood, 2006).

Disabled Students

1 You should be informed of any students who have disclosed a disability.
2 You will need to keep a check that appropriate and reasonable adjustments have been made for these students.
3 Liaise closely with your disability office.
4 Talk through the arrangements that have been made to ensure your supervisee is happy with them.
5 Some students have a 'hidden' disability such as diabetes and may, or may not, want other students/staff to know about this – be sensitive to this possibility.

Non-Resident Students

1 Second-year students in the UK can often move off campus – there is often considerable stress as they try to sort out both friendship groups and rental arrangements.
2 Non-residents may find it much harder to fully integrate if they are in a minority.

First-Generation University Students

1 May be alienated from families and friends at home.
2 More likely to be financial concerns.
3 May lack social confidence in seminar settings depending on previous exposure to debate and discussion.

Sexual Orientation

1 May be coming to terms with sexual orientation – a crucial part of life for many who are just leaving home.
2 May have issues relating to birth control, sexually transmitted diseases and so on – refer to health centre as appropriate.
3 Gay, lesbian or bisexual students may be taking the move away from home as an opportunity to 'come out' or to think through their sexuality.
4 Transgender students may meet opposition.

Phobias, Panic and Anxiety

1   Refer to counselling services or health centre for anything beyond 'normal' anxiety levels.

Health

1   Ensure your students are registered with a local doctor.
2   Keep a watch for common diseases such as meningitis, mumps and measles.
3   Short-term illnesses – ensure that the appropriate 'special case' provision is made, for example, in assessment.

Finances

1   Students who do not get direct or indirect parental support can be especially concerned about financial self-sufficiency.
2   International students can experience sudden and serious set-backs in receiving financial support.
3   Mature students can be under considerable financial pressure.

Most universities have staff who are specially qualified to advise on student finance issues and debt. This is a relatively specialist advice area and you should not be tempted to offer amateur advice. However, there are areas you should be aware of – especially as new students arrive. Does your institution have hardship funds or bursary schemes? To whom do you send your students who might benefit from advice on this (Hatt, 2005)? Student unions are often excellent sources of advice for students on many of the aspects above.

In general:

1   Ask open-ended questions as you talk to your supervisees.
2   Enhance your listening skills.
3   If you are unsure of what is being said or implied, you may need to pace their conversation, repeat, backtrack and summarise what you think has been said and agree any actions you both need to take.
4   Refer on to specialised help when necessary.
5   Keep a written record for yourself but place on student's file where relevant.

153

OUR GENERAL COLLEGIAL ROLE

Collegiality in a university can only arise when individual students and staff contribute to activities. This may, for example, involve us in extra-curricular societies or discussion groups in our disciplines. These may often be linked to teaching or research networking and enhancement and also to furthering career prospects. For some it may even mean participation in activities beyond our own discipline such as music or sports groups. Clearly the latter are not normally part of our job description. We need to determine first to what extent our employers require us to participate in out-of-classroom activities. Formally this is probably very little, unless we take on roles such as hall warden and so on as an additional duty, or unless we teach in a discipline such as music, where running an orchestra or choir may be part of our formal duties. However, the success of the student experience at university is built on the enthusiasm of staff as well as of the student body. There are many positive reasons for being involved in more peripheral activities with our students and it is often extremely informative. In relation to inclusivity and diversity, one fulfilling activity is to talk to student union representatives who represent various groups such as mature, international, women, lesbian, gay, bisexual groups and so on. The main decision about involvement in these areas is probably one that simply relates to your own priorities, preferences and available time.

There is no single correct approach to personal tutoring but, in summary, here are general points we should think about/include as appropriate:

1 Create an open and accessible relationship.
2 Tell them how we wish to be addressed.
3 Explain availability hours if we are concerned to protect time.
4 Will we be available via mobile? If we do give out mobile numbers, do we establish latest and earliest times for calling?
5 Try to find the balance between 'spoon-feeding' and lack of support/interest.
6 Set boundaries as to what we will and will not do. When we first meet our students make it clear how we see our role.
7 Articulate these boundaries to our students.
8 Try to get the student to take the first actions.
9 Make it clear who will do what.
10 Make it clear they can come back to us if the first action does not work or if we wish them to update us.

11 Find out where to send student to if they need expert advice from central welfare services or from other departmental/school/faculty colleagues.

12 Try to develop a 'sixth sense' about what is urgent and what is not.

13 Troubleshoot early to prevent escalation of incidents.

14 Try only answering e-mails once or twice per day and not as they come through.

15 Learn, out of hours, to mentally switch off from student problems.

16 If an issue is not urgent we may wish to give a holding or interim response and deal with the issue at our convenience.

17 Do not be pressured into overly quick reactions – take time to think, even in seeming emergencies.

18 Do not necessarily respond immediately, as students cannot expect instant turnaround.

19 Do not promise solutions that are beyond our remit to offer.

20 Do we need to arrange cross-cover with colleagues if we are absent?

21 Are our students aware of the arrangements for our cover and when we will/will not be around?

22 Keep a written record.

 FURTHER READING

Clements, P. and Spinks, T. (2000) *The Equal Opportunities Handbook: How to deal with everyday issues of unfairness*, London, Kogan Page.

Thomas, L. and Hixenbaugh, P. (2006) *Personal Tutoring in Higher Education*, Stoke on Trent, Trentham.

Wheeler, S. and Birtle, J. (1993) *A Handbook for Personal Tutors*, Buckingham: Society for Research into Higher Education and Open University Press.

 USEFUL WEB RESOURCE

Useful work by Tariq Modood and the Centre for Ethincity and Citizenship is available at www.bristol.ac.uk/sociology/ethnicitycitizenship/.

Chapter 8

Student Skills Agenda

This chapter will consider the issue of students' skills and how these relate to diversity issues in higher education. We will look first at undergraduate skills training and then at postgraduates as there are some specific requirements for the latter from funding councils.

In Chapter 3 we said that research into procedural knowledge suggested that there were three main phases to skills learning: cognitive (e.g. descriptions of the rules); associative (e.g. tuning methods, pattern-recognition, etc.); autonomous (skill becomes more rapid and automated). We stressed that practice was critical to the latter stage. As you read this chapter try to think how you would apply this process to the introduction of skills in your curriculum.

STUDENTS' SKILLS

The publication of the Dearing Report (NCIHE, 1997) renewed interest in the development of students' skills in higher education and, in particular, the recording of these skills through progress files. Various terms have been used to describe the skills that students acquire through their higher education experience, such as: transferable skills; key skills; academic skills; study skills; employability skills. The skills being discussed in these terms may include some or all of the following:

1 communication (written and verbal);
2 group work;
3 adaptability/flexibility;
4 networking;
5 time management;

6 leadership;
7 planning and organisation;
8 initiative;
9 decision-making;
10 negotiation;
11 creativity;
12 analysis and problem solving;
13 numerical;
14 computing;
15 self-awareness;
16 continuing personal/professional development.

 PAUSE FOR THOUGHT

■ Are there other specific skills that you would include in this list?
■ How do you support your students in developing these skills?
■ Would you consider there to be any specific diversity issues in relation to the development of these skills?

The topic of employability and career development is covered in more detail in Chapter 10. In this chapter we will discuss some issues relating to the development of students' skills, specifically communication and group work.

Personal Development Planning

The term personal development planning is often used within UK higher education and is defined as: 'a structured and supported process undertaken by an individual to reflect upon their own learning, performance and/or achievement and to plan for their personal, educational and career development' (QAA, 2000).

Depending upon your institution, students' engagement with PDP may be as an explicit process – for example, as a discrete module or course – or it may be integrated and delivered within the context of your discipline. Whichever approach is taken, and given the definition of PDP presented above, it is likely that there will be some requirement for students to record their achievements, possibly through a portfolio that can be developed and enhanced throughout the student's period of study.

157

Given the fact that for some students – for example, international students – this may be a very different approach to learning compared with previous studies and experiences, it may be useful to provide some examples of previous students' work. Students will need to see the benefit of developing a portfolio in order to provide the required motivation to continue compiling and maintaining this throughout their period of study. Linking this development with issues such as employability may provide a clear and tangible benefit for students. Although some students will not be particularly interested in considering employability options until the later stages of their course, it is important to start discussing these skills with students at an early stage and providing opportunities for them to consider:

1   what skills they currently possess;
2   what evidence they can show to demonstrate that they possess these skills;
3   what skills they do not yet possess;
4   strategies for filling the gaps.

In particular, we may have to help our students to recognise some of the skills that they already possess. In relation to diversity, some of the skills that could have been acquired are identified in Table 8.1.

The advice to give to students at this stage is to concentrate on the positive aspects of the skills that they possess and their achievements, rather than considering some of the negative reasons why they might have developed these skills in the first place.

Working with students to recognise skills that they have already developed will also assist in helping them to reflect on other activities that they may undertake and the skills that will be developed through such activities. It should also help in terms of assisting students to identify examples of evidence that they could include in their PDP portfolio. Perhaps a good lesson to promote in terms of portfolio development is the fact that the quality of the evidence presented is more important than the number of examples of evidence. Undertaking a general skills audit will help students to reflect on the abilities that they already possess, and will identify skills that may need to be developed further. As part of the audit it may be useful to provide specific examples of the way in which a skill could be demonstrated or obtained, in order to assist with the development of appropriate action plans designed to address any gaps in skill provision. By encouraging our students to create action plans that may allow them to obtain better examples of evidence, and perhaps to

158

▓ **TABLE 8.1** Possible employability skills that could be listed by students from particular groups.

Disabled student	• Flexibility • Problem solving • Determination • Persistence • Motivation
Disabled student assisted by a support worker	• Co-operation • Negotiation • Interpersonal skills
International students	• Persistence • Motivation • Language skills • Commitment • Flexibility • Willingness to learn • Self-management • Ability to adapt to change
Students managing family commitments	• Time management • Determination • Persistence • Organisational skills
Students who have 'come out' and declared their sexual orientation	• Determination • Risk-taking • Sensitivity • Commitment

consider examples that address multiple skills, we will be assisting them in focusing on particular tasks and reflecting upon the range of activities that they routinely undertake not only as part of their studies but also outside the classroom. For example, returning to the skills listed at the start of this chapter, many students should be able to find opportunities during their time in higher education that will help them to enhance many of these skills. This could be through work (either in parallel with the period of study or as a separate work placement opportunity – see Chapter 6), volunteering, social clubs or other activities such as helping out or teaching in a local place of worship.

As noted above, the practice of maintaining a portfolio and reflecting on activities may not be natural for some students, who may require some support in differentiating between *reflection* and *description*. Reflection can potentially be used as a useful tool for diversity awareness in all students, if they are encouraged to 'step back' and include other perspectives as part of their reflections. By getting students to consider their own viewpoints and actions in the context of a diverse student population, they may start to appreciate the views of other students and other cultures.

Some skills that students may have more trouble developing are communication and group working skills. At first sight, it may appear that the difficulties associated with acquiring these skills could be directly related to inclusivity issues. For example, group work may highlight discrimination issues from other students in relation to all aspects of diversity, particularly in relation to not wanting to work with particular students because of a perceived fear that this will reduce the final mark obtained from the activity (if assessed), while oral presentations may be difficult for students with language problems or acute anxiety. However, in a study of disabled and non-disabled students, Healey *et al.* (2006) found that 29 per cent of non-disabled students perceived that they had encountered difficulties when participating in group work, compared with 19 per cent for disabled students, and 33 per cent of non-disabled students felt they had experienced difficulties with oral presentations, compared with 28 per cent of disabled students. This is not to say that disabled students do not have a problem with these activities, but perhaps in relation to other areas of the curriculum the difficulties associated with acquiring group work and oral presentation skills may not be as apparent. The point that we are trying to make here is that by addressing the issue of skills acquisition through an agenda of inclusion and diversity we will be addressing the needs of other students at the same time.

Communication Skills: Written

The development of written communication skills will not simply involve assessed work such as essays and reports, but will also include skills such as taking notes — either from lectures, discussions and presentations or from books and journals — and writing for different audiences. Students therefore need access to opportunities that will allow them to develop such skills; for example, ask students to write essays and reports in styles that would be appropriate for a range of publications from academic journals to a popular discipline-based magazine aimed at the layperson, or a tabloid newspaper.

It is helpful to provide students with opportunities to reflect on the way in which they take notes, and to provide other examples of how this may be done. Encouraging students to move away from writing verbatim notes and to focus on recording important words, ideas and concepts will help many students to concentrate on the content of what is being said. Encouraging students to record accurately the source of the information, whether within a formal lecture session or through additional reading outside the classroom, will assist them when writing essays and reports for assignments and will highlight the importance of acknowledging sources.

It can be informative to ask students to compare their notes for a particular topic with each other. Also, if a topic is presented that has been prepared in advance and may, for example, have been videoed, it might be helpful to prepare some notes in different formats as exemplars for students; for example, linear examples versus creative methods of taking notes such as mind maps or concept maps. Some students with dyslexia find it easier to use mind maps rather than linear notes, and as well as being able to create hand-drawn mind maps there are several computer software packages that can assist with this process. Encouraging students to review, edit and if necessary annotate and enhance their notes as soon as possible after they were made will help to ensure that the notes make more sense when they are returned to, possibly for revision purposes.

The issue of assessment is covered in more detail in Chapter 9. However, some general points in relation to assisting students when writing essays or reports for assignment are as follows:

1 Are students clear about the assessment criteria for the essay or report?
2 Is it clear what style of writing is required for the assignment, and are there examples that we can provide that might assist some students by clarifying what we are looking for?
3 Are students aware of word limits and of any consequences if these are ignored, for example, a penalty that results in a reduced mark?
4 Is the essay title/assignment brief clear and unambiguous?
5 Are students aware of the correct style of referencing to be used in the assignment, and the potential implications if this is not used appropriately?

6   Does your institution provide additional support for students to improve their academic writing?

Reading written work aloud can be very useful at highlighting potential issues relating to the flow of information and the structure of the work, but this may be difficult for some students, for example, students with dyslexia. One way in which this might be overcome is by encouraging small groups of students to peer review each other's work. Another method is to use text-to-speech software to read written work if it has been produced electronically using a word processor. The benefit of this approach is that the text-to-speech voice is dispassionate and is guaranteed to read what has actually been written, rather than what someone thinks has been written.

Communication Skills: Verbal

Many students find it hard to give face-to-face presentations in front of an audience, particularly an audience comprising their peers.

As with written assessments, there are a number of questions that should be considered when supporting students with oral presentations:

1   Are students clear about the assessment criteria for the presentation?
2   Are students aware of time limits, and any consequences if these are ignored; for example, the fact that the presentation may be stopped even if the speaker has not finished? How will elapsed time be notified to the students?
3   Is the presentation title/assignment brief clear and unambiguous?
4   Are students aware of the equipment that will be available to them to assist with the presentation; for example, overhead or data projector, computer, available software packages and the version (this is important in terms of compatibility, particularly if the students have access to a later version of the software)?
5   How large will the audience be?
6   Is interaction with the audience permitted, or encouraged?
7   Does the time limit include time for questions?

It was suggested in Chapter 4 that one way in which we can improve our own teaching is to video ourselves, and the same can be true for students in their preparation for a presentation. Videoing a presentation may give a far more accurate estimation of the time it will take to give the presentation compared with an individual student rehearsing the script to themselves. It may be possible for the students to record their presentation in front of a few trusted colleagues, but even if the student is alone the fact that the presentation is being recorded may raise a student's adrenalin so that it may partially reproduce the nerves that will be felt when giving a face-to-face presentation. When viewing the film, a student could be advised to concentrate on:

1   *Language*. Is the language clear and appropriate for the topic and the audience?

2   *Structure*. Does the structure of the presentation make sense? Is the topic introduced appropriately and is there a suitable summary and conclusion?

3   *Body language*. Does the film highlight any distracting mannerisms? (One of the best ways to identify such mannerisms is to watch the film using the fast-forward option, as this can emphasise repetitive actions.)

4   *Eye contact*. Is there appropriate eye contact with the camera/audience?

5   *Speech*. Is the voice projected appropriately? Are there lots of unnecessary filling words, such as 'um' or 'OK'? Is the pace of the session appropriate and not too rushed? Is there some variation in the speed, pitch and tone of the voice, which will maintain interest?

6   *Visual aids*. If visual aids are being used, are they clear? Is there appropriate contrast between the text and the background?

7   *Notes and prompts*. Some students, but particularly students who are not studying in their first language and who may not be entirely confident about what they are saying, may write out a complete script. This approach should be discouraged; if the students have written out verbatim notes then it is likely that they will read the script word for word. The effect of this is that the students will tend to read with their head down (looking at their notes), which can restrict the projection of the voice, and will not make eye contact with the group.

Although it will be necessary for all students to have gained the experience of face-to-face presentations by the time that they have completed

163

their studies, you may feel that it would be appropriate in the early stages of students' studies to allow them to submit their presentation as a recording. The benefit to the students of this approach is that feedback can be given regarding the structure and nature of the presentation, rather than this aspect of the presentation being overpowered by nerves on the day. Also, if the presentations are played to the group as a whole, the students can themselves participate as part of the group in a critique of their own work.

Group Work Skills

As we have suggested in Chapter 3, the use of groups within higher education is fairly common and may involve students working together for an assignment. The use of such an approach to learning also reflects the importance of group work in most forms of employment. However, some students dislike group work, particularly when associated with an assessment activity, as there is a fear that members of the group who may be perceived to be weaker academically could contribute towards a lowering of the overall mark for the assignment.

Group work is an activity that has the potential to enhance awareness of diversity issues, particularly through the use of groups where the students represent a range of identities. The use of group work with groups comprising a range of student identities will often be initiated by the teacher, as if students are left to choose their own groupings they tend to restrict themselves to mono-identity groups. (We offer some practical suggestions in Chapter 3 for dealing with the formation of groups; see also Chapter 9 for a discussion on this issue in relation to assessed group work.) The success of multi-identity groups can be improved by:

1   ensuring that there is a reason for using group work; how will the use of group work enhance the output?

2   assigning an appropriate task, or choice of tasks, for the group to complete; the task needs to be something that it is not possible for an individual to complete, and may explicitly involve the identification of different points of view.

3   encouragement for the group to develop ground rules; for example, in relation to meeting deadlines, attending meetings, making decisions and assigning roles. In terms of assigning roles, it may be necessary for individual students to be assigned to particular roles in the early stages of group work, and for

particular tasks to be associated with these roles. This ensures that everyone is clear about what they should be doing at the start of the group work activity, and may assist in the early development of the group development.

4   assessing group work in a way that provides a clear indication of how the marks will be allocated to the group; for example, a group may be awarded a grade that is multiplied by the number of group members to produce an overall group mark; it is then up to the group to negotiate marks to reflect their contributions, but on the basis that the overall negotiated mark cannot exceed the group's pooled mark. (As a worked example, if a group with four members was awarded a mark of 62 per cent overall, then the total group mark would be 248, which could result in the following individual marks: 65 per cent; 55 per cent; 70 per cent; 58 per cent.)

5   a structure that allows for students to demonstrate their progress, perhaps through the use of weekly summaries of activity posted to an online discussion forum or blog.

As noted above, multi-identity groups can assist in raising awareness of diversity issues; however, if this is not handled carefully then it could lead to the enforcing of stereotypical views (De Vita, 2005). It is therefore important to ensure that, during the completion of the activity, the group has a chance to reflect upon the *process* as well as the *product* of the group work, and this might involve a personal reflection on the views and opinions expressed by other group members. If appropriate, this reflection could form part of the overall assessment of the task as a whole.

POSTGRADUATE STUDENTS AND SKILLS TRAINING

This section will focus on skills training provision in the UK, as it is likely to be very different worldwide. However, the general debates, principles and processes will be of comparative interest to academics from other nations. For postgraduate skills training there are potentially two very different groups of students. Masters-level students' skills training generally remains extremely varied and is often up to the particular institutional programme providers. Sometimes there will be requirements related to professional or funding bodies, but often there are not.

165

The extent to which the approach is an inclusive one will therefore depend entirely upon whatever the normal institutional or departmental approach is. Many of the issues that have been outlined above for undergraduates will be identical but will perhaps relate to higher-level skills (e.g. written communication). This means there are also some specific issues for such postgraduates. Perhaps the most practical problem is how we keep alive the interest of students who are now being offered transferable-skills courses from early school years, through first degree to postgraduate experience. Experiencing the same team-building exercises they did at school, for example, can be disaffecting for them! Enhancing written communication skills at this level can be more complex as errors may be more sophisticated and harder to correct. Students on a Masters course may find it harder to admit to deficiencies in basic skills. Group sessions can be more challenging to run since the language (and other skills) needs are likely to be very diverse at this level. It can be helpful to liaise with skills advisers to develop more sophisticated ways forward for Masters students as this has often been a neglected area.

Discipline-specific research skills are, of course, part of the Masters programme itself, and for a number the degree will be preparation for further research. The research skills will almost always be provided by the disciplinary experts, whereas the more general skills may well be provided by skills units or careers departments as with undergraduates. Some Masters programmes in the UK are specifically run as pre-PhD programmes (1+3 years), and these students will need to satisfy certain requirements in order that they be exempt from later skills training. The Economic and Social Research Council (ESRC) is one example of a funding council requiring training at this level. For example, the ESRC 1+3 award is as follows:

> This is an ESRC-funded studentship providing a training programme for full- and part-time students who have not previously completed substantive research training. Students are funded for a one-year research-training Masters (two years part-time), and then for three years (five years part-time) for a PhD, subject to satisfactory progress. The aim is to provide continuity of support, allowing progress and training to be planned with more certainty and to free up more time within the PhD for work on the thesis research and for submission of the thesis with a maximum of four years (full-time) or seven years (part-time) from the beginning of the PhD.

166

Thus the ESRC has a very clear guideline for skills training for such students.

Other funding councils have similar requirements. The ESRC requires 'broad-based' training. Research skills include: bibliographic and computing skills; teaching skills; language skills; ethical and legal issues; exploitation of research and intellectual property rights. Personal and employment-related skills include: communication skills (writing, dissemination and media skills); research management and team working skills and personal and career development skills. All councils will have information similar to that issued by the ESRC (e.g. www.esrcsociety today.ac.uk/ESRCInfoCentre/Images/Section_D_General_Research_Ski lls_and_Transferable_Skills_tcm6–9070.pdf).

In many cases such relatively recently introduced PhD requirements relating to skills training are having a 'knock-on' effect on other Masters students. Indeed there have been some troublesome equity issues about the potential difference in access to training for funded and non-funded students. Institutions have found themselves having to try to fund more access for all their students.

Where you are working with a professional body you will also need to map your own programme against their skills requirement – the British Psychological Society (BPS) for example, will have specific requirements. Indeed the BPS also maps its requirements to the National Qualifications Framework, which at Masters level requires degree holders to:

1 deal with complex issues both systematically and creatively, make sound judgments in the absence of complete data, and communicate their conclusions clearly to specialist and non-specialist audiences;

2 demonstrate self-direction and originality in tackling and solving problems, and act autonomously in planning and implementing tasks at a professional or equivalent level;

3 continue to advance their knowledge and understanding, and to develop new skills to a high level; and

4 have the qualities and transferable skills necessary for employment requiring:

■ the exercise of initiative and personal responsibility;

■ decision-making in complex and unpredictable situations; and

■ the independent learning ability required for continuing professional development.

167

The QAA Code of Practice for research supervision is also clear and is inclusive in intent:

> The precepts and explanations below are intended to cover the many different types of students undertaking research programmes in the UK, including full and part-time, students of all ages and with different needs, UK and international, and from all backgrounds. Not all precepts will be equally applicable to all students and wherever possible, the explanations recognise this.

Variation in funding streams, amongst many other factors, will continue to make this complex to apply however.

The recent changes in student funding are likely to continue to affect recruitment as students graduate with larger loans and as new bursaries change these patterns. Institutional bursaries to support postgraduates often apply to certain groups of students only, and this will continue to impact upon numbers of international, mature or disabled students on our programmes. Skills training for these and all students will need thinking through by both course teams and personal supervisors. The balance of time spent on disciplinary content and skills training can be a contentious issue. Many institutions have found that relating the skills training to the degree content has been a more credible way of introducing the generic skills – for example, helping students to manage the degree completion itself as a project – rather than sessions divorced from the actual course. On the whole, however, generic training is often provided by the central function of the institution. Many UK institutions have distributed the substantial funding for PhD skills training (often know as 'Roberts' money' after the Report author) in a way that combines central generic training and departmental specific training. Masters students may be able to access some of the centrally available courses but this access varies.

Research postgraduates studying for a PhD in the UK are in a completely different situation to undergraduates (expect perhaps those for whom there are professional-body requirements for skills training) since, as we have said above, there are now specific requirements relating to the provision of skills training for all research council-funded students. Since 2002 the results of the influential Roberts Report to the UK Treasury has meant that the research funding councils have created specific requirements regarding skills training. Constant criticism of the PhD purpose over the last twenty years or so led to initiatives that sought to make PhD graduates more employable. Over 50 per cent of PhD graduates do not go into

168

PAUSE FOR THOUGHT

- How is the skills training (research and transferable) run for your Masters students?
- How effective is the approach – do you link your course content to more generic skills in any way?
- Are there any specific issues around skills training for ensuring an inclusive approach? For example, if your students go on team building events are they designed to include students with physical disabilities?
- If you had a student with Asperger's syndrome how would you see the ESRC requirements about team-working skills applying?

academe, and so there was special concern to ensure that these students were equipped with skills for their employment. Thus since August 2003 all research council-funded PhD students have been expected to acquire a particular set of skills as part of the conditions for their funding. All institutions have had to develop a code of practice for ensuring this happens. As part of this, substantial programmes of skills training have been set up. You will need to check your institution's version.

There is little specific mention of issues relating to inclusiveness and diversity on these sites. However, the University of Warwick's provision includes a particular welcome to international students in its induction – as do many similar programmes. The programmes above and a majority of institutions with PhD students offer courses on:

1 academic writing;
2 time management;
3 working with your supervisor;
4 writing literature reviews;
5 upgrading from MPhil to PhD;
6 preparing for your viva;
7 personal development.

Some (e.g. the University of Warwick) even offer individual coaching on these topics, which, given the diverse needs at this level, can be very welcome.

169

The skills training requirement was originally met with some scepticism nationally by some students and supervising staff. However, others have embraced the idea and, as mentioned above, many positive training initiatives have been set up in the UK.

Wariness arose from concerns over conflicting priorities for students and the fear that they would not complete the thesis on time. Other academics felt that the role of the PhD was about research in a discipline and not about more generic skills acquisition. This was countered by champions such as UK Grad who argued that teaching students skills such as better time and project management should actually help address the poor completion rates. Once programmes were up and running, wariness was perhaps more about how good-quality and worthwhile programmes might be provided. The Roberts Report (Roberts, 2002) has thus led to a huge change in skills provision for PhD students, and staff new to supervising will need to be familiar with the relevant funding council requirements and with the local expectations and provision.

The QAA Code of Practice on research supervision makes it very clear that skills training is now on the postgraduate agenda, whatever staff may think:

> The importance of acquiring research and other skills during research degree programmes is recognised by students, academic staff, sponsoring organisations, employers and former students. These skills improve the student's ability to complete the research programme successfully. Development and application of such skills is also under-stood to be significant in the research graduate's capability for sustaining learning throughout his or her career, whether in an academic role, or in other employment. Research students are encouraged to recognise the value of transferable skills in enabling them to take ownership and responsibility for their own learning, during and after their programme of study.

And that the provision should suit a diverse student population:

> In providing research students with opportunities for developing personal and research skills, institutions will wish to pay particular attention to the differing needs of individual postgraduates, arising from their diversity. It is expected that a range of mechanisms will be used to support learning and that they will be sufficiently flexible to address those individual needs. For example, the development needs of research

students already employed to undertake research may be different from those of other students. The emphasis in formal training should be on quality, relevance and timeliness.

(QAA, 2004)

 PAUSE FOR THOUGHT

Do you know what central (as well as departmental/faculty) training provision is available for PhD students in your department?

The London School of Economics has a useful discussion of these debates on its website, *Teaching Matters: PhD*: lse.ac.uk/collections/ TLC/pdf/TM20_Mar06.pdf.

The UK Grad organisation has been at the centre of much of this development and in particular it offers 3–5-day residential training courses. Second- and third-year students funded by the main research councils are entitled to free places. These are designed to help postgraduates assess and develop their personal effectiveness, networking and team working, communication and career management skills. In the UK, the local hubs also offer events to students (e.g. www.grad.ac.uk/cms/ShowPage/ Home_page/p!eecddL). At the time of going to press this organisation is about to change name; however, it will continue to work in this field (alongside its partner CRAC, the career development organisation). The UK Grad website articulates very clearly the sorts of skills area that are being worked on in relation to postgraduates:

1 interpersonal skills development;
2 induction, review and reflective processes;
3 generic research skills development;
4 wider preparation for academic practice;
5 enterprise and innovation-related practices;
6 internships, placements and consultancy projects;
7 knowledge transfer and outreach activities;
8 career management/developing employability;
9 evaluation, feedback mechanisms and research relating to skills and career development;
10 strategic and management approach to practice.

The Lisbon strategy and the Bologna process are also set to introduce Europe-wide initiatives to address employability. (See the UK Grad site for summaries.)

Many institutions have very full programmes of workshops for their PhD students but most of this work, however, has not engaged in overt discussions about inclusion and diversity. If you are a supervisor and are thinking through this issue you are most likely to have to return to the websites and reading we have flagged up as useful for other supervisory issues. Perhaps the *Premia* website is one of the most helpful. This is aimed at disabled students and even this tends to focus on delivering small-group training when it addresses skills issues (www.premia.ac.uk/).

Some of the material aimed more at undergraduates may be useful material for postgraduates, for example, relating to employment skills (e.g. www.disabilitytoolkits.ac.uk/students/).

Many institution's sites for postgraduates offer specialist guidance for international students, mature students and so on, although they are not especially related to skills training and your students may need to follow up a range of links to arrive at relevant material (see, for example, www.bournemouth/ac.uk/careers/careers_advice/resources_postgrad.html).

In terms of inclusive approaches, we are likely to need to be sensitive to the requirements of particular groups/individuals. For mature students the skills agenda may mean very little – many have come to PhD study with very accomplished personal, transferable and employment skills. Further-more, they may see themselves as having little chance of an academic career even if they are still young enough to need/want employment. Deter-mining what skills enhancement is appropriate and/or desirable for such students may need some sophisticated and nuanced thinking rather than simply expecting them to attend existing courses on project or time man-agement. For example, one of the authors once found themselves leading a session on project management with a mature PhD student present who had managed many projects in his career, including the development of a local multimillion-pound shopping centre. He had been 'sent' on the course with the assumption that all the PhD students needed to enhance these skills. His experiences were very useful to the group, but such students need also to feel they are benefitting if training is mandatory.

Both Masters and PhD programmes are likely to include a considerable number of international students. For many of these the issues around integration can be considerable – particularly, for example, in a one-year Masters programme. They are also likely to be grappling with the shift in the understanding of the discipline from country to country. Some of the more generic skills training is actually likely to be very beneficial to such students – especially in terms of enhancing cross-cultural competencies. There are particular areas of skills training which will vary from culture to culture – one example from the QAA Code of Practice for research supervision is 'guidance on the ethical pursuit of research and the avoidance of research misconduct, including breaches of intellectual property rights'.

 PAUSE FOR THOUGHT

Think of one research-related skill that your students should possess (e.g. for a historian the effective use of archival documents). Think back to the three stages of procedural learning. How might you introduce your student to the:

1 **Cognitive phase?** Here the rules or patterns would need to be explained so as to describe the skill. Would it make a difference (in your particular example) if the student were an international student? If yes, how would you help?

2 **Associative stage?** Students should begin to recognise and associate patterns of what they should do with actually being able to do it. If you had a student with a hearing impairment would this make a difference at this stage and, if so, how?

3 **Autonomous stage?** This is the point where students can automatically do the tasks. If you have a student with mental health difficulty would that affect this stage in your particular example? If yes, what plans would you make?

The latter exercise is, of course, artificial but is aimed to make us think through issues we might not normally consider. We are meant to make anticipatory provision in our teaching so we need, at the very least, to remind ourselves not to potentially exclude any individual students.

The exercise might be more complex in the area of general and so-called transferable skills as concepts such as time management and leadership might contain subtle cultural differences, and practical exercises (e.g. physical exercises often used in team building) can prove more difficult/differentiating for some disabled students or for the different genders.

The concept of time also varies from culture to culture (see, for example, college.hmco.com/collegesurvival/ellis/master_student/10e/students/rcd/rcd_ch02.html or www.orvillejenkins.com/whatisculture/timecul.html). How does this affect the standard Western presentation of time or project management sessions? Concepts such as risk management have been said to be culturally specific (e.g. www.sciencedirect.com/science?_ob=ArticleURL&_udi=B6V9V-4PNMH2B-2&_user=10&_rdoc=1&_fmt=&_orig=search&_sort=d&view=c&_acct=C000050221&_version=1&_urlVersion=8&_userid=10&md5=7f69af27537ebacf643d4a19feb03717). Likewise, gendered or cultural notions of hierarchy will affect understanding of skills sessions relating to team building or leadership (Harris *et al.*, 2004; Lau Chin *et al.*, 2007).

In the UK, we have barely begun to consider such implications for student skills training in a globalised higher education, although one of the first areas being addressed in the name of more inclusive skills training may be that of enhancing cross-cultural competencies (e.g. www.york.ac.uk/services/careers/ya_courses.cfm?page=30).

It may be that those of us attempting to introduce skills elements into our curriculum will need to return to first principles in some cases to think how students from other cultures, of different ages, physical abilities and so on, will view the concepts and skills we are introducing.

 ## FURTHER READING

De Vita, G. (2001) 'The use of group work in large and diverse business management classes – some critical issues'. *International Journal of Management Education*, 1 (3): 27–35.

De Vita, G. (2005) 'Fostering intercultural learning through multicultural group work', in Carroll, J. and Ryan, J. (eds) *Teaching International Students: Improving learning for all*, London: Routledge, pp. 75–83.

Joint Funding Councils (2003) *Improving standards in postgraduate research degree programmes,* Bristol: Joint Funding Councils.

Quality Assurance Agency (QAA) Code of Practice, www.qaa.ac.uk/academic infrastructure/codeOfPractice/section1/default.asp.

 ## USEFUL WEB RESOURCES

www.skill.org.uk/
Skill: National Bureau for Students with Disabilities has skills-related material on its website – some of it for students in higher education.

www.premia.ac.uk/
  Premia 'making research education accessible'.

www.grad.ac.uk/cms/ShowPage/Home_page/p!eecddL
  UK Grad is a site with information for postgraduates, researchers,
  universities and employers 'dedicated to realising postgraduate talent'.

Chapter 9

Assessment Time

How Do We Attempt to Ensure Fairness for All?

In this chapter we will consider some of the particular issues relating to inclusive practice in assessment and feedback. The topic is vast, and the first thing to say is that there are many texts that focus on assessment and feedback that could be helpful. Some are listed at the end of the chapter, others are given as web links. Two previous volumes in this series relate to the assessment of written work and of skills and they could be a starting point for reading on this topic as they outline the principles of good practice in assessment and feedback (Haines, 2004; Pickford and Brown, 2006).

Key questions for early career staff are often:

1   How do I design assessment – to be fair and efficient?
2   How do I mark fairly and efficiently?
3   How do I support students in handling their assessment – fairly and effectively?
4   How do I give feedback effectively?
5   How do I find time to do it?

The words 'fair' and 'effective' are critical in relation to all students but especially so in a chapter on inclusive assessment. The key aim of this chapter is to think through approaches to assessment that do not penalise students for aspects of life and/or study that are *beyond their control*. We will also consider how and where there are sufficient grounds for making reasonable adjustments to redress inequities. But, beyond that, we wish to plead that all of us, wherever possible, approach assessment as a positive, inclusive part of learning for all students. It should never be merely a system where we tag on assessment as an afterthought. Nor should it be the case that, where a student has no control over their circumstances, we offer special adjustments for them based on a deficit model that implies any change needed is 'their fault'.

Changing existing assessment methods can be an extremely contentious area. First, many are wary of reducing standards by introducing more flexible assessment forms. Second, there is a danger that, by introducing new forms of assessment that make it fair for one individual, or group of students, we may introduce new inequities. Third, there are sometimes areas (for example, where assessment relates to 'fitness to practice' on vocational courses) where assessment cannot be tailored to students' requirements but must be matched with existing occupational standards and requirements.

WHAT ARE THE MAIN ISSUES FOR STUDENTS REGARDING ASSESSMENT?

Since 2005, a new form of higher education evaluation has been used in the UK, called the *National Student Survey* (NSS). In this, students are asked their views on the courses they studied. The results have suggested that a high proportion of students are generally satisfied with their experiences (so far as any such evaluation can ascertain – and, indeed, there were problems for many academics with the type and process of the questioning). However, according to this survey, the weakest link in the chain is in the realm of 'assessment and feedback.' There are many possible reasons for this but one is clearly that, for most students, assessment is likely to be the most daunting aspect of their academic experience at university. Problems with managing work loads, poor lectures, having to give seminar papers and so on can all cause anxiety, but the issues relating to assessment often relate to their fears for the ultimate performance and final results and, of course, it is the final assessment that may cause issues for future careers if poorer than hoped.

If that latter point seems obvious then we must ask ourselves why it has often been the case that on some courses the creation of the form and content of assessment has been treated as an 'add-on'. Of course some may maintain that is because we have wanted to discourage strategic learning – for example, students who only work for good exam results with little intrinsic interest in the knowledge or the learning. We want, we claim in higher education, to encourage genuine learning for learning's sake. In that case we must seek to integrate and consider our purposes for assessment from the very start of our course design. Assessment should be part of the repertoire of our teaching tools. We must be clear from the outset what we want our students to learn and what we will therefore 'test' (in the widest sense of the word) as part of the assessment processes. We must also think strategically about our use of feedback to the students as an integral part of the whole learning experience. Constructive alignment is a term often used for the aligning of teaching, learning and assessment, and the practical way of ensuring this is to check that both teaching and assessment relate clearly to the learning outcomes. (At www.johnbiggs.com.au/constructive.html, John Biggs, the originator of this term explains it in more detail.)

 PAUSE FOR THOUGHT

You are teaching a seminar series but other staff will set the end-of-course examinations – how do you ensure there will be no mismatch?

Check with those who are likely to set the papers and/or the member of staff in charge of your course that what you intend to do is what they intend to examine – the programme approval system in most higher education institutions should have ensured alignment, but it could be the case that individuals setting questions are not familiar with your programme learning outcomes. Make sure they have a copy and that you check that what you are teaching and what they are testing is aligned.

This chapter will focus on some of the key questions that concern staff in their earlier years of assessing in relation to inclusion and diversity. Thus, for reasons of space, it will not consider issues such as being an examinations officer or being an external examiner.

As we discussed in Chapter 3, our premise will be that, wherever possible, assessment should be fully 'inclusive' and not simply offer the compensatory 'contingent' or 'alternative' provisions for non-traditional students. However, we continue to recognise that this is not always possible. Indeed there is a genuine dilemma, and there are many pragmatic decisions to be made about this and about how much time we put into anticipatory provision for situations that might never occur. Furthermore, advice from experts on dyslexia, for example, makes it clear how individualised and particular the needs can be for students who have dyslexia. We must do our best to aim for inclusive provision as a best practice principle, but we will still have to check that provision for a particular individual is appropriate. At that later point we may still need to make alternative or contingency arrangements. This chapter will suggest very general principles for inclusive design, but specialist advice on individual situations will often be needed too.

A reminder of the definitions used above repeated from the HEFCE-funded SPACE project:

1 Contingent approach: special arrangements such as extra time, amanuensis [scribe], own room and so on, which is essentially a form of assimilation into an existing system.
2 Alternative approach: for example, a viva voce instead of a written assignment – offering a repertoire of assessments embedded into course design as present and future possibilities for a minority of disabled students.
3 Inclusive approach: for example, a flexible range of assessment modes made available to all – capable of assessing the same learning outcomes in different ways.

(Waterfield and West, 2006)

 PAUSE FOR THOUGHT

In the SPACE project the authors offer a case study (www.plymouth.ac.uk/pages/view.asp?page=10494) to demonstrate an inclusive approach in which it was felt that the same outcomes could be fairly assessed by offering students a choice of either: an end-of-module test; coursework; or a portfolio.

The result was clearly more student satisfaction. It must be said, however, that the increased resources demanded by this, such as additional staff to aid choice and support progress and marking time, would have to be demonstrated as offsetting time made for creating other special arrangements before departments and central examination officers would be convinced. Furthermore, the quality assurance office would have to be convinced of the equity and fairness and of the maintaining of academic standards before they would approve such flexible systems. We need to aim for inclusive design, but part of that will include considering pragmatic issues such as those mentioned and part of that is likely to be convincing other colleagues of its worth and practicality. What do you think?

The SPACE project reminds us of how untenable the thousands of special provision arrangements are becoming in the UK. This is a different issue from the question of the educational value or otherwise of compensatory assessment forms of assessment. It may be that, at the moment, you have no control over the institution's approach to this. But at this point we should at least think in principle of how and where we can create and embed more inclusive measures as we go about our business – be that creating marking schemes, examination types or new programme/module designs.

 PAUSE FOR THOUGHT

- Think about the courses you are about to teach. How will they be assessed? Does this form of assessment cater for all students with equity?
- If the answer is no, then can you think how the same outcomes could be assessed in different ways?
- To what extent do you have any opportunity to amend assessment practices? (This varies enormously for new staff, and postgraduates probably have very little say in this.)
- If you did wish to introduce new assessments, with whom would you discuss this and from whom would you need to seek approval?

The DRC, in partnership with HEFCE and other bodies, offers a guide that can help clarify how we approach this (www.dotheduty.org/files/HEIoverview.rtf).

They remind us that our questions for judging the equity in assessment are:

- Am I treating any students 'less favourably'?
- Am I making 'reasonable adjustments'?

In the UK, and indeed in other countries, in respect of students who are disabled, it is our statutory obligation to ensure equity. The DDA is clear that, if necessary, we may need to change institutional procedures, adapt the curriculum (including assessment) and/or modify teaching, provide additional services, train staff and/or alter the physical environment. In other words, pragmatic problems will not be seen as an excuse for a failure to 'reasonably' amend provision. Equally, the Race Relations Act in the UK means we cannot discriminate on grounds of race or ethnicity. Legislation protecting students against discrimination on grounds of gender, sexuality and age is less obvious and specific in relation to assessment and feedback. The two questions above are surely useful to ask in relation to all of our students.

The DRC guidelines suggest that we must maintain academic rigour in assessment and that all should be tested against the same academic benchmark. But, they suggest, it is the mode of assessment that we need to be flexible about.

WHAT IS ASSESSMENT?

Assessment drives learning, and feedback is an integral part of the process. The UK QAA Code of Practice describes assessment as 'any process that appraises an individual's knowledge, understanding, abilities or skills' (QAA, 2006). As they say, different forms of assessment will assess different types of things, and we need to ensure that we have the appropriate form of assessment for whatever it is we wish to assess. Reviewing this often helps us to see whether or not we are actually assessing what we think we are assessing and whether or not the form we are using is essential.

Traditionally assessment has been seen as either *formative* or *summative*. Summative assessment normally comes at the end of a module or programme, and the mark is used as a public measure of perceived ability or performance at that stage – for example, final degree classification. Formative assessment is staged throughout a programme and is used to help staff and students gauge their progress in learning and to determine how to develop towards the final goal. Formative assessment implicitly assumes that feedback to students is a part of the assessment process and that this is a key part of the overall learning experience. Often these two features of assessment have been perceived and handled as two separate issues.

However, there are forms of assessment that are a combination of both formative and summative, and it may be that these are not always as distinct as often suggested. For example, course work may well be continuous assessment and thus contribute to the final degree mark, but also be a part of the formative feedback process. In fact, all the above aspects of assessment are inextricably interwoven and should be part of the overall design of the learning process. In terms of offering an inclusive approach to

181

students, therefore, we must be consistent and ensure equity is embedded throughout. If it is not, then discrimination at any one point may affect the whole picture and the final outcome for the student.

GOOD DESIGN

How do we choose which assessment tool to use, assuming we have a choice? As we have said, the critical starting point in assessment is to think about it from the moment of inception in programme planning. We have already referred to the constructive alignment of the learning programme. How will the content, the desired learning outcomes and the teaching, learning and assessment processes be aligned? At times past courses have not always ensured this – we have all heard anecdotal stories of exam questions that ask about topics not included in the teaching course. It is also easy to muddy the waters by accident in our teaching; for example, it is exciting, in a seminar series, to follow particular interests as they arise. At one level this is surely one of the stimulating purposes of education! However, allowed to creep too far, this approach may not result in a fair final outcome for some students if it is not the material they thought they had signed on to the course for, or if the final examination is set according to the original proposal. We need to ensure that there are not large mismatches in expectations and in coverage as this can result in inequity. For some students – international students with less good English, or students with dyslexia needing more clarity of structure – it may be far more difficult to compensate and make up work if, for example, required reading suddenly and unexpectedly changes direction. Life would be dull without some spontaneity; however, we must always seek to assess precisely what it is we want to assess (not some incidental feature) and what we have stated we will assess. At degree level and with well-written outcomes, there will almost always be opportunity for pursuing exciting and unexpected avenues within the boundaries stated in the programme outline and in the outcomes seen by the students.

WHAT ARE WE ASSESSING?

An Oxford Brookes Briefing Paper has grouped categories of assessment into the following and given examples of types of assessment for each area. You may think of more. Fuller amplification of this is available at www. brookes.ac.uk/services/ocsd/2_learntch/pandp.html:

1   thinking critically and making judgments;
2   solving problems and developing plans;
3   performing procedures and demonstrating techniques;
4   managing and developing oneself;
5   accessing and managing information;
6   demonstrating knowledge and understanding;
7   designing, creating performing, communicating.

We must ensure that the test that has been chosen measures the required features and not some incidental factors. This is termed *validity* in the discourse of assessment. Thus, if we have said we wish to assess knowledge of a topic, we should not be giving debit or credit for incidental skills. This can often be where the inequities lie for students with a disability, for example. Equivalence is also, therefore, something to be sought: is any one student likely to be placed in a disadvantaged position for *reasons beyond their control*? For example, if a student has a considerably poorer grasp of the English language, will this be part of the assessment judgment made? If it will be, then this should be clear at the outset of the course and in the selection for it. In an English degree, for example, an excellent grasp of English will be critical and assumed, but in a Physics report we will need to make clear the extent to which command of the language will matter and will or will not be assessed. All of this is often far from easy in practice, as ascertaining levels of English ability before students arrive can be notoriously difficult. Standard test results (International English Language Testing System (IELTS), www.ielts.org/), for example, do not always match the reality. But once students have been accepted and have achieved the stated entry requirements, they cannot be merely penalised and/or left to their own devices. It is up to the university either to amend entry requirements or to provide appropriate support. Our job is likely to be to try to obtain language support for such students. The discussion of language skill is only used here as an example of the kinds of area where what we say we assess and what we actually assess can be slightly at odds.

Deciding what we assess should relate, not only to the expectations we have of the students' abilities at a particular point in the course, but also to our notions of what constitutes 'graduateness' in our departments, disciplines and institutions and nationally. We cannot today make arbitrary decisions about what content or skills we wish to asses in our modules without reference to the wider picture. QAA subject benchmarks may be of relevance (see www.qaa.ac.uk/academicinfrastructure/benchmark/honours/default.asp).

Many contentious hours have been spent trying to articulate 'graduate-ness' in the different disciplines – subject benchmarks are useful starting points for thinking through the content and the process for which we think our students should be assessed. They then need contextualising within our own departmental and institutional ideas.

A CHECKLIST FOR FAIR AND CONSISTENT ASSESSMENT FOR ALL

Am I clear about the following?

1   *What* I want to assess.
2   *How* I will actually assess this (mode/validity).
3   *Why* I wish to assess the particular content.
4   *Why* I wish to assess it in this particular way.
5   That this will be a reliable measure (i.e. could I replicate the tests to give similar results).
6   That *what and how* I want to assess are clearly articulated in the criteria and instructions.
7   That all the above relates clearly to the learning outcomes and that what I have claimed students will be able to learn has been possible.
8   That my learning outcomes use verbs that express the varying levels of sophistication of what I wish the students to learn.
9   That the outcomes are addressing different learning domains appropriately.
10 That the types of assessment available are as inclusive as possible – do I need/is it possible to offer more flexibility.
11 That my own particular assessment is in line with the overall aims of the whole programme.
12 – And also with the graduate or postgraduate notion of what students will have when they graduate.
13 That what I say is in line with local statements on this, such as the degree programme handbooks, to ensure that we are in line with what our students think they should study.
14 Whether the assessment is intended to assess skills as well as content – disciplinary, vocational or other general and transfer-able skills.
15 That my procedures are rigorous and equitable.

16 That my timetable for assessment is practical and achievable.

17 That all of the above is non-discriminatory (for example, have I checked for clashes with religious festivals? How does the timing affect carers of children? And so on . . .).

18 That my teaching methods will encourage the students to prepare appropriately for the above and for the learning not merely the assessment.

19 Where using increasingly difficult assignments/assessments might help increase confidence.

20 That the frequency of assessment is appropriate.

21 That feedback turn-round times are such that students can learn in time for the next assessment.

22 About my rationale for varying feedback and assessment intervals.

23 That the assessment methods are varied for different approaches and preferences – as far as is fair and practical.

Particular considerations for inclusive assessment might mean checking:

1 that all assessment is understood by all students;

2 that language skill does not influence the assessment of other skills unless that is a key and stated intent;

3 that any inequities as a result of gender, ethnicity, disability, have been redressed;

4 that potential discrimination is ruled out by rigorous marking procedures; for example, anonymous where possible;

5 that timetabling does not introduce discrimination;

6 that material examined is not unnecessarily/unwittingly Eurocentric.

Items 1–6 above do not necessarily ensure an inclusive approach to assessment but should help limit discrimination. A study of assessment in Australian universities from the Centre for the Study of Higher Education in Melbourne, Australia, concludes that students value 'unambiguous expectations', 'authentic tasks' and 'choice and flexibility' in assessment (McKinnis and Devlin, 2002: 10). Is this what we offer? It is only after having thought through the above general actions in relation to inclusive action that we should begin to think about catering for specific situations.

Our appeal for 'inclusive' assessment does not only relate to disabled students, international students, first-generation students or students

185

from a poor socio-economic background, but to all students, including, for example, those who have short-term illnesses. There is considerable literature to guide us where students have disabilities or are international students, but rather less has been written about short-term illness, an issue that can face staff frequently. Our institutions are almost certain to have guidelines for such situations, but these are not standard nationally (de Lambert and Williams, 2006).

HOW DO I MAKE FAIR DECISIONS?

In issues of inclusion and diversity we have to repeat again at this stage that there is often no clear right or wrong answer. How, therefore, do we make decisions regarding all this? The first port of call should be our university regulations. The UK law requires that we act in particular ways regarding disability and race. This is non-negotiable. Our institutions will also have a range of other mandatory requirements with regard to assessment. If we do not follow these regulatory arrangements we can find ourselves with complex problems if, for example, a student appeals a result. Our institutions all have different terms for the various offices, but you should be aware of, and consult as necessary:

1   the course leader/examination officer in charge of assessment;
2   any relevant staff handbooks on assessment and feedback (departmental/school/faculty/institution);
3   any subject-specific or professional body regulations or guidance;
4   any student handbooks/course outlines and so on;
5   examination office regulations;
6   any particular guidance from offices such as international office, disability office, etc.

However, the vast majority of our decisions do not fall into such clear cut areas. For areas where more discretion is allowed, discussion with other colleagues, with mentors and with others who are more senior or experienced can be a sensible option. We should not forget that, as well as having experts employed to handle student issues of inclusivity and diversity, many institutions are repositories of considerable academic knowledge and expertise built on research interests. For instance, you may have experts on women's issues, aspects of disability, globalisation, race and ethnicity and so on, in your academic departments. If you are interested in a topic then look for relevant articles by your colleagues – it may be cutting-edge research that offers guidance on fundamental principles.

If our queries relate to day-to-day procedure, then often the administrative staff can be best placed to answer them. They can often alert us to systems that have been evolved to ensure fairness and security in assessment – it is rare to need to invent everything from scratch! Course leaders, mentors, chairs of examinations boards, chairs of departments/schools or whoever the equivalent is in your institution should also be approached about more serious technical queries. Never attempt to make 'on the hoof' or ill-informed decisions about assessment matters that might lead to contention in appeals or legal challenges. We must always have our decisions verified/approved by the appropriate staff in matters of summative – and often formative – assessment.

Below, however, are some thoughts on making decisions where we do have some authority and discretion. These might well apply to all other decisions relating to inclusion and diversity and not only to assessment.

ENSURING EQUITY IN ASSESSMENT AND THE NOTION OF FAIRNESS

In assessment matters our students will want, almost above all other things, to perceive that the system is fair. Indeed, in the UK the QAA will also demand to see that university assessment is fair. Equity in practice will often, of course, be quite a different thing to having a system that is the same for everyone. How do we ensure fairness when not all students have the same opportunities? Notably, of course, life is not fair! But it is nonetheless up to us to make life as fair as we can for our students. We need to try to anticipate any potential inequities, not only because intrinsically that is for most of us the right thing to do but also because by law we must, at least in respect of disability, race and so on.

Why and when might assessment seem unfair?

■ Where conditions beyond the control of the student make 'normal' assessment conditions inequitable.
■ Where there is a sufficient degree of verifiable impairment to warrant different treatment.

SOCIAL JUSTICE – ENSURING FAIRNESS, EQUITY AND RIGOUR

Students want to receive fair treatment and to feel that their work has been fairly rewarded. The former we may be able to ensure more easily than the latter. Equity theory suggests that perceptions of fairness are derived, in part, from an individual comparing contribution to outcomes. If students consider grades do not match their effort they can become disaffected. A mismatch between expectation, ability and achievement is not uncommon, and we cannot be responsible for our students' 'raw/ natural' abilities, but we need to ensure that the system for assessment and the teaching and support that lead up to it are not inappropriately contributing to a mismatch. Where students possess what might be deemed to be a disadvantage they may appropriately feel aggrieved. *How* we then assure fairness is a matter of procedural justice. Is our system fair and transparent? People care about being within a fair system not simply because they wish to see clearly where and how to challenge decisions but also because such fairness communicates something to us about people's value and status – we all like to feel we matter to others. Recent studies have shown that students can be more concerned about *how* their work is processed than the actual nature/content/result of the original assessment (Lizzio *et al.*, 2007). Students want to feel there has been interpersonal justice – that is that they have been treated with respect. But they also want to feel they have received informational justice – that is that they have been given full and honest explanations or rationales for outcomes.

Psychological identification with the institution and/or staff has been shown to be a very important feature in student retention, and studies have demonstrated that, within that notion, the students' perception of fairness is critical. A study of 342 psychology students in Australia showed students wanted a 'respectful partnership' and 'systemic fairness'. Ultimately, it was argued that the most important feature was actually the respectful partnership, but in most circumstances a perception that there is a fair system is essential to the development of the respectful relationship (Lizzio *et al.*, 2007: 207).

In fact, many accepted and traditional forms of assessment have been demonstrated to possess inbuilt bias. For example, various articles have demonstrated gender bias in assessment or feedback (see, for example, Read *et al.*, 2005). A number of studies have illustrated the 'situatedness' of assessment practice and the possible challenges to the conception of 'reliability' of essay and other assessment (Shay, 2004). We should review

188

and trial new alternatives where we are in doubt as to the validity and reliability of our existing methods or seek to ensure that those methods are used as fairly as possible.

SPECIAL ARRANGEMENTS ARE NECESSARY

We all encounter situations where special arrangements need to be made in order to ensure fairness. Where there is to be any compromise in assessment it should always occur in *methods* not in rigour. One study of the use of 'special cases' suggests that, whichever of the main frameworks of moral philosophy we use, it is legitimate to make special arrange-ments from time to time. In other words, whether we are thinking of the 'common good' or of individual human rights, or of 'just', 'fair' or 'virtuous' approaches, there are grounds on which we can justify special treatment in particular circumstances. It must be admitted that these judgments are based upon Western philosophies but it appears to be hard to make a case for not doing so under most of the moral frameworks in which we might operate (de Lambert and Williams, 2006). In fact, research on 'rule making' has stressed how even the tightest of systems will still have been developed as a result of seemingly irrelevant charac-teristics of the people involved in developing the particular system and that a number of the underpinning rationales of that system are likely to be a result of interpersonal bias (Stangor, 2000). In other words, even our most tried and tested systems should be reviewed and scrutinised from time to time.

INSTITUTIONAL POLICY

Having decided we wish to try to ensure fair treatment in assessment for all our students we must decide what our legitimate options are when we need to make a decision:

1   What is the framework within which we must make the decisions?
2   What is in our power? What is not?
3   To whom must we go for help/permission?
4   Are we being fair to others who will be assessed?
5   When have we gone as far as we can in making alternative provisions?

We must:

1   check we that are aware of the institutional policies and requirements with regard to assessment;
2   double check the information our students have received in their student handbook so we are clear about their expectations and they are clear about ours;
3   check that we know what our institution expects in respect of 'reasonable provision' for disabled students relating to assessment;
4   check guidelines on international students;
5   check requirements such as the Race Relations Act; the Commission for Racial Equality (CRE) expects institutions to have a policy regarding assessment and race relations;
6   check we are not unfairly penalising students who are older, younger, carers, part-time or unused to university ways because of their cultural backgrounds; for example, first generation in higher education;
7   check that cultural diversity is both reflected and promoted – ask: would my assessment practices support this?

SENSITIVITY TO BACKGROUNDS

The typical experience of many international students will be different to UK students in assessment. For example, in Korea much assessment is multiple choice or rote learning and memorising (McGuire, 2007). Should we change our assessment practices to accommodate Korean students or should we offer support to the students as they adapt? In this example, the former option is probably not tenable, either because our institution would not approve or because we do not feel it is educationally appropriate. We must therefore offer support as they adjust to the required approach. We should articulate what is required in terms of mental and procedural ways forward. We should offer all students opportunity to ask questions. Offering examples of previously completed work may help. We could consider setting up peer/buddying or mentoring systems where students who are used to the system can explain what is required. This may sound dangerously like a deficit model for addressing this issue (Warwick, 2006), but in assessment this may be the most pragmatic option for new staff.

NEED TO ENSURE CLEAR ASSESSMENT CRITERIA AND MARKING SCHEMES

We cannot stress enough that our institutions all have numerous guidelines relating to assessment practices. We are obliged to adhere to those; if we do not it will be hard to obtain institutional support should something go wrong. Once we are sure we are about to act within guidelines and regulations, then we should seek to articulate to our students very clearly and precisely what we are expecting for their assessment. We need to make explicit the boundaries of knowledge and content that will be assessed. We need to ensure that they are very clear about the precise process of the assessment. They should know timescales for assessment, marking and feedback and to whom they should go for advice at any point. Disabled students should be advised to check with ourselves and with the appropriate university officer (e.g. dyslexia officer) if they are in doubt as to appropriateness. Students whose language competencies are in doubt should be advised to seek help from the language skills centre, international officer or whichever welfare staff are appropriate in our institution. Students' unions also have officers who can be extremely knowledgeable and helpful in these areas.

MARKING

Consistency is one of the key requirements for fair assessment. We are often one of a team marking for a course. If you are relatively new to the course and do not feel that the criteria alone make it clear as to level and standards, you should ask for a 'standardising' session with others or with those more experienced. In many sectors of education this would be routine, but in higher education it can be lacking – furthermore, despite the move to tighter assessment criteria, standards for degree classes vary from institution to institution. Your work may be double-marked or overseen by a co-ordinator or other markers, but ask before you submit final marks if you are unsure. Criterion referencing (marking against a predetermined set of criteria) is meant to give clearer guidelines for this, but in many subjects it is seldom adequately detailed for all queries regarding the marking. The Scottish Enhancement Themes initative on assessment found it to be uncommon for there to be any systematic oversight of feedback to ensure consistency (www.enhancementthemes. ac.uk/themes/Assessment/outcomes.asp). Do not feel it is your inadequacy if there is little support on this – feel free to ask! Often, and despite the theoretical shift from norm-referencing (how work compares with others in the group), there is an implicit or subliminal sense of norm-referencing within essay marking. In the marking of discursive texts there is often a notional idea of what top, bottom and middle scripts are/should be, and for the newcomer this is hard to determine. Once again, ask for guidance – there is no reason whatsoever why new staff should be inherently aware of this, but that often seems to be the assumption. Furthermore, if we are unsure of this, how much more must this be the case for our students and, for example, for international students or returners to education. Where staff have been familiar with standards for many years, it can take queries from newcomers for them to be reminded of the need for overt and explicit articulation of what is needed to meet a particular level.

Double-marking has often been used to ensure fairness, but increasing numbers of students also means this is becoming more burdensome and is being challenged as a norm. Often this is now done only as a sample. Anonymous marking is where the markers do not know the identity of the students, and this is standard practice in most institutions in the UK. It is often seen to be fairer in terms of limiting discrimination; however, it is not always possible. With portfolio work, for example, it is sometimes impossible to preserve anonymity, and in such cases it is probably better not to have the pretence of anonymity and to offer other safeguards (such as double-marking) instead.

A number of institutions use symbols to indicate where special regard should be paid to marking the work of disabled students. This means that the marker should then refer to the appropriate guidelines when marking. In certain cases, therefore, markers would specifically be asked only to mark for content and not 'mark down' for errors in literacy. Where this is the case, staff should indicate very clearly where correct spelling is essential (vocabulary on a foreign language course, drug names and so on). Other institutions do not feel that such all-embracing approaches are appropriate and expect different departments/schools to set their own approaches. Being aware of local rules is the first priority of a new member of staff in this.

MONITORING YOUR ASSESSMENT FOR INCLUSIVE PRACTICES

The Scottish Enhancement Themes advice on assessment mentioned above reminds us that it is critical for us to monitor our assessment practices.

In their review they found that many areas of assessment are surveyed regularly, but that a number of issues are frequently overlooked. In particular, they found that course experience questionnaires asked little about information regarding student backgrounds and prior knowledge of the subject concerned. We have noted in earlier chapters that this is a critical part of learning.

They also suggest that mid-semester/term questionnaires might especially help new students struggling to find their feet – intervention can come earlier than if we only use end-of-module questionnaires. Formative assessment and course evaluation can be used similarly. Conversely, of course, we need to remember that students can easily tire of filling in evaluation forms and we need to give thought to the ways in which we ensure a good response – this may be improved by offering electronic evaluation opportunities or it may be simpler to dedicate a short time in the classroom to ensuring returns.

MULTICULTURAL GROUPS

The QAA Code of Practice on assessment requires universities to 'encourage staff to be aware of cultural differences and the ways in which these may affect student perceptions of assessment and their ability to perform assessment tasks successfully'.

It is suggested (De Vita, 2001) that multicultural groups of students will take longer to achieve some final outcomes in assessment compared with monocultural ones, because identifying effective ways of communication takes longer to achieve. The author suggests that assessment of multicultural group work will be more effective if:

1 students know what will be assessed and how marks will be allocated;
2 difficult aspects such as cross-cultural communication or managing conflict effectively attract a percentage of marks to reflect effort involved;
3 marks are allocated for individual effort (criteria need to be clear);
4 novel or unusual methods of assessment (e.g. poster or oral exam) are rehearsed, with formative feedback on how to improve.

193

FORMAL ARRANGEMENTS FOR INCLUSIVE ASSESSMENT

Where students have disclosed a disability, your appropriate welfare office should have identified any specific needs and made appropriate arrangements for fair assessment. Most institutions will now have a special assessment committee in place to approve individual arrangements. Check with the student, personal tutor, course team leader or equivalent if you are unsure. Normally, students should complete all assessments as normal wherever possible (your inclusive arrangements should hopefully include flexible options to make the assessment as accessible as possible), but some will need particular arrangements.

Our priorities are to ensure security in assessment; however, we need to ensure that administrative arrangements are pedagogically sound, as sometimes convenience can seem to override good practice. (For example, an alternative room is provided in a location easy for invigilation but lacking in comparison with the better, high-quality physical environment of the main examinations rooms – a not uncommon location in times past, for example, has been behind the curtains on the poorly lit platform of a large examination hall.)

Ensure that everything you do in the way of special provision is protected by a paper trail so that there is a clear record of the provision that has been offered should results be appealed. There is a clear need to be accurate with all of the assessment-related paper trail and the marking records. Check too what your institutional arrangements are in relation to data protection and to the disclosure of records should it be requested.

INVIGILATING

Check regulations in your institution – some institutions require staff to attend training sessions on this. Ensure that you are comfortable about who to contact if you have students who need special arrangements. Think through all the issues above about equity and also about the possibility of stigmatising if you have to engage in discussion about alternative arrangements.

ASSESSMENT ADJUSTMENTS: ISSUES TO KEEP IN MIND

Individual arrangements often need to vary hugely even for the same condition (such as dyslexia), and students should always be consulted about what is appropriate.

Below are some possible adjustments and issues to consider for groups of students. It must be stressed that these lists are not comprehensive and also that each individual needs assessing. Many of the adjustments under the headings would be entirely inappropriate for some students with these impairments; they are given to suggest the range of possibilities. Most of these would need specific approval and expert facilitation from appropriate university support staff.

Adjustments to Consider

Blind and Vision-Impaired Students

1   Braille papers; tactile diagrams.
2   Personal computer – voice synthesiser.
3   Reader.
4   Oral examination.
5   Audio taped material.
6   Large print.
7   Additional time.

Deaf and Hearing-Impaired Students

1   It is common for many deaf students to have their English checked before they hand in essays. It is important for such students to know whether remaining errors in grammar and syntax are part of the marking scheme.
2   Practical exams (e.g. laboratory work) may need more preparatory work so that they are clear about instructions.
3   Hearing loop.
4   Dictionary or thesaurus.
5   Personal computer – spell check.

Students with Dyslexia

1 Allocated extra time (after a formal assessment of their dyslexia).
2 Scribe.
3 Oral examination.
4 Oral answers recorded.
5 Personal computer/spell check/dictionary.
6 Other technical aids (for example, Spell Master – see TechDis, www.techdis.ac.uk).
7 Multiple-choice papers/short answers.
8 Graphic presentation instead of sustained prose.
9 Demonstrations.
10 Portfolios.

Other Learning Difficulties

1 Numeracy – may need calculators.
2 See, for example, *Guidelines for marking work of students with SpLD* (Specific Learning Differences) at the University of Northampton (www.northampton.ac.uk/departments/studentservices/docs/spld-marking-guidelines.doc).

Physical Mobility

1 Scribe.
2 Oral account to examiner.
3 Recorded account.
4 Additional time.
5 Rest breaks.
6 Personal computer.
7 Specialist software (e.g. consult TechDis).
8 Personal assistant if unable to turn pages and so on.

Impaired Concentration Due to Pain or Fatigue

1 Additional time (this may compound problems such as fatigue).
2 Rest breaks.
3 Two sessions.
4 Separate venue.

Language and Speech Issues

(Does not relate only to international students or only to students with a speech impairment.)

1   Interpreter.
2   Personal computer/voice synthesiser.
3   Reader.
4   Additional time.
5   Graphic presentations.

Issues to Consider

The following are some of the symptoms that can affect assessment:

Mental Health Difficulties

1   Anxiety and panic attacks.
2   Low self-esteem and confidence.
3   Inability to concentrate or make decisions.
4   Memory problems.
5   Difficulty working with other people.
6   Severe mood swings.
7   Lack of participation.
8   Difficulties with motivation.
9   Changes in behaviour.
10 Inappropriate behaviour.
11 Effects of medication – can include: drowsiness; dry mouth; blurred vision; shakiness, etc.
12 Aggression.
13 Hallucination in more extreme cases.
14 Self-harm.

Oxford University and Sheffield University have two examples of websites with more information on supporting students with mental health difficulties:

■   www.admin.ox.ac.uk/shw/mhguide.shtml;
■   www.shef.ac.uk/disability/teaching/mental/3_he.html.

197

Gender Issues

Considerable work on gender and assessment has been carried out. Suggestions such as women being more suited to course work and men to closed examinations have been made. Recent work shows us that little of this is as yet certain (Woodfield *et al.*, 2005). A report undertaken by the Higher Education Academy and the Equality Challenge Unit (ECU), due in 2008, should shed further light on some of this.

Meanwhile there are practical areas where we could be sensitive. Carers of young children, for example, often but not always women, may well have complicated lifestyle arrangements. Care of sick children can prove complex on exam days, and course work can prove problematic over school holidays.

International Students

Consider:

1   familiarity with exam procedures/different cultures;
2   understanding of how plagiarism is defined and viewed in the UK;
3   different approaches to learning.

Jude Carroll of Oxford Brookes suggests that we need to explain the following assessment-related issues to international students:

1   Decode and discuss assignments and essay titles. How is 'evaluate' different from 'justify' or from 'analyse'?
2   Clarify the criteria that you will use when marking (but be aware that when you explain that the explanation may also contain assumptions).
3   Be explicit about the format you expect for students' submitted work and share examples they can see and read. Just being told to submit a report is a daunting task if your only clue is a dictionary definition.
4   Discuss how long the submission should be and explain why 'more is not necessarily better'.
5   When you mark, make it clear how much weight grammar and vocabulary will have compared with content and structure of the argument. Surveys of international students confirm they often misjudge the impact of language proficiency.

(See www.brookes.ac.uk/services/ocsd/2_learntch/briefing_papers/
international_students.pdf and www.shef.ac.uk/disability/teaching/
mental/3_he.html for advice.)

There are, of course, many factors that cause stress for our students
that are seen as part of normal student life: financial worries; having
to earn money; friendship problems; accommodation worries; drink
problems; drugs and so on. Our particular job is to ensure that our students
are not disadvantaged by events beyond their control and to determine
when these stress factors are beyond normal limits.

DIFFERENT TYPES OF ASSESSMENT

One of our jobs here is to flag up that there are many more types of
assessment than the commonly used essay or closed exam. Indeed most
of us are using a range of these already. (See Pickford and Brown (2006)
for a fuller explanation of different types of assessment.) The purpose of
this chapter is to ask if the modes we currently use are inclusive and to
enquire whether there are forms of assessment that will offer fairer access
to all students. If new approaches seem unviable for the sake of academic
rigour, or genuinely insurmountable practical difficulties, then we must
ensure we create alternative or contingency measures, but we must have
ruled out the possibilities of changing to a genuinely more inclusive
measure first.

Types of assessment commonly used in higher education include the
following (there will be many other factors needing attention, but the
purpose of the list below is to raise awareness and not to offer a
comprehensive guide):

- *Essay* – there is a lack of clarity and research as to the effect of
  gender difference on essay writing (Read *et al.*, 2005) but we
  may need to be alert to this.
- *Closed examination* – there is some question over closed
  examinations that rely entirely on memory and on quickly
  structuring information, which may be difficult for many
  students with dyslexia. This has become an oft-challenged mode
  of assessment in recent years. However, quick
  recall/processing of facts and ideas may actually be a job-
  related skill for some.
- *Open book examination* – the candidate is allowed to take into the
  examination a clean text. This is often believed to be more

199

appropriate for students with dyslexia and can be a better test of critical analysis rather than memory.

- *Take away* – students are given a set period of time, for example, a week, to submit an examination paper and can use resources. This can cause more concern over plagiarism, and so the expectations with regard to this must be explained, especially if there may be different cultural understandings about quoting text. For carers, with responsibilities for children or sick relatives, this can be a difficult form of exam if they do not have adequate support.

- *Reports (including laboratory reports)* – students unfamiliar with the style of report writing will need training in what is required.

- *Objective structured clinical examinations* (OSCEs) – are assessments that take place in practical clinical scenarios. Clearly disabled students will need special provision in these circumstances; students who are not first-language students will need to be able to communicate clearly in these situations. These can be very stressful for students with certain mental ill-health conditions. 'Fitness to practice' issues may also arise. Setting up repeat examinations for students who are ill can also be necessary, and equity will need to be ensured.

- *Multiple Choice Questionnaires* (MCQs) – students with dyslexia may need more time for these. International terms can be different – for example, drug names – so use in MCQ should be consistent with teaching material and course work.

- *Letters / case presentations* – as above; written / oral English may be an issue for second-language speakers.

- *Briefing papers* – as above but may be less pressured.

- *Book / article review* – command of written language; structuring issues possible.

- *Oral presentation* – second-language speakers, hearing- and language-impaired students may need additional support.

- *Posters* – as above, and vision-impaired students will need special arrangements.

- *Portfolio / journal* – may be easier for students with dyslexia if order and structure are not as critical as in some written work.

- *Peer assessed presentations* – students need to know each other's names; criteria for assessment need to be extremely clear; contingency arrangements would need to be clear to all if language-impaired students; be aware of any possible gender or inter-cultural issues.

■ *Online* – see Chapter 5 for issues relating to accessibility of technology; for older students there may issues of lack of familiarity and sometimes gender issues.

■ *Video exercise* – as above and particular attention to physical and cultural factors.

■ *Problem scenarios* – general awareness of any special inclusivity and diversity issues needed. International students will need to understand any culturally specific features.

■ *Group tasks* – students with communication difficulties will need support and guidance and special arrangements as appropriate. Students with any type of autistic spectrum disorder will particularly have to be considered.

■ *Work-based problem* – as above.

■ *Draft bid* – all students would need task explaining very clearly and practice attempts. There may be cultural differences in approach on this.

■ *Learning contract document* – if individually negotiated, any special features can be accommodated.

■ *Dissertation* – sustained prose and long, complex documents can be difficult for some students with dyslexia to structure.

■ *Applied task* – manual dexterity, vision, etc. may all be issues.

The SPACE project offered a range of case studies where new forms of assessment had been tried. How practical/useful are any of these to you?:

1   video portfolio (instead of written);
2   portfolio (instead of extended essay);
3   use of British Sign Language (BSL) and voice-over;
4   design report (instead of essay);
5   viva with supporting portfolio;
6   taped seminar report;
7   oral presentation of research proposal;
8   end-of-module test or coursework or portfolio as assessment choice.

The complex issue is that, as has been said of students with dyslexia, each student's needs will be different. Thus, the DRC guidelines explain,

PAUSE FOR THOUGHT

Attempt to think through the application of a new (to you) assessment method from the list of commonly used assessment types (pp. 199–201).

- What might be the issues with regard to inclusivity?
- Would it be better or worse than your current systems? Why?
- Is it truly inclusive or might you need contingency measures for certain students?
- If you did wish to amend assessment what flexibility would you have?
- Who would you need to consult with first in your institution?
- What would be the practical implications for the department/ school/institution?
- How might you evaluate its effectiveness as a new measure?

one student with dyslexia may need additional course work instead of an examination; another may need extra time in the exam; another may need to use a keyboard and so on. They therefore suggest needs should be individually tailored and monitored. The difficulty that then arises is that there seems little point making mass change to ensure inclusive assessment if we are then still going to need to make alternative and contingent arrangements for individuals.

So what can we do?:

1 Check there is a policy that ensures changes can be made to exams to ensure fair treatment for all – in the UK higher education institutions should now have these in respect of race, ethnicity and disability.

2 Consider accessibility (include other areas not mentioned above as mandatory, such as age, socio-economic background, etc.) when the course and the assessment are in planning stage.

3 Make our students aware that appropriate arrangements can be made for exams and assessments.

4 Ensure that the policy can respond to needs of all disabled students and not just 'standard' ones.

5 Involve students in discussion about the appropriate adjustments.

6 Involve appropriate academic staff to ensure rigour is maintained.

7 Do we apply arrangements to all occasions of assessment?

8 Are the disability-related needs verified to prevent abuse of system?

Many students are disadvantaged in written exams (language itself, stamina, etc.). Slightly adapted from the DRC guidelines are the following suggestions:

1 Check the wording is clear and straightforward.

2 If needed provide a reader.

3 Offer large print or Braille if needed.

4 Allow extra time for deaf students or students with dyslexia as assessed as appropriate.

5 Allow rest break for students who suffer chronic fatigue, back or other problems with sitting/working for prolonged periods.

6 Provide an amanuensis (scribe) – students may need practice in using these, and amanuenses may need some familiarity with subject area.

7 Allow submission of scripts by computer (make sure computer is 'clean' and technician on hand if needed).

8 Handle 'extra time' sensitively, so that others are not disturbed (separate room and invigilator?) and that, if separate room, it is suitable.

9 Adjust exam timetable if needed where rest breaks (and/or) 'isolation' required.

FEEDBACK

Giving students good feedback is a core part of our job. It is also an integral part of teaching. That much seems obvious; however, in the UK NSS this is one of the areas – with assessment – where our students are least satisfied according to the survey. Our feedback should be:

1 clear (and written so that it can be read!);

2 regular;

3 timely;

4 prompt;

5   specific;
6   realistic;
7   constructive – aimed at improving future performance;
8   not so demoralising as to make performance worse.

If we build on the NSS questions – problematic though they are in some respects – we can create a self-check list:

1   Have I made it clear ahead of submission what I will be looking for?
2   Am I seen to be fair? Is the exercise valid, reliable and transparent? Fit for purpose?
3   Do they understand what the feedback will be (i.e. is it linked to assessment criteria)?
4   Do I give feedback promptly?
5   Do I make clear what the timescale is for feedback?
6   Do I keep to it?
7   Am I clear to the student about the level of detail they can expect in my comments; for example, will I pick up all errors? Will I just comment on key areas? Will I flag up areas for them to pursue or just correct errors? Do I vary my approach and do they understand that?
8   Do I check that they use my feedback?

For all our students, but particularly international students, we will need to articulate precisely how our system works. Hopefully our approach to all students will satisfy the requirements of disabled students, but there may be particular areas to watch; for example, BSL students may have a more limited vocabulary. During 2007, 250 scientific words have been added to the BSL glossary by a team at the University of Edinburgh, but this only serves to highlight its limitations. Many of the difficulties of disabled students become more apparent under timed conditions. Students with dyslexia and some mental health difficulties may have low self-esteem; for example, a number of students with dyslexia experience years of being told they are lazy before the diagnosis is made, and feedback may be especially painful.

A common method of feedback is the 'feedback sandwich'. We should give students good news – being positive about what has been done well – then the bad news (constructively) – or suggestions as to where the work could have been improved; finally a note of encouragement – and offer the option of discussing issues raised if the comments are not given personally.

Another common method in medical circles is to follow *Pendleton's Rules*. This approach can be more time-consuming and is for face-to-face situations. Generally this approach means: clarifying matters of fact; letting the learner identify and articulate what has been done well; the lecturer doing the same; the student then suggests what could be improved, followed by the lecturer/and perhaps others in the group – with options for changing deficiencies clearly identified. This method can work well in that it helps the student to learn to self-assess in a positive environment. It can seem patronising if not carefully done and, although it is excellent to ensure the positive feedback, the lecturer needs to offer learning points too. However it is given, always ensure that feedback has been understood.

Think *what* you say, *how* you say it and *when* you give it.

Is the way we give feedback efficient for us as well as the students? For example, do we pick up common errors and deal with them in the whole group rather than repeating ourselves many times?

It may be that students do not always understand when they are being given 'feedback', and so we need to be clear about how the students can use what we tell them. Oral feedback can be excellent but do they remember it? We can all recall situations – the PhD viva might be a common one – where it has been difficult to recall accurately all the points of feedback in accurate fashion.

As appropriate:

1   Encourage students to write down what you have told them if you are in doubt.
2   Get them to summarise back to you what you have said.
3   Get them to articulate likely changes.
4   Try exercises where students submit a memo with an assessment to say how they have built on previous feedback.
5   Get them to mark their own work – they could try using 'track changes' to comment on their own work and submit this.
6   Where feedback forms are given to them they could resubmit with responses ticked or annotated.
7   They could discuss with peers how to address tutor's comments.
8   Aim to get students to self-correct.

REFLECTIVE PRACTICE

This chapter cannot go into the detail of what is now a common term in education and indeed in professional practice, that of 'reflective learning'. We referred to it in Chapter 2 as we discussed the aspiration for students to become better learners. Learning to receive feedback and use it effectively is a critical part of this process for students – they must reflect upon and build on their own experiences and their own learning. Self-critique and analysis are essential parts of becoming an independent learner. Cultural background and prior learning will frequently be critical factors in this process. There is some suggestion that the notion of reflective practice is a particularly Western approach. Some international students may find it more difficult to speak of their learning in the intensely personal way that this notion demands (Burnapp, 2006). Disregarding cultural differences in the context of learning and teaching can, we are told, 'create unintended mischief'. Assessment that does not take this into account is likely to fail with regard to some students.

HAVE WE DONE ENOUGH?

It is very important for our own sanity and survival that we ask ourselves at what point we must stop trying to help. We must recognise that we cannot always create the perfect situation in our arrangements. Having explored all the reasonable possibilities and arranged assessment as appropriately as we can, we must then take a step back. If we have satisfied legislative and institutional requirements to the best of our ability and if we are content that we have done all that is pragmatically possible – taking into account our workloads and our obligations to other students and staff – then we must learn to say 'at this point I have made my contribution and will stop'.

FURTHER READING

Angelo, T. and Cross, P. (1993) *Classroom Assessment Techniques: A handbook for faculty*, 2nd edn, San Francisco, CA: Jossey-Bass.

Brown, S. and Knight, P. (1994) *Assessing Learners in Higher Education*, London: Kogan Page.

Bryan, C. and Clegg, K. (2006) *Innovative Assessment in Higher Education*, London: Routledge.

Carroll, J. and Ryan, J. (eds) (2005) *Teaching International Students: Improving learning for all*, Abingdon: Routledge.

De Vita, G. (2001) The use of group work in large and diverse business management classes – some critical issues, *International Journal of Management Education*, 1 (3), 27–35.

Haines, C. (2004) *Assessing Students' Written Work*, Abingdon: Routledge.

Irons, A. (2008) *Enhancing Learning through Assessment and Feedback*, Abingdon: Routledge.

McDowell, L. and Sambell, K. (2005) 'Negotiating academic assignments: the experiences of widening participation and traditional students', in Rust, C. (ed.) *Improving Student Learning: diversity and inclusivity*, Oxford: OCSLD, 149–158.

Mole, J. and Peacock, D. (2005) *Learning, Teaching and Assessment: A guide to good practice for staff teaching d/Deaf students in science and engineering*, Wolverhampton: University of Wolverhampton.

Waterfield, J. and West, B. (2006) *Inclusive Assessment in Higher Education: A Resource for Change*, Plymouth: University of Plymouth (The Staff–Student Partnership for Assessment Change and Evaluation, SPACE, project).

 ## USEFUL WEB RESOURCES

www.celt.mmu.ac.uk/ltia/issue4/wray.shtml
'How to assess disabled students without breaking the law', an online article written by Mike Wray (2003).

www.qaa.ac.uk/academicinfrastructure/codeOfPractice/section6/default.asp
QAA Code of Practice on Assessment of Students.

Chapter 10

'After the Ball is Over ...'

HOW DO WE HELP PREPARE OUR STUDENTS FOR LIFE AFTER THE COURSE HAS ENDED?

In the previous chapter we thought through what is perhaps the most critical academic issue for many students. The worries about assessment particularly come to a head in the final year, and there are clearly a number of other matters that press hard on final-year students. In particular, of course, the rather large question of what they will do for the rest of their lives! As staff we are likely to be involved in supporting these students as they think through these developments. Our involvement may be peripheral if we are only meeting them in teaching situations, but it may be more significant if we are personal tutors. Even if we are only involved as teaching staff there are things we need to keep in mind. There has, perhaps understandably, been far more attention paid in academic circles to the 'first-year experience' than to the transitional stage that students experience at the end of their university lives (perhaps with the exception of the focus on final assessment). Often the approach to this 'final stage' has been simply to 'send' students to the careers service. However, approaches are changing. Student employment services are generally extremely keen to embed their work into the curriculum at the earliest stage possible and not to be a mere adjunct at the end. See, for example, the suggestions on the Geography, Earth and Environmental Sciences (GEES) network on this (www.gees.ac.uk/pubs/planet/index.htm #PSE1). Although this information is aimed at academics in the GEES and related disciplines, the principles and implications are transferable. For our institutions, the policy, practical implications and the responsibility may seem more routine at the final stage (since retention is perhaps the key institutional interest in the initial years). Yet for most students this is likely to be one of the most critical years of their lives.

For some of the students we have focused on in this volume, the issues may be even more complex. If you are a mature student with childcare responsibilities or if you are a disabled student, job opportunities may seem more restricted. If you are an international student it may be more difficult to find employment while not in your home country. The Careers and Student Employment (CaSE) website at the University of Westminster is one of a number that offer specific webpage support for such students. (See their FuSION equality and diversity website: www.wmin.ac.uk/page-886.) This site has specific links headed: women; mature students; ethnic minority students; disabled students; students with previous convictions; gay, lesbian and bisexual students; class issues; religion and belief; and transsexuals.

LEGISLATION

In the UK much of the legislation mentioned in Chapter 1 applies to the world of work. Some protective legislation is now quite longstanding. In 2003, for example, it became illegal to discriminate in employment and vocational training on the grounds of religion or belief, or sexual orientation. In 1999, an amendment to the Sex Discrimination Act of 1975 made it illegal to discriminate against transgendered people, and further legislation in 2004 offered protection to those who wish to be entered in the Gender Recognition Register after full transition. Direct discrimination is unlawful on the grounds of gender or sexual orientation whether it is intentional or not. In theory our students are well-protected; however, in practice there still remain a number of problems. Barriers might include low confidence and lack of opportunities for some students. Whatever the reason, UK black and Asian graduates, for example, are twice as likely to be unemployed as white graduates and half as likely to be offered jobs in their first year (see CaSE website: www.wmin.ac.uk/page-886).

APPROACHES TO TEACHING AND SUPERVISION WITH FINAL-YEAR STUDENTS

As well as being aware of the critical employment issues for our students we need to think through specific final-year issues in our teaching. We need to ensure that the curriculum, and the students' learning, have spiralled upwards as they approach the close of their degree programmes.

Some universities in the US and Australia have introduced end of pro-gramme 'capstone' courses to try to ensure increased complexity and the necessary sophistication associated with academic progression. These courses are generally designed to tie together key learning objectives from the whole programme.

In the UK we do not use this model, but its existence prompts us to think further about the culmination of a student's programme of study. Although many curricula are carefully planned to ensure that the exit-level knowledge of a graduate has been built up with care, there can be a problem for our students with fragmented modular programmes. If we do not ensure an overview and careful linking of the whole degree pro-gramme, it is hard to guarantee a spiral curriculum. The spiral curriculum was proposed by a Harvard professor, Jerome Bruner, who felt that an optimal learning process went through certain stages. We may or may not subscribe to a particular technical model of the spiral curriculum, but at its most basic it makes sense to ensure that we introduce concepts in increasing order of difficulty and that we review these and add more sophisticated elements as our students progress. At least within our courses we should keep this in mind as we develop, review and summarise material in the final year of a degree programme. It might be useful to remind ourselves of the expected levels of skills and knowledge of a graduate in our subject. For example, we could check to see if our subject benchmarks or other disciplinary literature offer guidance on this. It can be particularly helpful to students whose first language is not English, or who were new to the institutional cultural traditions, to have a very clear summary and overview; but all students benefit.

ENCOURAGING INDEPENDENT STUDY IN FINAL-YEAR STUDENTS

On many programmes the final year will be geared towards more inde-pendent learning for students. For this reason, for example, a huge number of final-year courses involve project work. The Internet offers many institutional programme guidelines for the support of final-year students involved in such project work, so it may be worth looking at some of these and comparing the ideas with the support that is offered to our students. The move towards independence in learning is critical whether it is for PhD or first-degree students. Building on our earlier discussion about pedagogy and andragogy, it may be worth briefly thinking about a third type of 'ogy' that is now being discussed more frequently – especially in the field of e-learning – that is 'heutogogy'. (See: ultibase.rmit.edu.au/Articles/dec00/hase2.htm#heutagony for a short but readable and useful amplification of this.) This is a further development of the notion of adult learning that proposes a model to try to develop totally student-directed learning. It asks us to make sense of the learner's world rather than expecting the learner to make sense of the teacher's world. In university learning it is probably not normally possible – or even desirable – for the learner totally to determine what and how learning takes place. At the end of the day there would be no point providing experts in the field in universities if no guiding, inspiring, enthusing and transmission of recently researched knowledge took place. However, it may well be that, at times, we do need to consider moving closer to this model to help develop more fully independent learning (usually, after all, a stated aim of universities). And, we certainly need to help our students move more towards this kind of learning as they are weaned off our support. In many subjects this is precisely the process that students experience during a PhD. This is also the direction that is being actively discussed in medical education, as our future doctors will have to constantly update and retrain. In an age of rapidly changing knowledge, all our students will have to continue to be good learners. They are very likely to have to direct their own learning in their jobs. This is even more reason to encourage self-directed learning in our final-year students.

Academics are themselves examples of successful independent learners – the students who successfully made this transition. We owe it to as many of our students as possible to lead them to similar independent learning. An essential step in this is that, by the final year, students need to have been inspired by love of the subject if they are to continue future independent learning in it. This transcends any student differences and applies to every student, whatever age, gender, cultural, ethnic or economic background and whether disabled or not.

OFFERING PRACTICAL SUPPORT

Encouraging independent learners does not mean leaving students to fend for themselves inappropriately. We should make it clear, perhaps via a web/noticeboard and/or an oral message, how we see our support roles and how and when our students can have access to us. Scheduling regular meetings with those for whom we have specific responsibility is important. Students need to be encouraged to keep us informed as to any difficulties experienced – prevention is better than last-minute attempts at cure.

We should make sure that our students have read and understand the requirements regarding submission. Where disability might mean special arrangements, we need to ensure these well ahead and reassure the student that they are under control.

Where we have students with dyslexia, they may need more help in organising and structuring project work because of the large volume of information to manage in such a project (for example, a dissertation). Furthermore, and as we have said previously, students who are struggling with academic work will frequently have a number of reasons for the difficulties. A case study of a student at the University of Nottingham offers some principles for decision-making with regard to final-year supervision in these contexts. In this case study the personal tutor discusses how one student with dyslexia was helped to identify and progress a dissertation after experiencing time off with depression. With creative thinking and much support from all concerned the student gained a 2:1 degree. (See www.nottingham.ac.uk/teaching/resources/methods/assessment/identify 105/ for details.)

One of the critical points of this study is to highlight the need to get the support of the institution in such cases. Student, assessment officers, study support staff, disability office and academic staff need to work in partnership. The author of this case study also returns us to the question of equity in assessment for all students by asking if the special arrangements would be deemed fair by other students.

INTERNATIONAL STUDENTS IN THE FINAL YEAR

In a survey of final-year international students by the University of Melbourne, the 'culture shock', homesickness and loneliness identified as common problems in the first years were generally diminished. However, another set of problems were identified as continuing problems. English language skills and financial problems remained as issues, but the biggest continuing concern identified by final-year students was how they could socialise with Australian or non-international students. Clearly this issue links to language skills but is also associated with more sophisticated issues of general cultural integration and the inter-cultural competencies of host-nation students. It does mean, however, that it may not be appropriate to assume that our final-year international students feel well integrated, even if they give the impression of understanding their way around the academic system.

SPECIAL ATTENTION TO UNDERSTANDING OF NOTIONS OF ACADEMIC MISCONDUCT

We need to make sure students are very aware of rules on academic misconduct as they approach final assessments – especially plagiarism. It is to be hoped that any cultural differences in approaches to this have been long sorted out, and indeed our efforts in this should start from their early days. However, it is worth double-checking to make sure that they are absolutely clear about local conventions – having to resit exams or course work at this late stage has even more severe consequences. We should spell out, once again, that penalties for any plagiarism can be very severe – for example, a student's degree class could be reduced. This issue may also catch out mature students whose experience of working in industry has left them more used to the ideas of working on collaborative projects without the need to encourage individual ownership of material. Explanations of academic misconduct and plagiarism should have been be introduced at the start of the course, but extended work such as final year projects may bring new complexities into this area and should always be clarified. Jude Carroll's helpful guidance on plagiarism can be accessed via www.brookes.ac.uk/services/ocsld/books/plagiarism/index.html.

FINAL EXAMINATIONS/ASSESSMENT

Clearly the pattern of assessment varies hugely from institution to institution, and the number of programmes with a heavy emphasis on final-year examinations is now much reduced. However, courses still exist that do place a very high importance on final closed examinations. This can make the final year the most stressful one for those students. Even where there is less emphasis on this system, the pressure on final-year students doing relatively large-scale projects can be very great. Suddenly they are more aware of the serious stakes that may affect future employment.

A number of institutions run special support classes/groups for those undergoing final-year stress, and some have Internet support material dedicated to this; the University of Portsmouth, for example, has some online course material relating to self-esteem. And the *AskStudent* portal has links to various stress support tools (see www.askstudent.com/tips/ how-to-handle-end-of-semester-final-exam-stress/). These tools tend to be aimed at students in general and not particularly at any of the groups we are especially concerned with in this book.

213

THE EMPLOYMENT HUNT

We have already stressed that where we are involved in any careers discussions with students, in an ideal world these would have started well before the final year. We should direct students to the student employment office and the Internet for advice. It is not our job, as academics, to give careers advice; however, it is our job to support the students as they find this. We should encourage personal tutees to attend CV writing training sessions as appropriate – poorly presented CVs will immediately impair their job prospects. In the final year, if not before, students will be able to avail themselves of a range of workshops from the careers service in the institution. A number of institutions have opportunities such as the York Award (www.york.ac.uk/services/careers/skills.cfm), which offer students opportunities to participate in courses that will enhance their employability skills and also help them to articulate the skills they already possess in a marketable fashion.

Alarming figures quoted by the Higher Education Academy revealed that, at the summer recruitment fairs for final-year students, 58 per cent of student were still ' just getting a feel' of the job market, with 54 per cent still 'considering further study'. As 78 per cent of these same students said they were worried about competition for jobs, and 90 per cent said they wanted to start earning as soon as possible, there are likely to be very confused feelings in the final-year students we meet!

Many universities have links with particular companies, and these attend the various recruitment fairs. Occasionally departments will have staff with specialist knowledge of the industrial and commercial links, but normally students should go to the careers service to discuss such issues. Almost all institutional websites are full of advice on these matters. International students may find it particularly complex to pursue jobs at home while not in their own countries. Many large companies offer internship experience for final-year students, and some of these are seeking to attract their own nationals once they have finished university. It may be worth pointing out this careers information and guidance for our students.

DISABILITY SPECIALIST ADVICE

We should not be tempted to offer the very specialist advice needed with regard to employment and disability unless, as can happen, our academic expertise covers this area. But there may be subject-specific issues that students want to talk through with personal tutors or subject experts. The careers and disability services will help point out the specialist advice, but there is information for academic staff on some of the appropriate sites. For example, *Toolkits for Success: managing off campus learning for students with disabilities* (www.disabilitytoolkits.ac.uk) has information that can help with discussions about work placements. The DfES has produced a document, *Providing Work Placements for Disabled Students*, which has some hints on using placements (www.lifelonglearning.co.uk/placements/).

This is something for personal tutors to discuss earlier than the final year with disabled students so that appropriate links can be made sufficiently early; for example, the UK Bar Council offers a 'matching' process to link students with barristers with a similar disability.

INTERNATIONAL STUDENTS' ISSUES

Most international students in the UK return to their home country to start or continue their careers. Be particularly careful if asked for advice on work permits to remain in the country. In the UK, we must refer all international students who need visa advice to trained and recognised immigration advisers, it is illegal to do otherwise. But for background information our students can go to the website of the UK Council for International Affairs, for example, for general advice (www.ukcosa.org. uk/student). The student employment services will, of course, be able to give expert advice on these issues to our students.

OLDER STUDENTS

A number of older students will not be looking for new, long-term careers – indeed some may be closer to retirement and others will need to combine any new job with family commitments. This does not mean, however, that the final year will not bring emotional turmoil for some. Many will be wondering what will happen after the course has finished. A number will have experienced radical changes in relationships during their study years. Such life-cycle changes may need close guidance, as we have discussed in earlier chapters. And such students who are job hunting may need careful advice from the careers office. Age discrimination is technically illegal in the UK (see Chapter 1 for more detail), but this may not always help individual students in practice.

DIRECTING OUR STUDENTS TO THE CAREERS SERVICE: INCLUSIVITY AND DIVERSITY ISSUES

The University of Bristol careers service is another example of a website (www.bris.ac.uk/cas/focuson/) that has a list of relevant links relating to diversity, with specialist links on the topics of deaf students, disability, ethnicity, mature students, offenders, sexual orientation, women and vision-impaired students.

The Higher Education Academy, amongst other groups, claims that there is evidence of discrimination in progression opportunities for students from under-represented groups, and so it is clear that some students may need more specialised guidance. Encourage them to use it.

 PAUSE FOR THOUGHT

One of the authors muses:

> As my (normally quite well-motivated) student son walked through the front door in his second year he disdainfully picked up the letter from his university careers service and asked, in apparent astonishment, 'Why are they writing to me?'. He threw it in the rubbish bin. Now in his final year he is greatly exercised by the lack to time to sort out his future. This must be being repeated in student rooms throughout the country!

It is the case that our students are less likely to spend their lives in one career for forty years than previous generations were. Furthermore, they may well be more likely to work with short-term contracts. Higher education institutions are thinking through the impacts of these changes – both on curricula and support. Such ongoing shifts may not be as easy for disabled students or those who have less financial background family support.

STUDENTS WISHING TO GO ON TO FURTHER STUDY

As personal tutors, it may help to ask students who discuss the possibility of further study with us to think through a series of questions:

216

1   Why do they want to do this?

    (a) Is it because they love the subject?

    (b) Is it related to a career they aspire to? If yes, is it the best/appropriate course for that job?

    (c) Do they need a vocational postgraduate course (e.g. law, etc.)?

    (d) Do they want to change direction/specialise more?

2   Why a particular location and not elsewhere?

3   Does their academic record suggest they can successfully complete the course?

4   How will they fund it?

5   Have they been to the careers service?

6   Have they discussed with family or other people from whom they may need emotional or practical support?

It is not the best idea to use postgraduate study because of a lack of clear career ambitions – if this seems to be the case, suggest more discussion with careers service, friends and family.

Prospects website is one amongst many useful sites that can help students consider what courses are available and what the funding issues are (see www.prospects.ac.uk).

Many international students do stay on in the UK to pursue postgraduate study. It is probably not wise to encourage any of our international students to stay on to study simply in order to get a job in the UK. If we supervise students who are already doing this, then it is essential that they realise that the postgraduate degree alone will not open up job opportunities. They will need a well-rounded CV that includes extracurricular activity as well as demonstrating academic achievement. The university's international or graduate office should be able to offer advice on funding.

WRITING REFERENCES

Students can require a number of references from us, and their requests may continue for many years. Check your institution's advice on reference writing, as different universities have different guidance and regulations. There is no legal obligation on academics to provide references; however, most institutions would see it as a 'positive obligation', and many universities state that it is indeed a staff obligation to provide references.

217

For example, see the University of Warwick's guidelines on this at www2. warwick.ac.uk/services/careers/staffadvice/reference/. Much of the useful information below is repeated from that and similar sites. Their guidelines (and others) point out that failure to provide a reference could disadvantage a student and could be deemed discriminatory on the grounds of race, sex, age or disability and be the subject of legal action. They tell staff that, if they are unwilling or unable to provide a reference, they should discuss with the appropriate senior member of the department. It is good practice, we are told, to give clear and transparent reasons to the person whose request we feel we must decline. We must remember that refusing to give a reference, whatever the explanation, can be taken by any involved as a negative comment.

Where we think our students will require references, we should ask them to give us as much advance notice as possible. With our personal supervisees it may be best discussed just before the final year – although, in fact, students may well want references for summer or term-time employment before this. It is always useful to have a copy of the student's CV to work with as a prompt. The department will possess other appropriate records such as grades, reports, personal tutor comments and so on. We should use official paper if the reference is written by us as a member of staff. Clearly the obvious point is to save any references that we write for future, amended use.

Reference writing in the UK is covered by the Data Protection Act, and this is the main reason why we advised above that any guidelines available in our universities should always be consulted – if these are not available many other institutions have them on their websites. Any reference writer has personal liability for the things they say. Liability can occur regarding either 'fact' or 'opinion' given in references. We are required to 'use due care' and to ensure that our comments are accurate. The author actually has a 'duty of care' both to the person about whom a reference is written and to the recipient. Some information is deemed sensitive under the Data Protection Act, for example, information about health, mental welfare, ethnic origin and religious belief and/or defamation, malicious falsehood or negligently provided information. Permission is needed to disclose sensitive information, and it is better to direct any enquirers about these areas to the individual concerned. We are not required to give information about previous convictions (Rehabilitation of Offenders Act), although a number of our students may be entering professions that are exempt areas from this restriction (for example,

Medicine, Law and Accountancy). If we are in doubt as to sensitive – or indeed any other – content, it is always as well to seek advice from a more senior member of staff or appropriate university officer.

The person for whom we write a reference cannot demand to see it from us; however, they can ask the potential employer to show it to them. Therefore, we should only write what we are happy for the student in question to read. Staff should discuss any issues that give concern in references with those about whom the reference is being written. As personal tutors, for example, our responsibility – moral or academic – is for the student's development, and it would seem best practice to try to help them where there are issues. However, that is sometimes easier said than done!

References should not be supplied in response to unsolicited requests without the consent of the student (although this does not necessarily apply to students who have left the institution). A central office such as the registry will be the appropriate office to supply employers with proof of attendance or qualifications. Indeed some universities (e.g. Heriot Watt) require that staff do not hold their own files on students but store them centrally. Some universities also require that references are deposited centrally. Other useful guidelines include:

- www.hw.ac.uk/policy/students/student_references.pdf;
- www.bristol.ac.uk/cms/go/handbook/legal/references.html;
- ittraining.lse.ac.uk/documentation/Files/Guide-to-Sensitive-Information.pdf.

Increasingly employers take up references after a provisional job offer has been made, but some ask for them at interview stage. Telephone references are more open to confused interpretation, and great care should be taken if these are used. It may be wise to seek for a delay and ring back using notes and having verified facts. It goes without saying that we should only ever write or give facts that we can verify and opinion that we can substantiate.

A student will normally approach their personal tutor for a reference but may ask any of us. When we are away for any length of time we need to make sure that our mail is not neglected – students could lose jobs because of unopened letters. There is often a list of specific skills that are needed for a post and, with a CV and the job specification to hand, it should be possible to make the reference appropriate. However, the extent to which you feel able to do this will depend upon your volume of business and on the importance of the reference. The length one can go to in making amendments may be limited. Many employers use standard forms, but many do not. If forms are offered we should use them and not simply send any existing letter version. We should comment on suitability for the post in question so far as we can from the evidence we have.

We should include clear information about basics: name; dates of registration; programme and so on. Comment on: the academic record and on extracurricular activity; include work experience where we are aware of it; relationships with staff and students; key academic and transferable skills – verbal and written abilities and skills such as team-working, leadership, critical thinking, initiative and so on. Where we wish to support the student we need to make sure that we emphasise strengths. We should make clear what our relationship with the student is, so that the extent to which we are able to make a judgment is clear.

It may be wise to put in a disclaimer about the information being given in good faith, stating that it is without liability and may not be disclosed without written consent. Some institutions require this and offer a form of wording. This will not protect against negligence however. If legal action is taken, both the individual and the institution may be liable if found guilty. Because of this, and in some cases because of an interesting sense of equity, many referees are now limiting responses to factual information only, but clearly this begins to call into question the point of references.

We should try to be consistent with length and effort so that we do not favour any students unreasonably. Coded messages can be difficult to interpret. We should reply to named individuals. We must be careful how we use subjective opinion but also remember that employees are interested in potential and not simply past abilities.

WHAT TO DO IN DIFFICULT CASES

The guidance offered by most universities suggests that it is thought best not to mention matters relating to bad standing unless it is directly relevant to the duty of care that we owe to the recipient – that is to say, directly relevant to the job that has been applied for. We should not raise issues that students have not previously been made aware of. Where there are issues such as this, we should normally discuss them with the students concerned. Careers services can often offer advice on such situations.

If we are ever challenged about a reference we have provided we should respond with great care. We should not admit liability. It is advisable (and indeed some universities insist upon it) to contact the registry or appropriate university office for advice in such cases.

 PAUSE FOR THOUGHT

My student has asked me for a reference but has had a number of periods of leave for reasons of mental illness. What are the key issues?

- The reason for the leave is sensitive information under the Data Protection Act and you cannot disclose it without the consent of the student.
- However, you have a duty of care to both student and recipient.
- You should not make positive statements regarding future potential unless you can verify them.
- Stick to the facts of previous performance and, if you offer opinion about potential, make it clear that it is opinion.
- If you wish to offer mitigation, for example, regarding low results on grounds of the ill-health you will need to have the student's consent.
- The way that the student handled the ill-health may have demonstrated strengths, for example, particular coping or adapting skills.
- If you feel unable to give a reference, make it clear to the student why, but ensure you do not discriminate on the grounds of disability.
- If you are at all uncertain consult the appropriate office in your university.

A student who left three years ago has asked me for a reference – he/she actually appeared lazy and disinterested and did poorly.

Options:

- Tell the student you cannot offer a strong reference and say why – suggest that there may be other situations in his life where he could use a referee who has seen more strengths.
- Write a purely factual reference – concentrating on results and actual evidence of performance.
- Discuss with more experienced colleagues.

Finally, we will need to remember to keep student records for several years if we are likely to be asked for references and where adequate information is not kept centrally. Some universities recommend five years, but we can be approached well beyond this, especially where we have had a strong relationship with the student concerned.

PREPARING STUDENTS FOR A GLOBAL WORLD

By the time our students enter their final year it is perhaps rather late to think about preparing them for a global world! This is one more task that should have been done from year one, but programmes are packed and life is hectic. Furthermore, even in the three or four years in which current students have studied, approaches to globalisation have changed. For example, in the last three or four years the use of electronic communication has burgeoned for our students and made the world increasingly smaller. Perhaps the start of the students' final year is a good time to review progress on how well our institution is equipping them for the world to come. A text book on enhancing inclusion is not premised simply upon the need to ensure lack of discrimination amongst our international students, for example. It is about far more – such as embedding a more global vision in all aspects of the curriculum and student experience. In a discussion of global position-taking in Australian higher education, for example, Simon Marginson comments that research universities were always involved in cross-border activities at their margin, but (in spring 2007) for the first time, he says, a 'single system of worldwide HE can be identified' (Marginson, 2007). He points out that instant messaging and data transfer now run through the centre of institutions and governments and are integral to day-to-day practices.

As we are writing this chapter, the death of a British student on a placement in Italy has generated media comments from some students in the UK about not going abroad. While such fears are understandable – and while parents will continue to find 'gap years' an anxious time – an insular attitude will not serve students well in the twenty-first century. Although the student debt situation is constantly a factor that is unhelpful in this debate, it may also be that the likely future employment patterns of many of our students will be less stable and less localised than was previously the case. Overseas employment will not be for all, but it may be worth encouraging our students to have a larger vision of the world if we do not think this has developed in their previous years. In our final-year curriculum we should make doubly sure that, as appropriate, we are offering a truly internationalised approach and that we are not encouraging Anglocentrism, eurocentrism or insularity.

Former US College Principal and President of the US MacArthur Foundation (a wealthy private US grant-making foundation dedicated to fostering 'lasting improvements in the human condition'), Jonathan Fanton, offers the following imperatives (in the US) for global education:

1 Our graduates are going to live their lives fully in a globalized world where the private market, civil society, and international agencies pull along national governments. The most interesting jobs will go to students with a global perspective.
2 Second: students will be attracted to colleges with cosmopolitan campuses and an international curriculum.
3 Third: it is in our national interest that our students know and care about the rest of the world. At a time when anti-American attitudes are growing, it is important to show the world the real face of America through contact with its people.

The above is not without contention and its own political agenda, but the issues raised need to be considered by all – and the lessons are very likely to apply to those of us elsewhere in the world. Some of Fanton's solutions for this are:

1 A curriculum so infused with international content that a student can't escape. I am not talking about a new version of distributional requirements with a few courses set up to satisfy them: rather, a comprehensive rethinking of the curriculum.
2 The second is to cultivate a way of thinking about the world that is not US (or UK or Europe?) –centered – a way of looking at an issue, problem, opportunity, or conflict from multiple perspectives.
3 The third is comfort with difference – diverse cultures and traditions, as well as respect for people of different races, ethnicities, classes, and ideologies.
4 The final element is the practical ability to work in radically different cultures. It requires more than a knowledge of other places learned on campus. A meaningful study or work experience abroad is essential.

Not everyone will agree with all of this, but we should at least consider our position on these statements because, at the very least, they remind us of some essential values. Key amongst them is the need to develop tolerance within and amongst our students.

Find out about opportunities such as Erasmus and Socrates if you are reading this in the UK; for example, see:

- www.erasmus.ac.uk/;
- ec.europa.eu/education/programmes/socrates/socrates_ en.html.

One academic unit dedicated to global citizenship (www.kingston.ac.uk/ global-citizenship/who-we-are/), says:

> Our framework for global citizenship involves supporting people and institutions in our network to develop partnerships and curricular developments that:
>
> 1   engage responsibly with complex local/global processes and diverse perspectives;
> 2   negotiate change, to transform relationships;
> 3   make accountable, informed and conscious choices;
> 4   develop inter-cultural skills, to live with and learn from difference and conflict and to prevent conflict from escalating to aggression and violence;
> 5   establish ethical and responsible relationships within and beyond their identity groups.

These are surely aspirations we hold for all our students, aren't they?

LAST BUT NOT LEAST: PERSONAL ISSUES

In their final year, our students will probably not be thinking about global citizenship so much as the myriad of personal changes that they need to process! They may need to review their close personal relationships – whether their romance will continue beyond university being an issue for many. They will need to come to terms with losing other friends with whom they have spent a great deal of time. The future may be either/both daunting and exciting in all these respects. Emotions may be in turmoil.

Other students will be attempting to grapple with parental expectations relating to employment, further study or marriage. Perhaps some will be forced to think about returning to the family home after some years of independence; others may wish that were possible. There are some cultural traditions where this is more likely to be the case than others. Accommodation and finance all remain large issues. Remind them of loan and other financial support arrangements if needed. Here we may need to be especially aware of the cultural differences amongst our students.

 PAUSE FOR THOUGHT

Think back to Chapter 1.

■ Am I aware of the barriers to employability for my students in the same way as I was when I considered their barriers to learning earlier?

■ Have I been aware of the particular final year issues for those students who may find study or job applications more challenging than their peers?

 FURTHER READING

Arksey, H. (1994) *Juggling for a Degree*, Lancaster: Lancaster University.

Carver, J. and Sharman, J. (2006) *How to Cope with Exam Stress*, London: MIND.

Knight, P. and Yorke, M. (2003) *Assessment, Learning and Employability*, Maidenhead: Society for Research into Higher Education and Open University Press.

Maynard, L. (2001) *Mature Students' Guide*, Richmond: Trotman.

Race, P. (2005) *How to Win as a Final-Year Student: Essays, exams and employment*, Milton Keynes: Open University Press.

 USEFUL WEB RESOURCE

Handling Discrimination (Prospects)
An overview of jobseeking issues relating to different groups of students, that includes: age; disability; gender; mental health; political and ethical issues; race; religion and belief; sexual orientation; social and class issues; transsexual and transgender issues: www.prospects.ac. uk/cms/ShowPage/Home_page/Handling_discrimination/p!eacfg.

Bibliography

Adams, M. and Brown, S. (eds) (2006) *Towards Inclusive Learning in Higher Education: Developing curricula for disabled students*, Abingdon: Routledge.

Adrian-Taylor, S.R., Noels, K.A. and Tischler, K. (2007) 'Conflict between international graduate students and faculty supervisors: toward effective conflict prevention and management strategies', *Journal of Studies in International Education*, 11 (1): 90–117.

Agnew, C. and Elton, L. (1998) *Lecturing in Geography*, Cheltenham: Geography Discipline Network.

Allen, E.J. and Madden, M. (2006) 'Chilly classrooms for female undergraduate students: a question of method', *The Journal of Higher Education*, 77 (4): 684–711.

Anderson, L.W. and Krathwohl D.R. (eds) (2001) *A Taxonomy for Learning, Teaching, and Assessing: A revision of Bloom's taxonomy of educational objectives*, New York: Longman.

Angelo, K.A. and Cross, K.P. (1993) *Classroom Assessment Techniques: A handbook for college teachers*, San Francisco: Jossey-Bass.

Apthorp, H., Kinner, F. and Enriquez-Olmos, M. (2006) *A Teachers' Tool for Reflective Practice: Racial and cultural differences in American Indian students' classrooms*, Aurora, CO: Mid-continent Research for Education and Learning.

Arksey, H. (1994) *Juggling for a Degree*, Lancaster: Lancaster University.

Arshad, R. (2006) 'Race Equality Toolkit: learning and teaching', Edinburgh: Universities Scotland. Available at www.universities-scotland.ac.uk/race equalitytoolkit/.

Asmar, C. (2005) 'Internationalising the students: reassessing diasporic and local student difference', *Studies in Higher Education*, 30 (3): 291–309.

Avramidis, E. and Skidmore, D. (2004) 'Reappraising learning support in higher education', *Research in Post-Compulsory Education*, 9 (1): 63–82.

Bartram, B. (2007) 'The socio-cultural needs of international students in higher education: a comparison of staff and student views', *Journal of Studies in International Education*, 11 (2): 205–214.

Basit, T.N., Roberts, L., McNamara, O., Carrington, B., Maguire, M. and Woodrow, D. (2006) 'Did they jump or were they pushed? Reasons why minority ethnic trainees withdraw from initial teacher training courses', *British Educational Research Journal*, 32 (3): 387–410.

Baume, C. and Baume, D. (1996) *Learning to Teach: Running tutorials and seminars*, Oxford: Oxford Centre for Staff and Learning Development.

Baxter, A., Tate, J. and Hatt, S. (2007) 'From policy to practice: pupils' responses to widening participation initiatives', *Higher Education Quarterly*, 61 (3): 266–283.

Biggs, J. (2003) *Teaching for Quality Learning at University*, 2nd edn, Buckingham: The Society for Research into Higher Education & Open University Press.

Birnie, J. and Grant, A. (2001) 'Providing Learning Support for Students with Mental Health Difficulties Undertaking Fieldwork and Related Activities', Cheltenham: Geography Discipline Network. Available at www2.glos.ac.uk/gdn/disabil/mental/.

Bostock, S. (2007) *e-Teaching: Engaging learners through technology*, SEDA Paper 119, Birmingham: Staff and Educational Development Association.

Boud, D., Keogh, R. and Walker, D. (1985) *Reflection: Turning experience into Learning*, London: Croom Helm.

Brown, S. and Knight, P. (1994) *Assessing Learners in Higher Education*, London: Kogan Page.

Bryan, C. and Clegg, K. (2006) *Innovative Assessment in Higher Education*, London: Routledge.

Buckridge, M. and Guest, R. (2007) 'A conversation about pedagogical responses to increased diversity in university classrooms', *Higher Education Research Development*, 26 (2): 133–146.

Burnapp, D. (2006) 'Trajectories of adjustment of international students: U-curve, learning curve, or third space?' *Intercultural Education*, 17 (1): 81–93.

Butcher, C., Davies, C. and Highton, M. (2006) *Designing Learning: From module outline to effective teaching*, Abingdon: Routledge.

Campbell, A. and Norton, L. (eds) (2007) *Learning, Teaching and Assessing in Higher Education*, Exeter: Learning Matters.

227

Cannon, R. and Newble, D. (2000) *Handbook for Teachers in Universities and Colleges: A guide to improving teaching methods*, London: Kogan Page.

Carroll, J. (2005) '"Lightening the load": teaching in English, learning in English', in Carroll, J. and Ryan, J. (eds) *Teaching International Students: Improving learning for all*, London: Routledge, pp. 35–42.

Carroll, J. and Ryan, J. (eds) (2005) *Teaching International Students: Improving learning for all*, Abingdon: Routledge.

Carver, G. (2002) *How to Cope with Exam Stress*, London: MIND.

Cassidy, S. (2007) 'Assessing "inexperienced" students' ability to self-assess: exploring links with learning style and academic personal control', *Assessment and Evaluation in Higher Education*, 32 (3), 313–330.

Chalkley, B. and Waterfield, J. (2001) 'Providing Learning Support for Students with Hidden Disabilities and Dyslexia Undertaking Fieldwork and Related Activities', Cheltenham: Geography Discipline Network. Available at www2.glos.ac.uk/gdn/disabil/hidden/.

Chalmers, D. and Fuller, R. (1996) *Teaching for Learning at University*, London: Kogan Page.

Chin, J.L., Lott, B., Rice, J. and Sanchez-Hucles (2007) *Women and Leadership: Transforming visions and diverse voices*, Malden: Blackwell Publishing.

Chin, P. (2004) *Using C&IT to Support Teaching*, Abingdon: RoutledgeFalmer.

Clegg, S. (1999) 'Professional education, reflective practice and feminism', *International Journal of Inclusive Education*, 3 (2), 167–179.

Clements, P. and Spinks, T. (2000) *The Equal Opportunities Handbook: How to deal with everyday issues of unfairness*, London: Kogan Page.

Coffield, F., Moseley, D., Hall, E. and Ecclestone, K. (2004) *Learning Styles and Pedagogy in Post-16 Learning: A systematic and critical review*, London: Learning and Skills Research Centre.

Cooper, M. (2003) 'Communications and information technology (C&IT) for disabled students', in Powell, S. *Special Teaching in Higher Education: Successful strategies for access and inclusion*, London: Kogan Page, pp. 37–56.

Croucher, K. and Romer, W. (2008) *Inclusivity in Teaching Practice and the Curriculum*, Guides for Teaching and Learning in Archaeology, No. 6, Glasgow: The Higher Education Subject Centre for History, Classics and Archaeology.

de Groot, J. (1997) 'After the ivory tower: gender, commodification and the Academic', *Feminist Review*, 55: 130–142.

de Lambert, K. and Williams, T. (2006) In sickness and need: the how and why of special consideration for students, *Assessment and Evaluation in Higher Education*, 31 (1), 55–69.

228

De Vita, G. (2001) 'The use of group work in large and diverse business management classes – some critical issues', *International Journal of Management Education*, 1 (3), 27–35.

De Vita, G. (2005) 'Fostering intercultural learning through multicultural group work', in Carroll, J. and Ryan, J. (eds) *Teaching International Students: Improving learning for all*, London: Routledge, pp. 75–83.

Disability Rights Commission (2004) *Disability Discrimination Act 1995. Code of Practice: Employment and occupation*, London: TSO.

Disability Rights Commission (2007a) *Disability Discrimination Act 1995. Code of Practice Post-16: Code of Practice (revised) for providers of post-16 education and related services*, London: TSO. Available at http://83.137.212.42/Site Archive/drc_gb/pdf/COP_Post16.pdf.

Disability Rights Commission (2007b) *Understanding the Disability Discrimination Act: a guide for colleges, universities and adult community learning providers in Great Britain*, London: Disability Rights Commission.

Edirisingha, P. and Salmon, G. (2007) 'Pedagogical models for podcasts in higher education'. Draft paper for presentation at the European Distance and e-Learning Network (EDEN) conference 'New Learning 2.0? Emerging digital territories, developing continuities, new divides', Naples, Italy, 13–16 June 2007. Available at http://hdl.handle.net/2381/405.

Elwood, E. (2005) 'Gender and achievement: What have exams got to do with it?' *Oxford Review of Education*, 31 (3), 373–393.

Entwistle, N. (1981) *Styles of Learning and Teaching: an integrated outline of educational psychology for students*, teachers and lecturers, Chichester: John Wiley.

Equality Challenge Unit (2006) *The Employment Equality (Age) Regulations 2006: General guidance note on age and student issues*, London: Equality Challenge Unit.

Exley, K. and Dennick, R. (2004a) *Giving a Lecture: from presenting to teaching*, Abingdon: RoutledgeFalmer.

Exley, K. and Dennick, R. (2004b) *Small Group Teaching Tutorials: seminars and beyond*, Abingdon: RoutledgeFalmer.

Feast, V. and Bretag, T. (2005) Responding to crises in transnational education: New challenges for higher education, *Higher Education Research and Development*, 24 (1), 63–78.

Fell, B. and Wray, J. (2006) Supporting disabled students on placement, in: Adams, M. and Brown, S. (eds) *Towards Inclusive Learning in Higher Education: Developing curricula for disabled students*, London: Routledge, pp. 164–175.

229

Fischer, M. (2007) 'Settling into Campus Life: Differences by race/ethnicity in college involvement and outcomes', *The Journal of Higher Education*, 78 (2), 125–161.

Fleming, N. (2001) 'VARK: a guide to learning styles. Available at www.vark-learn.com/English/index.asp.

Freire, P. (1972) *The Pedagogy of the Oppressed*, Harmondsworth: Penguin.

Fry, H., Ketteridge, S. and Marshall, S. (2003) *A Handbook for Teaching and Learning in Higher Education: Enhancing academic practice*, 2nd edn, London: Kogan Page.

Gardiner, V. and Anwar, N. (2001) 'Providing Learning Support for Students with Mobility Impairments Undertaking Fieldwork and Related Activities', Cheltenham: Geography Discipline Network. Available at www2.glos.ac.uk/gdn/disabil/mobility/.

Gardner, H. (1993) *Frames of Mind: The theory of multiple intelligences*, 2nd edn, London: Fontana.

Good, G. (2000) The new sectarianism and the liberal university, in Kahn, S. and Pavlich, D. (eds) *Academic Freedom and the Inclusive University*, Vancouver: University of British Columbia Press.

Gravestock, P. (2006a) 'Developing an Inclusive Curriculum: a guide for lecturers', Cheltenham: Geography Discipline Network. Available at www2.glos.ac.uk/gdn/icp/ilecturer.pdf.

Gravestock, P. (2006b) 'DisabilityCPD: continuing professional development for staff involved in the learning and teaching of disabled students', Cheltenham: Centre for Learning & Teaching. Available at www.glos.ac.uk/adu/clt/dcpd/guide.cfm.

Habermas, J. (1984) *The Theory of Communicative Action: Reason and the rationalization of society*, trans. Thomas McCarthy, vol. 1, Boston: Beacon.

Habeshaw, S., Habeshaw, T. and Gibbs, G. (1992) *53 Interesting Things to do in Your Seminars and Tutorials*, 4th edn, Bristol: Technical and Educational Services.

Haggis, T. (2006) 'Pedagogies for diversity: Retaining critical challenge amidst fears of "dumbing down"', *Studies in Higher Education*, 31, 5, 521–535.

Haines, C. (2004) *Assessing Students' Written Work*, Abingdon: Routledge.

Hall, T., Healey, M. and Harrison, M. (2002) Fieldwork and disabled students: discourses of exclusion and inclusion, *Transactions of the Institute of British Geographers* NS, 27, 2, 213–231.

Harris, P.R., Moran, R.T. and Moran, S.V. (2004) *Managing Cultural Differences: Global leadership, strategies for the twenty-first century*, Burlington MA: Butterworth–Heinmann.

Hatt, S. (2005) 'Bursaries and student success: a study of students from low income groups at two institutions in the South West', *Higher Education Quarterly*, 59 (2), 111–126.

Hatt, S., Hannam, A., Baxter, A. and Harrison, N. (2005) 'Opportunity knocks? The impact of bursary schemes on students from low-income backgrounds', *Studies in Higher Education*, 30 (4), 373–388.

Healey, M., Bradley, A., Fuller, M. and Hall, T. (2006) 'Listening to students: the experiences of disabled students of learning at university', in Adams, M. and Brown, S. (eds) *Towards Inclusive Learning in Higher Education: Developing curricula for disabled students*, London: Routledge, pp. 32–43.

Healey, M., Jenkins, A., Leach, J. and Roberts, C. (2001) 'Issues in Providing Learning Support for Disabled Students Undertaking Fieldwork and Related Activities', Cheltenham: Geography Discipline Network. Available at www2.glos.ac.uk/gdn/disabil/overview/.

Heidemann, T. (2000) 'Organisation culture and intercultural competence', *Sprogforum*, 6 (18): 31–35. Available at http://inet.dpb.dpu.dk/infodok/sprogforum/Espr18/heidemann.html.

Honey, P. and Mumford, A. (2006) *Manual of Learning Styles*, revised edn, Maidenhead: Peter Honey.

Hopkins, C., Jackson, D., Tennant, J., Wilson A. and Arlett, C. (eds) (2005) *Engineering Subject Centre Guide: Working with disabled students*, 2nd edn, Loughborough: The Higher Education Academy – Engineering Subject Centre.

Howes, A., Booth, T., Dyson, A. and Frankham J. (2005) 'Teacher learning and the development of inclusive practices and policies: framing and context', *Research Papers in Education*, 20 (2), 133–148.

Humphrey, R. (2006) 'Pulling structured inequality into higher education: the impact of part-time working on English university students', *Higher Education Quarterly*, 60 (3), 270–286.

Irons, A. (2008) *Enhancing Learning through Assessment and Feedback*, Abingdon: Routledge.

Jackson, C. (2003) 'Transitions into higher education: gendered implications for academic self-concept', *Oxford Review of Education*, 29 (3), 331–346.

Jaques, D. (2000) *Learning in Groups: a handbook for improving group work*, 3rd edn, London: Kogan Page.

Jarvis, P. (1987) *Adult Education in the Social Context*, London: Croom Helm.

Kember, D. (1999) 'Integrating part-time study with family, work and social obligations', *Studies in Higher Education*, 24 (1), 109–132.

Knight, P. and Yorke, M. (2003) *Assessment, Learning and Employability*, Maidenhead: Society for Research into Higher Education and Open University Press.

Knowles, M.S. (1990) *The Adult Learner: A neglected species* (4th edn), Houston: Gulf Publishing.

Kolb, D.A. (1984) *Experiential Learning: Experience as the source of learning and development*, New Jersey: Prentice-Hall.

Lahteenoja, S. and Pirttila-Backman, A. (2005) 'Cultivation or coddling? University teachers' views on student integration', *Studies in Higher Education*, 30 (6), 641–661.

Laurillard, D. (2002) *Rethinking University Teaching: A framework for the effective use of educational technology*, 2nd edn, London; RoutledgeFalmer.

Lave, J. and Wenger, E. (1991) *Situated Learning: Legitimate peripheral participation*, Cambridge: Cambridge University Press.

Leask, B. (2006) 'Plagiarism, cultural diversity and metaphor: Implications for academic staff development', *Assessment and Evaluation in Higher Education*, 31 (2), 183–199.

Leong, F.T.L. and Sedlacek, W.E. (1986) 'A comparison of international and US students' preferences for help sources', *Journal of College Student Personnel*, 27, 426–430.

Lewis, M. (2005) 'Moving Tales: acculturation experiences of migrant women staff entering a New Zealand polytechnic', *Higher Education Research and Development*, 24 (1), 95–108.

Light, G. and Cox, R. (2001) *Learning to Teach in Higher Education*, London: PCP Publishing.

Littlejohn, A. and Higgison, C. (2003) 'e-Learning Series No.3: a guide for teachers', York: Learning & Teaching Support Network. Available at www.heacademy.ac.uk/assets/York/documents/resources/resourcedata base/id323_A_Guide_for_Teachers_e-Learning_Series_No3.pdf.

Lizzio, A., Wilson, K. and Hadaway, V. (2007) 'University students' perceptions of a fair learning environment: A social justice perspective', *Assessment and Evaluation in Higher Education*, 32 (2), 195–213.

McDowell, L. and Sambell, K. (2005) 'Negotiating academic assignments: The experiences of widening participation and traditional students', in Rust, C (ed.) *Improving Student Learning: Diversity and inclusivity*, Oxford: Oxford Centre for Staff and Learning Development, pp. 149–158.

McGuire, J. M. (2007) 'Why has the Critical Thinking Movement not come to Korea?' *Asia Pacific Review*, 8 (2), 224–232.

McKinnis, J.R.C. and Devlin, M. (2002) *Assessing Learning in Australian Universities*, Melbourne: Centre for the Study of Higher Education, The University of Melbourne.

McLean, P. and Ransom, L. (2005) 'Building intercultural competencies: Implications for academic skills development', in Carroll, J. and Ryan, J. (eds) *Teaching International Students: Improving learning for all*, London: Routledge, pp. 45–62.

McNickle, C. (2003) 'The Impact that ICT has on how we learn: Pedagogy, andragogy or heutagogy?', in 16th ODLAA Biennial Forum Conference Proceedings, 'Sustaining Quality Learning Environments'.

Manheimer, R.J.(2005) 'The older learner's journey to an ageless society: Lifelong learning on the brink of a crisis', *Journal of Transformative Education*, 3 (3), 198–220.

Man Ling Lee, T. (2005) 'Intercultural teaching in higher education', *Intercultural Education*, 16 (1), 201–215.

Marginson, S. (2007) 'Global position taking: The case of Australia', *Journal of Studies in International Education*, 11 (1), 5–32.

Marton, F. and Säljö, R. (1976a) 'On qualitative differences in learning – 1: Outcome and process', *British Journal of Educational Psychology*, 46, 4–11.

Marton, F. and Säljö, R. (1976b) 'On qualitative differences in learning – 2: Outcome as a function of the learner's conception of the task', *British Journal of Educational Psychology*, 46, 115–27.

Marton, F., Hounsell, D. and Entwistle, N. (eds) (1997) *The Experience of Learning*, 2nd edn, Edinburgh: Scottish Academic Press.

Maslow, A. (1987) *Motivation and Personality*, 3rd edn, New York: Harper & Row.

Maynard, L. (2001) *Mature Students' Guide*, Richmond: Trotman.

Mezirow, J. (1991) *Transformative Dimensions of Adult Learning*, San Francisco: Jossey-Bass.

Modood, T. (2005) *Multicultural Policies: Racism, ethnicity and Muslims in Britain*, Edinburgh, University of Edinburgh Press.

Modood, T. (2006) 'Ethnicity, Muslims and higher education entry in Britain', *Teaching in Higher Education*, 11 (2), 247–250.

Mole, J. and Peacock, D. (2005) *Learning ,Teaching and Assessment: A guide to good practice for staff teaching d/Deaf students in science and engineering*, Wolverhampton: University of Wolverhampton.

Moon, J. (1999) *Reflection in Learning and Professional Development: Theory and practice*, London: Kogan Page.

Morrison, J., Merrick, B., Higgs, S. and Le Metais, J. (2005) 'Researching the performance of international students in the UK', *Studies in Higher Education*, 30 (3), 327–337.

National Committee of Inquiry into Higher Education (1997) 'Higher Education in the Learning Society', Norwich: HMSO. Available at www.leeds.ac.uk/educol/niche/.

National Society for Epilepsy (2005) 'Brainstorming is not offensive says leading epilepsy charity', Press Release. Available at www.epilepsynse.org.uk/pages/whatsnew/pr/show_pr.cfm?id=271.

Neville, L. (2007) 'Learning skills in HE', *Times Higher Education Supplement*, 1, June: 4.

Newland, B., Boyd, V. and Pavey, J. (2006) 'Enhancing disabled students' learning through virtual learning environments', in Adams, M. and Brown, S. (eds) *Towards Inclusive Learning in Higher Education: Developing curricula for disabled students*, London: Routledge, 143–153.

Newland, B., Newton, A., Pavey, J., Boardman, K. and Murray, M. (2004) 'duo (Durham University Online) VLE Report 2003', Bournemouth: Bournemouth University. Available at www.bournemouth.ac.uk/eds/documents/duo_vle_report-2003.pdf.

Newland, B., Pavey, J. and Boyd, V. (2005) 'Accessibility in Learning Environments and Related Technologies (ALERT)', Durham University and Bournemouth University. Available at www.bournemouth.ac.uk/alert/.

Office for National Statistics (2003) 'How do you define ethnicity?' Available at www.statistics.gov.uk/about/ethnic_group_statistics/how_define/default.asp.

Oliver, M. (1996) *Understanding Disability: From theory to practice*. Basingstoke: Macmillan.

OpenLearn (2006) 'K205_1: Diversity and difference in communication'. Available at http://labspace.open.ac.uk/course/view.php?id=1864.

Palmer, J.A. (2001) *Fifty Modern Thinkers on Education: From Piaget to the present*, London: Routledge.

Pearson, E. and Koppi, T. (2006) 'Supporting staff in developing inclusive online learning', in Adams, M. and Brown, S. (eds) *Towards Inclusive Learning in Higher Education: Developing curricula for disabled students*, London: Routledge, pp. 56–66.

Pearson, J.C., Turner, L.H. and Todd-Mancillas, W.R. (1991) *Gender and Communication*, 2nd edn, Dubuque, IA: William C. Brown.

Pennell, H. and West, A. (2005) 'The impact of increased fees on participation in higher education', *Higher Education Quarterly*, 59 (2), 127–137.

Pickford, R. and Brown, S. (2006) *Assessing Skills and Practice*, Abingdon: Routledge.

Pike, G.R. and Kuh, G.D. (2005) 'First and second-generation college students: a comparison of their engagement and intellectual development', *The Journal of Higher Education*, 76 (3), 276–300.

Pyvis, D. (2007) 'Why university students choose and international education: A case study in Malaysia', *International Journal of Educational Development*, 27, 235–246.

Quality Assurance Agency for Higher Education (2000) 'Guidelines for HE Progress Files'. Available at www.qaa.ac.uk/academicinfrastructure/progressFiles/default.asp.

Quality Assurance Agency (2004) 'Code of practice for the assurance of academic quality and standards in higher education'. Available at www.qaa.ac.uk/academicinfrastructure/codeofpractice/section1/default.asp.

Quality Assurance Agency (2006) 'Code of practice for the assurance of academic quality and standards in higher education: Assessment of students'. Available at www.qaa.ac.uk/academicinfrastructure/codeOfPractice/section6/.

Quality Assurance Agency for Higher Education (2007) 'Code of Practice for the Assurance of Academic Quality and Standards in Higher Education Section 9: Work-based and placement learning', Gloucester: QAA. Available at www.qaa.ac.uk/academicinfrastructure/codeOfPractice/section9/PlacementLearning.pdf.

Quarshie Smith, H. (2007) 'Globalisation and desire: a case study of international graduate student education', *Journal of Studies in International Education*, 11 (1), 54–72.

Quinn, J., Thomas, L., Slack, K., Casey, L., Thexton, W. and Noble, J. (2005) *From Life Crisis to Lifelong Learning: Rethinking working-class 'drop out' from higher education*, York: Staffordshire University for Joseph Rowntree Foundation.

Race, P. (2000) *2000 Tips for Lecturers*, London: Kogan Page.

Race, P. (2001) *The Lecturer's Toolkit: A practical guide to learning, teaching and assessment*, 2nd edn, London: Kogan Page.

Race, P. (2005) *Reading to Win as a Final-Year Student: Essays, exams and employment*, Milton Keynes: Open University Press.

Ramsden, P. (1992) *Learning to Teach in Higher Education*, London: Routledge.

Read, B., Francis, B. and Robson, J. (2005) 'Gender "bias", assessment and feedback: Analyzing the written assessment of undergraduate history essays', *Assessment and Evaluation in Higher Education*, 30 (3), 241–260.

235

Roberts, G. (2002) 'SET for Success'. Available at www.hm-treasury. gov.uk/documents/enterprise_and_productivity/research_and_enterpris e/ent_res_roberts.cfm.

Robson, J., Francis, B. and Read, B. (2004) 'Gender, student confidence and communicative styles at university: the views of lecturers in history and psychology', *Studies in Higher Education*, 29 (1), 7–23.

Rodd, M. and Bartholomew, H. (2006) 'Invisible and special: young women's experiences as undergraduate mathematics students', *Gender and Education*, 18 (1), 35–50.

Rogers, C.R. (1980) *Freedom to Learn for the 80s*, New York: Free Press.

Ryan, J. (2000) *A Guide to Teaching International Students*, Oxford: Oxford Centre for Staff and Learning Development.

Ryan, J. (2005) 'Improving teaching and learning practices for international students: implications for curriculum, pedagogy and assessment', in Carroll, J. and Ryan, J. (eds) *Teaching International Students: Improving learning for all*, London: Routledge, 92–100.

Sahdra, B. and Thagard, P. (2003) Procedural knowledge in molecular biology, *Philosophical Psychology*, 16, 477–498.

Salmon, G. (2000) *E-moderating: The key to teaching and learning online*, London: Kogan Page.

Schön, D.A. (1983) *The Reflective Practitioner: How professionals think in action*, London: Temple Smith.

Shakespeare, T. (2006) *Disability Rights and Wrongs*, Abingdon: Routledge.

Shay, S. (2004) 'The assessment of complex performances: A socially-situated interpretive act', *Harvard Educational Review*, 74 (3), 307–329.

Shepherd, I. (2001) 'Providing Learning Support for Blind or Visually Impaired Students Undertaking Fieldwork and Related Activities', Cheltenham: Geography Discipline Network. Available at www2.glos.ac.uk/gdn/ disabil/blind/.

Shumar, W. (1997) *College for Sale: A critique of the commodification of higher education*, London: Falmer Press.

Smith, V. and Armstrong, A. (2005) *Beyond Prejudice: Inclusive learning in practice*, London: Learning and Skills Development Agency.

Stangor, C. (2000) *Stereotypes and Prejudice*, Philadelphia, PA: Psychology Press.

Star, J. (2005) 'Research commentary: Reconceptualizing procedural knowledge', *Journal for Research in Mathematics Education*, 36 (5), 404–411.

236

Strauss, P. and U, A. (2007) 'Group assessments: dilemmas facing lecturers in multicultural tertiary classrooms', *Higher Education Research and Development*, 26 (2), 147–161.

Steele, C.M. (1997) 'A threat in the air: How stereotypes shape intellectual identity and performance', *American Psychologist*, 52, 613–629.

Steele, C.M. (1998) 'Stereotyping and its threats are real', *American Psychologist*, 53, 680–681.

Steele, C.M. and Aronson, J. (1995) 'Stereotype threat and the intellectual test performance of African Americans', *Journal of Personality and Social Psychology*, 69, 797–811.

Talbot, C. (2004) *Equality, Diversity and Inclusivity: Curriculum matters*, SEDA Special 16, Birmingham: Staff and Educational Development Association.

Tannen, D. (1996) *Gender and Discourse*, New York: Oxford University Press.

Taras, M. (2006) 'Do unto others or not: Equity in feedback for undergraduates', *Assessment in Higher Education*, 31 (3), 365–377.

Teachability (2000) 'Teachability: creating an accessible curriculum for students with disabilities', Scottish Higher Education Funding Council. Available at www.teachability.strath.ac.uk/originalteachabilitypage.html.

Thomas, L. and Hixenbaugh, P. (2006) *Personal Tutoring in Higher Education*, Stoke-on-Trent: Trentham.

Tinklin, T., Riddell, S. and Wilson, A. (2004) 'Policy and provision for disabled students in higher education in Scotland and England: The current state of play', *Studies in Higher Education*, 29 (5), 638–657.

Tinto, V. (1975) 'Drop out from higher education: A theoretical synthesis of recent research', *Review of Higher Education*, 45 (1), 89–125.

Tinto V. (1993) *Leaving College*, Chicago, IL: University of Chicago Press.

Turner, Y. (2006) 'Chinese students in a UK business school: Hearing the student voice in reflective teaching and learning practice', *Higher Education Quarterly*, 60 (1), 27–51.

Turney, L., Law, I. and Phillips, D. (2002) 'Institutional Racism in Higher Education Toolkit Project: Building the anti-racist HEI', Leeds: Centre for Ethnicity and Racism Studies. Available at www.leeds.ac.uk/CERS/toolkit/toolkit.htm.

Tym, C., McMillion, R., Barone, S. and Webster, J. (2004) *First Generation College Students: a literature review*, Austin, TX: TG research and Analytical Services.

Tynan, A. (ed.) (2005) *Time to Take Stock: Disability and professional competence*, London: The Royal Veterinary College (Diverse: The UK Veterinary Medicine Disability Project).

237

University of North Carolina at Chapel Hill (1997) *Teaching for Inclusion*. Available at http://ctl.unc.edu/tfitoc.html.

UPIAS (1976) *Fundamental Principles of Disability* (London: UPIAS).

Wagner, A.E. (2005) Unsettling the academy: Working through the challenges of anti-racist pedagogy, *Race, Ethnicity and Education*, 8 (3), 261–275.

Waller, R. (2006) 'I don't feel like "a student", I feel like "me"!': The over-simplification of mature learners' experience(s)', *Research in Post-Compulsory Education*, 11 (1), 115–130.

Wareham, T., Clark, G. and Laugesen, C. (2001) 'Providing Learning Support for d/Deaf or Hearing Impaired Students Undertaking Fieldwork and Related Activities', Cheltenham: Geography Discipline Network. Available at www2.glos/ac.uk/gdn/disabil/deaf/.

Warwick, P. (2006) *International Students in the UK : How can we give them a better experience?* Working Paper No. 26, York: Department of Management Studies, University of York.

Waterfield, J. and West, B. (2002) *SENDA Compliance in Higher Education: An audit and guidance tool for accessible practice within the framework of teaching and learning*, Plymouth: University of Plymouth (South West Academic Network for Disability Support, SWANDS, project).

Waterfield, J. and West, B. (2006) *Inclusive Assessment in Higher Education: A Resource for Change*, Plymouth: University of Plymouth (The Staff–Student Partnership for Assessment Change and Evaluation, SPACE, project).

Watts, R. (2007) 'Whose knowledge? Gender, education, science and history', *History of Education*, 36 (3), 283–302.

Weaver, M. (2006) 'Do students value feedback? Student perceptions of tutors' written responses', *Assessment and Evaluation in Higher Education*, 22 (3), 271–288.

Westland, A. (no date) 'How to Prevent PowerPoint Panic'. Available at www.creativekeys.net/PowerfulPresentations/article1056.html.

Wheeler, S. and Birtle, J. (1993) *A Handbook for Personal Tutors*, Buckingham: Society for Research into Higher Education and Open University Press.

Wilcox, P., Winn, S. and Fyvie-Gauld, M. (2005) '"It was nothing to do with the university, it was just the people": The role of social support in the first-year experience of higher education', *Studies in Higher Education*, 30 (6), 707–722.

Wood, P., Landry, C. and Bloomfield, J. (2006) *Cultural Diversity in Britain: A toolkit for cross-cultural co-operation*, York: Joseph Rowntree Foundation.

Woodfield, R., Earl-Novell, S. and Solomon, L. (2005) 'Gender and mode of assessment at university: Should we assume female students are better suited to coursework and males to unseen examinations?' *Assessment and Evaluation in Higher Education*, 30 (1), 35–50.

Wray, J., Fell, B., Stanley, N., Manthorpe, J. and Coyne, E. (2005) *Best Practice Guide: Disabled social work students and placements*, Hull: University of Hull.

Wray, M. and Houghton A. (2007) 'Disability: A Rough Guide for Widening Participation Practitioners', Ormskirk: Action on Access. Available at www.actiononaccess.org/download.php?f=277.

Yorke, M., and Longden, B. (eds) (2004) *Retention and Student Success in Higher Education*, Buckingham: Society for Research into Higher Education and Open University Press.

Index